Aspects of
Assemblies of God Origins

Aspects of Assemblies of God Origins

Exploring Narratives, Theologies, and Issues from the Early Years

By DANIEL D. ISGRIGG

☙PICKWICK Publications • Eugene, Oregon

ASPECTS OF ASSEMBLIES OF GOD ORIGINS
Exploring Narratives, Theologies, and Issues from the Early Years

Copyright © 2024 Daniel D. Isgrigg. All rights reserved. Except for brief quotations in critical publications or reviews, no part of this book may be reproduced in any manner without prior written permission from the publisher. Write: Permissions, Wipf and Stock Publishers, 199 W. 8th Ave., Suite 3, Eugene, OR 97401.

Pickwick Publications
An Imprint of Wipf and Stock Publishers
199 W. 8th Ave., Suite 3
Eugene, OR 97401

www.wipfandstock.com

PAPERBACK ISBN: 978-1-6667-6097-2
HARDCOVER ISBN: 978-1-6667-6098-9
EBOOK ISBN: 978-1-6667-6099-6

Cataloguing-in-Publication data:

Names: Isgrigg, Daniel D. [author].

Title: Aspects of Assemblies of God origins : exploring narratives, theologies, and issues from the early years / by Daniel D. Isgrigg.

Description: Eugene, OR: Pickwick Publications, 2024 | Includes bibliographical references and index.

Identifiers: ISBN 978-1-6667-6097-2 (paperback) | ISBN 978-1-6667-6098-9 (hardcover) | ISBN 978-1-6667-6099-6 (ebook)

Subjects: LCSH: Assemblies of God—History. | Pentecostal churches—History. | Church history—20th century. | Assemblies of God—United States—History. | Pentecostalism—United States—History.

Classification: BX6198.A7 I84 2024 (paperback) | BX6198.A7 (ebook)

VERSION NUMBER 082224

Cover Photo Credit: Holy Spirit Resource Center, Oral Roberts University.

Contents

Abbreviations | vii

Chapter 1
Aspects of AG Historiography | 1

Chapter 2
Aspects of the Name | 12

Chapter 3
Aspects of the Finished Work Stream | 27

Chapter 4
Aspects of Evangelical Identity | 42

Chapter 5
Aspects of Eschatological Influences | 59

Chapter 6
Aspects of Eschatological Variety | 79

Chapter 7
Aspects of Theology and Education | 114

Chapter 8
Aspects of Social Engagement | 138

Chapter 9
Aspects of Further Research | 152

Bibliography | 155

Index | 171

Abbreviations

AG	Assemblies of God (U.S.)
C&MA	Christian & Missionary Alliance
CBC	Central Bible College
CBI	Central Bible Institute
COGIC	Church of God in Christ
CPT	Centre for Pentecostal Theology
EA	Evangelical Alliance
EPTA	European Pentecostal Theological Association
GC	General Council of the Assemblies of God
GPH	Gospel Publishing House
JPTS	*Journal for Pentecostal Theology Supplement*
NAE	National Association of Evangelicals
ORU	Oral Roberts University
PTMS	Princeton Theological Monograph Series
SFT	Statement of Fundamental Truths
WCCF	World Conference on Christian Fundamentals
WMFA	World Missionary Faith Association

Chapter 1

Aspects of AG Historiography

INTRODUCTION

IN APRIL 2014, THE Assemblies of God U.S. (AG) celebrated its centennial. As one of the largest Pentecostal denominations, it has enjoyed the privilege of several popular denominational and academic histories by Pentecostal scholars. Because of this prominence and broad exposure, much of the AG story is well-rehearsed. With the proliferation of narratives on AG history, why is there a need for this volume?

When the first academic AG histories were published in the 1960s and 1970s, primary sources for Pentecostalism were still being discovered and made accessible to researchers. Because of this, early scholars had limited access to the number of primary sources available today. Instead, they relied upon popular accounts of the movement for details of historical events and people. Many of these early histories gave simplistic or hagiographical accounts of the denomination's early years.[1] While valuable and groundbreaking for their time, the early histories often struggled to critically assess the effects of that history from any perspective except for the majority. This trend made a critical turn in 1993 with Edith Blumhofer's critical AG history, *Restoring the Faith*.[2] Blumhofer raised new questions about issues that have not been adequately addressed. As an academic exercise, scholarship

---

1. Hagiography refers to the biography or history of a saint that usually paints the most flattering picture of the subject. Historical accounts of this nature typically have the goal of giving honor to venerated persons, groups, or events. The lack of critical and objective evaluation typically produces biased historical accounts.

2. Blumhofer, *Restoring the Faith*.

should always investigate, refine, and correct old narratives as new information surfaces. These critical reassessments are vital to the growth of AG scholarship, adding nuances to the understanding of history.

Since it has been three decades since the last history was published, there is a growing need for critical reflections on the AG's past beyond the simplistic or hagiographical accounts of the past. The priority for AG historiography is not documenting what happened, as that has been covered, but revisiting those events with a new critical lens to understand those narratives. Important questions about theological and social developments of the past half-century need fresh investigation by employing new methodologies.

Revisiting established narratives is only sometimes welcomed by stakeholders within a community as these questions can be seen as threatening to the status quo. But since the first academic histories of the 1950s and 1960s, historians have unearthed so much more about the development of Pentecostalism as scholarship has increased significantly and brought about new questions for scholars to answer today. Re-examining the narratives about the AG's origins is not intended to criticize or weaken the community; instead, it is a necessary process that allows the understanding of the AG to continue to develop and mature. As Blumhofer mentioned, there are many more questions to answer beyond what she did in her time. She says, "The Assemblies of God will be strong when it finds the courage to raise theological questions for which it may not have ready answers."[3]

This volume is an effort to raise new questions about the AG's origins by looking again with new lenses prompted by access to new materials. Because of the development of technology that allows us to search keywords in periodical literature digitally, researchers can give new insights that could not be known in previous generations. The goal is not to retell the whole AG story. Instead, it is an attempt to delve deeper into gaps in the narrative that need to be filled or explore blind spots in the narrative that need to be illuminated. This process must begin with a review of the previous accounts of the AG story as a starting point for the chapters ahead.

WAYS OF TELLING THE PAST

Over the past one hundred years, there have been multiple histories of the AG using different methodological approaches. In 1997, Augustus Cerillo

3. Blumhofer, *Restoring the Faith*, 273.

Jr. documented four major interpretive approaches to Pentecostal history: providential, historical roots, multicultural, and functional.[4] For Cerillo, each approach told the Pentecostal story through a unique methodological lens or horizon. Cerillo's interpretive framework represents the progression of Pentecostal historical reflection from its infancy of self-description to a more critical reflection by trained historians. The first approach, the providential approach, sees history as God's plan and attributes events and people to the direct action of God in the story. The historical roots approach offers a more objective view of history by identifying historical and theological developments rather than divine causation. The multicultural approach developed much later as an approach that attempts to better understand the narratives from the perspective of margins rather than from the perspective of the majority. It prioritizes the perspectives of those who perhaps were excluded from consideration in earlier accounts due to social or political realities. Finally, the functional approach was developed to understand the sociology of the movement and how cultural and sociological factors shaped history. It focuses on the human realities at work in religious or faith contexts. While AG histories have tended to adopt providential and historical roots approaches, there is a lack of the latter two critical approaches that tend to reveal aspects of history that are more painful to confront. However, these approaches are necessary to uncover new ways to understand the story. Here, we explore what insights might come from this volume by first exploring how previous histories have approached the narratives of the past based on these four approaches.

Providential History

The first wave of AG histories exhibited the characteristics typical of the providential approach. Prominent first- and second-generation AG ministers developed these popular histories internally. As such, these are ultimately insider histories in which the narratives usually give a favorable account of the denomination. In some cases, insider histories are viewed as apologetics because they must align with already accepted narratives rather than allow them to be shaped or reshaped by historical data.

Providential histories explain the origins of the denomination through the providence of God. For the earliest AG historians, God created the Pentecostal Movement and the AG. Cerillo notes that this approach provides

---

4. Cerillo, "Interpretive Approaches," 29–54.

a "supernaturalistic understanding of social and cultural causation."[5] The problem with providential approaches to history is that they often fail to acknowledge the theological and historical antecedents that influenced the movement. Instead, these accounts view the movement as a providential work of restoration back to apostolic Christianity.[6] The appeal to God's sovereignty to explain history may give some sense of internal validation. Still, it is a difficult position to prove to those outside the community.[7] As William Kay explains, the problem with this approach is that "attributing events to Providence is that we can end up without any proper explanation at all."[8]

The first AG history was *The Apostolic Faith Restored*, written by B. F. Lawrence in 1916.[9] Originally published as a series of articles in the *Pentecostal Evangel* in early 1916, Lawrence's account of the outpouring of the Spirit was compiled into a book by May 1916. A decade after the Azusa Street Revival, he sought to give "A History of the Present Latter Rain Outpouring of the Holy Spirit known as the Apostolic or Pentecostal Movement." For Lawrence, the Pentecostal Movement (and ultimately the AG) resulted from a sovereign move of God to revive apostolic Christianity in the last days. This providential approach is fueled by the "latter rain" historical paradigm that argues for the restoration of gifts of the Spirit and speaking in tongues that were lost from the apostolic days. He documents the stories of charismatic gifts and outpourings of the Spirit worldwide to prove that the latter rain has come. However, these occurrences are not explained as historical factors that gave birth to the movement; instead, they provide a defense for the legitimacy of the Pentecostal Movement.[10]

A decade later, Stanley Frodsham developed a more eschatologically centered providential history in *With Signs Following*, published in 1926.[11] In Frodsham's account, the Pentecostal movement is also portrayed as a sovereign, worldwide, last days, "latter rain" outpouring of the Spirit.[12] The purpose of the outpouring was not just to restore apostolic Christianity,

---

5. Cerillo, "Interpretive Approaches," 31.
6. Cerillo, "Interpretive Approaches," 32.
7. Kay, *Pentecostalism*, 18–19.
8. Kay, *Pentecostalism*, 22.
9. Lawrence, *Apostolic Faith Restored*.
10. Lawrence, *Apostolic Faith Restored*, 52.
11. Frodsham, *With Signs Following*.
12. Frodsham, *With Signs Following*, 353.

but it was also a precursor to the eschatological judgments that were to accompany the return of Christ.[13] Frodsham understood history as an eschatological event that culminated in the restoration of the Holy Spirit upon the church. While providential in orientation, his approach was animated by an eschatological timeline that explained its historical realities. God acted to create the Pentecostal Movement because it was the "last days" of prophetic fulfillment. This has a deterministic emphasis in arguing that whatever historical factors led to the movement were also part of that plan.

The next AG history was published nearly forty years later in 1961, when Carl Brumback wrote *Suddenly . . . From Heaven*.[14] Brumback's modern account of the AG's origins became an important text for AG ministers and church members.[15] Brumback's providential history orientation is set out from the beginning when he declares, "We Pentecostalists regard the absence of a progenitor of our own Movement as an indication that this mighty revival was begotten directly by an extraordinary outpouring of the Holy Spirit."[16] The fact that history has no antecedents is seen in the title because it is a providential event that happened "suddenly" as an act from "heaven." Brumback's popular history is filled with firsthand stories and quotes from Pentecostal pioneers who experienced the movement's birth.[17] Although Brumback takes a providential approach, he has a more open view of causation than he admits in that he notes the outpouring of the Holy Spirit with signs following was the result of fervent prayers of previous generations of pastors, teachers, and believers who asked for revival.[18]

What is unique about Brumback's providential approach is that he sees the movement as a revival rather than a last-day outpouring of the "latter rain." Brumback views revival as cyclical and repeatable rather than simply an initiatory event that founded the movement. Writing in the early 1960s, his shift in emphasis resulted from a sense that the movement was losing its fervor. To account for this, he adopts the possibility that the Pentecostal revival is cyclical like previous revivals. He opens his account with this

---

13. Frodsham, *With Signs Following*, 353.

14. Brumback, *Suddenly . . . From Heaven*.

15. The second half of *Suddenly . . . From Heaven* was republished in 1977 as a shorter popular history called *Like a River* and was mainly focused on the AG history. Brumback, *Like a River*.

16. Brumback, *Suddenly . . . From Heaven*, 48.

17. Brumback, *Suddenly . . . From Heaven*, viii.

18. Brumback, *Like a River*, 1.

preface: "Every revival is a coming again of the Lord Jesus Christ ... His coming in revival is not in the same literal, physical manner of the Second Coming, but it is, in a very definite sense, a coming by the omnipresent Son of God to judge the disobedient and heretical and to revive the spirit of the humble."[19] Though the revival could end in his mind, God could again open the windows of heaven if his people would only pray.[20] He says, "One thing which we trust has been made clear by this historical record is that *however this revival may end, it began in the Spirit!*"[21] This move from seeing the latter rain as a chronological and eschatological sign-event to seeing it as a refreshing or restoring of zeal and power is a clear reinterpretation of the earlier concept of Pentecostalism. The outpouring that started the movement is also repeatable based on human action. He says, "The revival that is in the Assemblies of God in foreign lands is a splendid reason for believing in *The Revival That Is To Come.*"[22] So, while the movement is providential in origin, that divine action is dependent and contingent upon human action.

Academic History

The second wave of histories came during the 1960s and 1970s when several AG educators were pursuing graduate and post-graduate education.[23] This new wave of academic studies were descriptive historical accounts that downplayed the providential perspective. They subjected AG history to critical investigation based on the conventions of academic history. Because their theories had to be more precise in proving causation, the studies lack the providential paradigm explaining the movement as a "latter rain" revival.[24] Therefore, these histories focus on two areas: theological development that led to Pentecostal beliefs and historical events that led to denominational developments.

---

19. Brumback, *Suddenly ... From Heaven*, 1.
20. Brumback, *Suddenly ... From Heaven*, 352.
21. Brumback, *Suddenly ... From Heaven*, 349.
22. Brumback, *Suddenly ... From Heaven*, 354, emphasis original.
23. Cerillo, "Interpretive Approaches," 37.
24. Kay, "Three Generations On," 58–70. Kay recognizes that it is impossible to tell the story of the movement without including Providence since the primary sources reveal how the original participants believed that they were part of a sovereign move of God in the last days.

The first AG educator to write an academic history was Irvine J. Harrison, who wrote his ThD thesis at Berkeley Baptist Divinity School in 1956.[25] Harrison was the president of Southern California Bible College (today Vanguard University) from 1945 to 1958.[26] Harrison pieced together a narrative that begins with the Pentecostal movement and then transitions to the AG story. Like those who came after him, he was interested in presenting the doctrinal issues, departmental developments, and challenges to the denomination from its infancy to its maturity in the post-WWII era. Harrison, who later joined Oral Roberts University's first faculty, was very interested in the AG's cooperation with the broader Pentecostal movement and the emerging Charismatic Renewal.[27] Harrison's dissertation was never published as a book, but it was an important study that was instrumental in establishing the narrative about the AG for later histories.

Shortly after, Klaude Kendrick completed his PhD dissertation from the University of Texas in 1959. GPH published his AG history as *The Promise Fulfilled* in 1961, placing AG history within the context of the broader Pentecostal movement.[28] Kendrick was the first historian to explain the AG's origins by pointing to theological and historical antecedents from various evangelical streams that came into the movement.[29] Rather than focus on theological distinctives, such as speaking in tongues, he takes an ecclesiological approach to focus on factors of two types of people that shaped the movement. The first type was ministers or congregations that had withdrawn from other denominations and established new independent Pentecostal churches and missions. Many of these churches held Baptist views of sanctification and began to organize after the finished work controversy of 1910, ultimately resulting in the AG's founding. The other Pentecostal groups comprised churches within the Holiness Movement that embraced Pentecostal theology.[30] Kendrick paved the way for

---

25. Harrison, "History of the Assemblies of God."

26. "With Christ," 28. He also served as head of the Education Committee of the General Council, where he led the denominational effort to begin converting the AG's Bible colleges into liberal arts colleges to meet the educational needs of Pentecostal youth, not just ministers. *GC Minutes* (September 4–9, 1947), 16–21. Unless otherwise noted, all periodicals and newspapers can be found on the Consortium of Pentecostal Archives at https://pentecostalarchives.org/.

27. Isgrigg, "The First ORU Seminary," 187–89.

28. Kendrick, *Promise Fulfilled*.

29. Kendrick, *Promise Fulfilled*, 43.

30. Kendrick, *Promise Fulfilled*, 71.

discussions of the widely held view of two streams of Pentecostalism that will be discussed later in this volume.

In 1971, William Menzies published his denominational history, *Anointed to Serve*, based on his PhD at the University of Iowa. Menzies was one of the AG's most notable early scholars and educators, having taught at Central Bible College, Assemblies of God Theological Seminary, and Asia Pacific Theological Seminary. Like Kendrick, his history minimizes the providential orientation found in the earlier histories. Instead, it focuses on the historical antecedents and the organizational development of the AG.[31] Menzies is particularly interested in the theological antecedents of the AG by rooting them in evangelical, fundamentalist, and Reformed roots.[32] He also identifies the dominant characteristics of Pentecostalism that led to its early appeal and growth, including the belief in the supernatural, evangelistic fervor, holiness, and an eschatological message.[33] Menzies is more aware of the controversies and potential issues that come from the AG's theological influences. Menzies is the first to recognize the problems with Parham, controversies over doctrine, and the problematic association of Pentecostalism with Fundamentalism, particularly concerning dispensational eschatology. These critical assessments show that Menzies was more objective in his evaluation of AG history.

Each of these early academic historians began the trajectory toward deeper questions about origins, theology, and the problems that come with a revival movement that is not only institutionalizing as a denomination but is also emerging from the margins of society. However, much of this scholarship had yet to grapple with various social issues confronting the nation and the movement in the changing cultural landscape of the 1960s and 1970s. There is little mention in this era about race, gender roles, and other issues of social engagement that have become highlighted in more recent scholarship.

Critical History

Following these early histories, Pentecostal scholarship expanded considerably as more AG ministers pursued higher education and terminal degrees.

---

31. Menzies, *Anointed to Serve*.

32. Menzies, "Reformed Roots of Pentecostalism," 78–99; Menzies, "Influence of Fundamentalism," 199–211.

33. Menzies, *Anointed to Serve*, 77–78.

Aspects of AG Historiography

This brought about the third phase of AG historiography in the 1990s, which focused on critical research of the movement's different historical, social, and cultural aspects. These modern critical accounts reassess the AG's legendary narratives using improved methods of historical research. This section will focus these critical studies in order to understand the development of the AG theological culture from a historical perspective.

The most notable modern AG history is Edith Blumhofer's *Restoring the Faith*, which gives a historical account of AG through the eschatological perspective of restorationism.[34] This Harvard-trained historian objectively examines the significant controversies, theological influences, and prominent historical figures.[35] Using a historical roots approach to Pentecostal doctrine, Blumhofer identifies four early Pentecostal theological themes inherited from radical evangelicals at the turn of the nineteenth century.[36] First, she recognizes the prevalence of providential narratives about the restoration of New Testament primitivism as the full gospel. Second, she notes the revival of prophetic expectation of the blessed hope through evangelical premillennialism. Third, she points to the strong emphasis on the doctrine of divine healing that emerged out of the nineteenth-century healing revival. Finally, she notes the "latter rain" metanarrative that fueled the belief in the end time restoration of the Holy Spirit and charismatic gifts. All four of these restorationist impulses contributed to the ethos of early Pentecostalism. The two most important restorationist concepts were premillennialism and the concept of latter rain restoration of the baptism in the Spirit and speaking in tongues. These twin doctrines have been the cardinal distinctives of AG theology throughout its history.[37]

Blumhofer's history is rooted in the main thesis that the AG is an example of a Pentecostal denomination whose restorationist roots have been challenged as it has expanded and settled into cultural relevance. While Harrison, Kendrick, and Menzies viewed organizational advances as positive developments of growth for the denomination, Blumhofer scrutinized the effects it had on the spiritual vibrancy of the movement. She describes

---

34. Blumhofer, *Restoring the Faith*. See also her denominational history: Blumhofer, *Assemblies of God*, vols. 1–2.

35. In *Restoring the Faith*, Blumhofer is more critical than she was allowed to be in the earlier two-volume history published by GPH. Blumhofer received criticism from the AG over her critique of the fellowship and some of its claims about the "Decade of Harvest," which is included as the last chapter.

36. Blumhofer, *Restoring the Faith*, 12–29.

37. Blumhofer, *Restoring the Faith*, 270–71.

the shift in identity as progressing from "pilgrims" to becoming "citizens" of the world.[38] A pivotal moment in the movement toward the mainstream came by identifying with Fundamentalism during the 1920s to 1930s, which she believes was the beginning of the quest to gain acceptance into the broader evangelical world.[39] She says, "Deemphasizing restorationism and millenarianism, they opted, rather, to perceive Pentecostalism as a 'full gospel' fundamentalism with a difference."[40] That progression continued with the AG's prominence with the National Association of Evangelicals in the 1960s. Blumhofer argues that what resulted was the "evangelicalization" and "institutionalization" that has undermined the AG's Pentecostal identity and contributed to the abandonment of its restorationist roots. Blumhofer also tackled some of the questions of origins, the treatment of women, and the less flattering aspects of the AG story.

Another study focusing on AG origin stories from an ethical perspective is Howard N. Kenyon's *Ethics in the Age of the Spirit*.[41] Kenyon explores the ethical pulse of the AG regarding attitudes toward race, the role of women, and shifting positions on war. While some histories engage these issues, Kenyon carefully follows these issues from the beginning of the AG into the modern day. He argues that while early Pentecostalism maintained its theological commitments, its ethical commitments have been subject to cultural accommodation as it matured toward legitimacy. The AG took a primarily "reactive" position regarding race relations, women in ministry, and participation in war.[42] Kenyon argues that the ethical impulses of the early years had threads of liberation, reconciliation, and justice while maintaining eschatological fervor and passion for the Spirit. A few other critical historical works have been published in recent years that also look at some of these particular aspects of AG history, including the role of women, ecumenism, and pacifism.[43]

The only other academic study to explore AG origins is Terry Minter's unpublished PhD thesis, where he revisits the theological and historical

---

38. Blumhofer, *Restoring the Faith*, 4–9. This shift has four stages: restorationist beginnings, association with Fundamentalism, mid-century institutionalization, and identification with the mainstream Evangelicalism.

39. Blumhofer, *Restoring the Faith*, 5–6.

40. Blumhofer, *Restoring the Faith*, 137.

41. Kenyon, *Ethics in the Age*.

42. Kenyon, *Ethics in the Age*, 293–94.

43. Alexander, *Peace to War*; Qualls, "God Forgive Us"; Ziefle, *David du Plessis*.

contributions of Charles Parham to the theology of the AG.[44] He argues that the nucleus of Pentecostal ministers that eventually became the AG were drawn from Parham's Apostolic Faith network and the Christian and Missionary Alliance rather than Azusa Street Mission. While these connections are not necessarily new contributions, his study is a deeper dive into these trajectories in an attempt to recenter the narrative of the AG's origins from Azusa back to Topeka.

THE TASK AHEAD

The task ahead for this project is to bring to light specific aspects of the origins of the AG that have emerged in the decades since these previous studies. While not a comprehensive retelling, this book is a series of essays that explore different historiographical issues that will clarify or correct historical narratives with new research. First, from a multicultural roots perspective, chapter 2 will revisit the early relationship with the Church of God in Christ and the AG and will explore the issues related to interpreting that history. Chapters 3 and 4 will explore how the AG's theological identity as an evangelical body was formed and will attempt to clarify the finished work stream and theology that differentiated the AG among early Pentecostal streams. Chapters 5 and 6 add details on the eschatological influences and eschatological varieties from AG-published books in the early years. The final two chapters will explore several social-political perspectives on the AG's early ethos, including attitudes toward education, social engagement, and theological methods. Some three decades since the last AG history, this volume will shed new light on these important theological and cultural issues to better understand its roots. Perhaps these conversations will help the AG understand its history to better approach the issues facing the denomination today.

---

44. Minter, "Antecedents to the Assemblies of God."

Chapter 2

Aspects of the Name

INTRODUCTION

THE CIRCUMSTANCES SURROUNDING THE formation of the Assemblies of God in 1914 have been scrutinized in recent years. Specifically, there are questions about why a group of primarily white Pentecostal ministers led by Howard Goss and E. N. Bell was named "Churches of God in Christ," the same name as C. H. Mason's black Pentecostal denomination that began in 1897. This association was first noted in 1950 by J. R. Flower, who claimed the white group was named "Church of God in Christ" because of an early agreement between C. H. Mason and Howard Goss.[1] From 1912 to 1914, this group organized in that name until several other Pentecostal networks joined together to form the Assemblies of God. This claim of association has become the basis for the belief that these white Church of God in Christ ministers broke away from Mason's leadership to start a white organization.[2] This chapter will explore the historiographical issues surrounding these claims and will seek to understand the early relationship between these two important Pentecostal denominations

---

1. Flower, *In the Last Days*, 8. Several earlier typed manuscripts were distributed in CBC classes in 1938, 1944, 1947, 1950, and 1952.

2. Daniels, "Charles Harrison Mason," 254–70.

Aspects of the Name

BECOMING THE WHITE CHURCH OF GOD IN CHRIST

Between 1906 and 1912, considerable shifts occurred in Charles Parham's Apostolic Faith Movement. In 1907, Parham was accused of sexual immorality and self-aggrandizement by declaring himself the head of the Pentecostal Movement.[3] By May 1907, the Apostolic Faith Movement in Texas, led by W. F. Carothers and Howard Goss, disavowed Parham as the leader of the movement.[4] Over the next few years, leadership in Apostolic Faith circles in the South shifted to Howard Goss, E. N. Bell, and M. M. Pinson. For a short time, this group rallied around William Durham and the finished work message. After Durham passed, Bell and Goss reasserted their leadership over the networks of ministers by publicly disavowing Parham for not repenting and confessing his sins.[5] Bell and Goss also wanted to distance themselves from the name "Apostolic Faith" and sought a new name to refer to the Pentecostal network they were leading.

In February 1911, a small group of ministers in Alabama led by H. G. Rodgers and M. M. Pinson adopted the name "Church of God" but were not affiliated with A. J. Tomlinson.[6] Pinson claims that he and Rodgers met with Tomlinson about using the name (possibly in 1908). Tomlinson approved of them using the name but "did not need to be connected to him" since it was the biblical name for the true church wherever it met.[7] In 1910, Rodgers and Pinson were ministering in Church of God (Cleveland, Tennessee) circles in Alabama.[8] Rodgers held an interstate convention in November 1911 at Montgomery, Alabama, but they did not mention the name they used.[9]

In July 1912, Howard Goss hosted a regional interstate camp meeting in Eureka Springs, Arkansas, where "Churches of God in Christ" was first used. Bell reported that about five hundred ministers of the "Churches of God in Christ of the Apostolic Faith" had gathered.[10] Pinson, Goss, Opperman, and Bell were appointed leaders over the group of ministers. A roster

3. See Martin, *Charles Fox Parham*, ch. 9.
4. "Parham Is Rallying Forces," 5.
5. Bell, "Notice about Parham," 3.
6. "Minutes of Church of God, Slocomb, AL."
7. M. M. Pinson to J. R. Flower, December 19, 1950; M. M. Pinson to J. R. Flower, January 10, 1951, 3.
8. Standifer, "Testimony for Jesus," 5.
9. "Convention Notices," 2.
10. "Glory and Unity," 1.

Aspects of Assemblies of God Origins

of ministers from Texas, Oklahoma, Alabama, Missouri, Iowa, and Arkansas was created to register with the clergy bureau.[11] From that point, the COGIC name was used for the various state associations across the South. In August 1912, W. T. Gaston announced that the Oklahoma "state camp meeting of the Church of God in Christ" was held in Tulsa.[12] In February 1913, D. C. O. Opperman announced the "Interstate Campmeeting of the Churches of God in Christ" in Meridian, Mississippi, to be held in June.[13] By October 1913, Rodgers (who had previously used Church of God) led the annual convention of the "Church of God in Christ as assembled at Dothan, Ala," where they passed a resolution to send delegates to the upcoming "General Assembly," referring to the General Council being planned in Hot Springs in April.[14]

In December 1913, Goss, Bell, Pinson, Opperman, and A. P. Collins signed a call for the "General Convention of the Pentecostal Saints and Churches of God in Christ" to be held in Hot Springs, Arkansas, in April 1914.[15] The call includes a list of over three hundred ministers ordained in this white COGIC group. When the Hot Springs meeting began, ministers from the white COGIC and several other Pentecostal groups from the upper Midwest from Christian and Missionary Alliance and Zion City backgrounds joined together to cooperate in Pentecostal ministry.[16] Also present at the Council was C. H. Mason, who was invited to preach a message. There were also a number of other black ministers in attendance, although it is unclear if they were ministers from the region or if they traveled with Mason.[17] During the meeting, the Council decided to adopt a new name, "Assemblies of God," which was intended to be an umbrella name for all the groups that were present, including all "Churches of God in Christ, Assemblies of God, and various Apostolic Faith Churches and Full

---

11. "Ordained Ministers," August 1, 1912.
12. "State Camp Meeting," 7.
13. "Interstate Campmeeting to Be Held," 1.
14. "Minutes of the Annual Convention." Also see Tomlin, "Dothan Camp Good," 1.
15. Pinson et al., "General Convention of the Pentecostal Saints," 1.
16. Flower's roots go deep, but he was not part of the white COGIC group before the AG was formed; rather he was part of another group from Indiana called "Association of Christian Assemblies." Brumback, *Like a River*, 17.
17. Burnett, "Forty Years Ago," 13. However, Burnett notes that the "colored" ministers were segregated into the balcony, but fully participated and even led in song from the balcony.

ASPECTS OF THE NAME

Gospel Pentecostal Missions, and Assemblies of like faith."[18] Bell notes that the decision to adopt the name was accompanied by "the glory of the Lord" and a message in tongues in which God said, "I have guided all in this."[19] The account of that meeting includes the statement that Mason "blessed the council for this action."[20] Thus, the AG was formed as a cooperative fellowship of Pentecostal ministers, missionaries, and churches.

THE ORIGINS OF THE NARRATIVE

What was the nature of the relationship between this white group and Mason's COGIC group? None of the early histories of the Pentecostal movement mention any connection between the two bodies. The first person to mention this relationship was J. R. Flower, who wrote a course on AG history for Central Bible College in 1949. Since the call to Hot Springs invited the "Churches of God in Christ," and it was widely known that this was also the name of Mason's group, Flower needed to research the history to understand the nature of the relationship for himself. In this history, Flower first claimed that the name "Church of God in Christ" came from an early agreement between Mason and Goss in 1910. Flower wrote that he read in Goss's diary the following: "With the consent of Elder C. H. Mason a white organization was formed, using the name 'Church of God in Christ.'"[21]

Flower's claim was instrumental in the first wave of academic histories clarifying the relationship between the two, but each had different ways of characterizing it. In 1961, Klaude Kendrick cites Flower's document to claim Goss "received permission to issue credentials to other minsters of his association in the name of the Church of God in Christ."[22] But, Kendrick adds that "no association existed between the two bodies." Similarly, Carl Brumback claims Goss "received permission to borrow the name" but that "there was to be no organizational union."[23] In 1971, Menzies quotes Vinson Synan's 1971 published dissertation that "many of the men who founded the white 'Assemblies of God' church in 1914, were thus ordained

---

18. *GC Constitution and Bylaws* (April 2–12, 1914) 1.
19. "Hot Springs Assembly," 1.
20. Bell, "General Council Special," 1.
21. Flower, "History of the Assemblies of God" (1949) 17.
22. Kendrick, *Promise Fulfilled*, 79–80.
23. Brumback, *Like a River*, 4.

in the Church of God in Christ by Bishop Mason."²⁴ However, Menzies does not address Flower's document or reference his assertion about Goss, as Kendrick did. By claiming it was Mason himself that ordained "many" of the founders, Synan asserts a more substantial connection than was previously stated. However, Synan provides no additional evidence for this assertion, citing only Kendrick (who cited Flower).²⁵ In 1971, Leonard Lovett followed Synan's characterization and claims "many white ministers from Pentecostal fellowships, including the Assemblies of God, were ordained by the late Bishop Charles H. Mason."²⁶ However, Lovett too cites no source for this claim. Two decades later, Edith Blumhofer takes a much less certain position and claims that "Goss had apparently visited C. H. Mason of the Churches of God in Christ and received credentials from that group. . . . Goss recorded in his diary that he obtained from Mason permission to issue papers."²⁷ Yet, Blumhofer's source is Flower's 1950 claim, not Goss's diary. Since Flower's first mention, no additional evidence of this association has been discovered.

By 2012, Ithiel Clemmons expanded on Synan's assertion of "many leaders" ordained by Mason to claim, "Bishop Mason ordained some 350 white ministers who later withdrew from the Church of God in Christ to form the Assemblies of God."²⁸ It is clear from Clemmons's characterization that the narrative had greatly expanded to say that Mason credentialed all those who became the AG in 1914. Estrelda Alexander is uncertain about the nature of the agreement between Mason and Goss but notes that either way, the ministers were ready to disassociate from the "agreement" with Mason by forming their own white group.²⁹ This assumption is clearly in Raybon Newman's book *Race and the Assemblies of God*, which definitively concludes that the AG was "formed" by the racial separation from Mason as an act of intentional segregation.³⁰ Today, this narrative has become almost universally accepted and is used to assert that the AG abandoned the "parentage" of Mason to form a white organization.

---

24. Menzies, *Anointed to Serve*, 64.
25. Synan, *Holiness-Pentecostal Tradition*, 153–54.
26. Lovett, "Black Origins of the Pentecostal Movement," 138–39.
27. Blumhofer, *Assemblies of God*, 1:132–33; Blumhofer, *Restoring the Faith*, 83.
28. Clemmons, *Bishop C.H. Mason*, 70.
29. Alexander, *Black Fire*, 269.
30. Newman, *Race and the Assemblies of God*.

INTERROGATING THE NARRATIVE

As the review has shown, every claim of the association between Mason and Goss can be traced back to one source: Flower's 1950 claim. Yet, there are several historiographical issues with this origin story. First is the uncertain nature of what Flower claims about the relationship between Goss and Mason.[31] The first mention is in Flower's 1949 history that claimed, "with the consent of Elder C. H. Mason a white organization was formed, using the name 'Church of God in Christ.'"[32] This can be read in several ways depending on what was consented to. Flower could be saying Mason gave consent for Goss to form a white organization under him using the name. However, it could also be saying that Mason gave consent for Goss to "use the name" for his white organization. The former interpretation implies that it is the same group (Mason's) with the same name (COGIC) but a different constituency (white). The latter interpretation suggests it was another group using the same name. It is not surprising, then, that the narrative of shared origins was built by this claim. But it is unclear precisely what Flower meant.

Clarity was added to this claim in a series of letters between Flower and M. M. Pinson in 1950 and 1951 as Flower sought confirmation of these facts. Flower told Pinson that he got the information about Mason from Goss's diary. He claimed that Goss "obtained from Elder Mason permission to issue papers using that name 'Church of God in Christ' for the white work in Texas."[33] This is a slightly different claim than in 1949. Here, he phrased it as Mason gave permission to "issue papers using the name" rather than "form an organization." Brumback, who also had access to these letters, interpreted Flower's words accordingly. He rewords this to say Goss had permission to "borrow the name" from Mason.[34] By 1962, when GPH published a formal booklet of Flower's history, it does not name Mason; it only says the group "changed its name to the Church of God in Christ, in agreement with the leaders of the Colored Church with the same name."[35]

---

31. Flower's first attempt at telling the AG's origin story was a 1938 pamphlet published by GPH with a brief history called *Origin and Development of the Assemblies of God*. This account makes no mention of this relationship. A decade later, Flower had added to his AG history notes for a class he taught at Central Bible College.

32. Flower, "History of the Assemblies of God" (1949), 17.

33. J. R. Flower to M. M. Pinson, January 4, 1950.

34. Brumback, *Like a River*, 4.

35. Flower, *In the Last Days*, 8.

Here, the emphasis is also on using "the same name," not forming an organizational affiliation, but the language is admittedly somewhat ambiguous. Based on Flower's account, the only clear thing is that Flower understood that Mason allowed Goss to "use the name." This could imply that these ministers were part of Mason's organization but a separate white branch, but it could also be Goss wanting the courtesy of using the name Church of God in Christ.

The second major issue is the testimony of M. M. Pinson, one of the core leaders of the white COGIC, who specifically denies this relationship ever happened. As mentioned, Pinson was a leader with Rodgers's Church of God group in Alabama and was part of the group that called the General Council. When Flower presented this narrative to Pinson in 1950, Pinson commented that he did not know anything about the white COGIC group being under Mason's COGIC.[36] Not only had Pinson not heard that story, but he also found it difficult to believe because Jim Crow laws in the South would require a separate charter to be a legal entity that the government would recognize. It should also be noted that Pinson is not the only person to deny this relationship. COGIC scholar Elton Weaver notes that one of the living COGIC bishops of that era, Bishop David Hall, claimed that no one in the COGIC knew of any such association.[37] The first-hand knowledge that there was no association should give substantial weight to doubts about the validity of Flower's claim and perhaps indicates that how it has been interpreted should be reconsidered.

The third problem is that Flower's statement that he got that information from Goss's diary is also problematic. Flower claimed Goss's diary states that he visited with Mason in 1907, where he received ordination and got permission to form the white COGIC group. Yet, Robin Johnson, Goss's biographer, is unclear where Flower could have learned that information in Goss's diary. He notes, "none of his diaries from 1907 through 1913 record any meetings between him and C. H. Mason."[38] Also, Goss's COGIC papers are signed by Bell, Collins, Opperman, and S. D. Kinne on July 25, 1911, not by Mason in 1907.[39] The fact that the diary does not make such a claim

---

36. M. M. Pinson to J. R. Flower, January 10, 1951. See also Rodgers, "Assemblies of God and the Long Journey," 55.
37. Weaver, *Bishop Charles H. Mason*, 192–93.
38. Johnson, *Howard A. Goss*, 76.
39. Johnson, *Howard A. Goss*, 76.

as Flower asserted and Goss's COGIC credentials are not signed by Mason is a significant piece of evidence to undermine the whole narrative.

Though the diary does not mention Mason, it is possible that Flower could be referring to Goss's biography *The Winds of God* (written by his wife), where he commented:

> For some years now, we had no organization beyond a "gentleman's agreement," with the understanding for the withdrawing of fellowship from the untrustworthy. There was, however, an association of ministers called "Church of God in Christ" to which a few of us belonged from 1910–1914, mainly for the purpose of business.[40]

It mentions using the COGIC name but does not mention any meeting with Mason or receiving credentials in 1907 from him, as Flower claimed. Still, based on the information in the biography, it seems more plausible that this is the source Flower read that he used to make his assertion, not his diary.

If the above quote from Goss's biography is the source for Flower's claim, there are more issues with this account's plausibility. Notice that the passage does not claim Goss met with Mason to be credentialed or receive permission to "use the name." Instead it appears that Flower assumed the "gentleman's agreement" was referring to an assumed agreement with Mason to use the name. This is a mistake also made by later historians as they describe this relationship as a "gentleman's agreement" or "courtesy" on Mason's part.[41] But that is beyond what Goss was saying here. The "gentleman's agreement" mentioned here describes the nature of the voluntary association of ministers in the Apostolic Faith Movement that "had no organization" before the 1910–14 association.[42] Howard Kenyon sees the vague language as Goss intentionally trying to "downplay the actual association" between him and Mason.[43] If this account does not claim an association between Goss and Mason, and Johnson is correct that it nowhere appears in Goss's diary, it appears that Flower misconstrued Goss's claim of

---

40. Goss, *Winds of God*, 163.

41. Weaver, *Bishop Charles H. Mason*, 192; Newman, *Race and the Assemblies of God*, 63; Synan, *Holiness-Pentecostal Tradition*, 153–54, Kenyon, *Ethics in the Age*, 59.

42. Blumhofer, *Restoring the Faith*, 83, makes this connection correctly, which I believe is more accurate.

43. Kenyon, *Ethics in the Age*, 57–59. But he also notes that it is "extremely difficult" to know the actual nature of that agreement.

a "gentleman's agreement." Yet the whole narrative and all of the scholarship asserting this origin story is based upon this mischaracterization.

How could Flower have read into this account such an association that is not mentioned? One explanation could be that Flower may have conflated the stories of Pinson's group using the name Church of God with Goss's supposed testimony in his diary or biography. Consider that Flower wrongly claims that Goss met with Mason in Arkansas in 1907, where he was credentialed. However, there is no record in Goss's diary or biography that he ever met with Mason. By contrast, Pinson told Flower that he met Mason at a meeting in Memphis with G. B. Cashwell in 1907, where he received the baptism in the Holy Spirit.[44] In addition, Flower claimed Goss got permission from Mason to "use the name" in 1907. This is remarkably similar to Pinson's story that he got "permission" from Tomlinson to "use the name" "Church of God" in 1908.[45] Considering it was Rogers and Pinson who first named their group "Church of God" in Alabama in February of 1911, rather than Goss or Bell, who were still using Apostolic Faith,[46] it is plausible that Flower's whole account was flawed to begin with. This is the difficulty of creating a narrative from oral histories decades after the events happen. Details get conflated, and sometimes evidence is read in a way that may not be historically accurate. Interestingly, Flower seems to have backed off this claim after his correspondence with Pinson. This is demonstrated as the 1962 published version did not mention the relationship between Mason and Goss but maintained it was in "agreement with the leaders of the Colored church."[47]

The doubt cast upon this narrative is not limited to white or AG scholars. COGIC historian Elton Weaver also doubts there was an agreement between Mason and Goss to "use the name" in any formal sense. He notes that from 1907 to 1911, Mason was fighting in court against C. P. Jones for his rights to use the name.[48] Therefore, there could be no way for Mason to "lend" the name to Goss to form a new organization in any formal way. Weaver believes the lack of Mason signing credentials for white ministers

---

44. M. M. Pinson to J. R. Flower, January 10, 1951, 3; Burnett, "Forty Years Ago," 13.

45. M. M. Pinson to J. R. Flower, December 19, 1950, 3; M. M. Pinson to J. R. Flower, January 10, 1951, 3.

46. Goss and Bell, "State Encampment," 10. There are no other records of Goss using name Apostolic Faith or Church of God in Christ until the July 1912 camp meeting.

47. Flower, *In the Last Days*, 8.

48. Weaver, *Bishop Charles H. Mason*, 193.

was part and parcel of the racist ideas of the time. He asserts, "whites did not want Mason to sign their credentials. Instead, they had the white leadership sign them."[49]

On the other hand, COGIC scholar David Daniels does believe there was a formal relationship between Goss and Mason since Mason allowed other white groups to form under his fellowship. He notes that Mason was open to having white branches of his COGIC fellowship.[50] The problem with this is that his examples are Goss and Pinson (which is under question) and L. P. Adams, who was already associated with Goss and was on the 1912 white roster.[51] There was a formal move to establish a white COGIC fellowship initiated by Mason that took place in 1916, led by William Holt.[52] While this does demonstrate Mason's interracial impulse, and could suggest the possibility that an agreement with Goss was an earlier attempt, there is no evidence that Mason was allowing Goss to do in 1910 what he asked Holt to do in 1916.

The final problem is the plausibility that this finished work group of ministers would be open to associating with Mason's Holiness-Pentecostal fellowship. If an association took place in 1907, that could be plausible because it was before the finished work debate. If it was 1910, as Goss's biography says, that would be more plausible as it was right at the beginning of the controversy.[53] Weaver claims that Goss and the white group used the finished work controversy to remove the group from under Mason's leadership.[54] However, Goss's credentials were signed by Bell and Collins in July 1911, in the middle of the controversy. There is only one record of ordination under the COGIC signed by Goss before June 1912.[55] The first recorded use of COGIC in advertisements was at the end of the contentious finished work controversy after Durham died in July 1912. After such

---

49. Weaver, *Bishop Charles H. Mason*, 193.

50. Daniels, "Charles Harrison Mason," 254–70.

51. Daniels notes that L. P. Adams was ordained by Mason. He also notes that Adams led a white COGIC group; however, Adams was on the 1912 list of white COGIC led by Goss and Bell but did not join the AG.

52. Daniels, "Charles Harrison Mason," 266.

53. Goss, *Winds of God*, 163.

54. Weaver, *Bishop Charles H. Mason*, 189. This is somewhat of an inconsistent position considering that later he claims no association occurred.

55. Burnett, "Forty Years Ago," 13; Warner, "Call for Love, Tolerance," 4. Goss's wife, Ethel, was ordained in the Apostolic Faith in December of 1911. If Goss was ordaining under COGIC in 1911, surely his wife would have those credentials.

consternation and advocacy about finished work theology from 1911 to 1912, it seems unlikely that finished work ministers would affiliate with a second work group in July 1912 and then disassociate months later. To do so would alienate the very constituency they were trying to organize. Instead, perhaps Goss felt at liberty to "use the name" because of his early association with Mason (if it happened). It is more plausible, perhaps, that Goss felt liberty to use the name (without consent) because of Mason's interracial impulse or a sense of racial privilege. Still, if that were the case, it would not explain why Mason was willing to come to the General Council in 1914 and "bless the action" of adopting the name Assemblies of God.[56] Ithiel Clemmons argues that the "blessing" Mason gave was to "bid them farewell" and allow them to leave his COGIC to start their denomination. Still, there is no citation or documentation of this inference from his account.[57]

Consequently, the uncertainty about the validity of Flower's claim should call into question the larger narrative of an association between Goss's group and Mason's. I agree with Darrin Rodgers that there is a lack of evidence that the AG was born by separating from Mason's COGIC. He argues, "There is little, if any, evidence known to exist that suggests that Mason and the founders of the Assemblies of God were once part of the same organization. Instead, they were members of different organizations both using the same name."[58] Rodgers is right to note that it is the name that they shared, not an ecclesiological relationship. Simply put, the origin story that the AG split off from under Mason does not appear correct.

CHOOSING THE NAME

If the white ministers led by Goss and Bell were not ordaining as a white branch of Mason's COGIC and were a separate group, then why did they want to "use the name" of the Church of God in Christ? A key piece of evidence that was missed by previous studies may bring clarity to this debated question. During the transitional time from 1910 to 1912, a series of incremental name changes took place for this association of ministers. Flower notes that to get out from under the name Apostolic Faith, they first started using the name "Church of God," with the "permission" of A. J. Tomlinson from the Church of God in Cleveland, Tennessee. Pinson notes

56. "Hot Springs Assembly," 1.
57. Clemmons, *Bishop C.H. Mason*, 71.
58. Clemmons, *Bishop C.H. Mason*, 54.

that he and H. G. Rogers had met with Tomlinson, and he allowed them to use the name.[59] But as not to confuse their group with Tomlinson, the trio of Pinson, Bell, and Goss instead started using "Churches of God in Christ," with some places adding "in unity with the Apostolic Faith" or "of the Apostolic Faith."[60]

The critical evidence for the motivation behind the change comes from the July 1912 convention in Eureka Springs, Arkansas. Bell testifies that a preacher (unnamed) gave a sermon on "the Church, the body of Christ, and how one gets into it."[61] Bell claims that this sermon "cleared up some difficulties" and the "friction" over the proper name for the body of Christ. This sermon inspired Bell and the Eureka Springs camp meeting leaders to begin using the name "Churches of God in Christ." The rationale was as follows, according to Bell:

> Nowhere in the Bible is a congregation of believers in Christ called a "mission" nor an "Apostolic Mission," but we read of "the church of God at Corinth" ... or the "churches of God" (2 Thes. 1:4), or the "Churches of God ... in Christ" 1 Thes. 2:14.... Why not all join with the Bible and with many of the Pentacostal [sic] and apostolic saints everywhere and call them "churches of God" and "Churches of God in Christ" as we are doing?[62]

Bell argued that Pentecostal bodies should be called by the biblical name "Churches of God" (which they had already abandoned to avoid confusion with Tomlinson) or "Churches of God in Christ." Although it is speculation, it is possible that Goss or Pinson gave this sermon, as they were already using the name. This sermon, not an association with Mason, led them to adopt the name.

The idea of Pentecostals adopting a "biblical name" to differentiate from other Christian groups was not novel. Seemingly, every new group sought out the most "biblical" name for Pentecostal believers, whom they believed to be the true body of Christ. A. J. Tomlinson led the Christian Union to adopt "Church of God" as its name in 1907.[63] Mason also testified that he received the name "Church of God in Christ" in a revelation in

---

59. "Minutes of Church of God, Slocomb, AL."
60. "Glory and Unity," 1. See also Rodgers, "Assemblies of God and the Long Journey," 56.
61. "Glory and Unity," 1.
62. Bell, "Not Missions," 2.
63. Roebuck, "Church of God, Cleveland."

Little Rock before he became Pentecostal.⁶⁴ According to the first COGIC General Secretary, Elder Justus Bowe, the Church of God in Christ wrestled with many of the same sentiments as Bell did in 1912. He says, "As to its name: In the New Testament the general name we find was 'Church of God,' 'Church of Christ,' 'Church of the saints.'"⁶⁵ Similarly, a group of Parham-associated Apostolic Faith churches that chose not to join the Assemblies of God formed in 1914 as the Church of God of Apostolic Faith.⁶⁶ In each of these cases, the name was an attempt to classify the true body of Christ, not give a name to their particular group, since nearly all early Pentecostal fellowships shunned denominationalism. Instead, they used this name to register with the Clergy Bureau to purchase property and receive clergy benefits legally. This suggests that the choice to use the name Church of God in Christ did not mean they were forming a white group under Mason; instead, they were using a biblical name, even as others adopted the same or similar names.

BECOMING THE ASSEMBLIES OF GOD

If the name Church of God in Christ was an attempt to adopt a biblical name, why the shift just a year and a half later in Hot Springs to "Assemblies of God"? First, it is important to note that the two names are essentially the same with different words. The Greek term *church* means "assembly." As a biblical name, "assembly of God" was considered an alternative expression of "Church of God," which Bell believed to be a more biblically accurate name. Second, is the influence of A. S. Worrell's *New Testament*, a Bible widely used by Pentecostals because he had a Pentecostal experience in 1891. One of the distinctive features of this Bible was the translation of the term *ecclesia* as "the assembly" instead of the term "church."⁶⁷ Worrell commented on his choice in the appendix, where he argued that the real problem with modern denominationalism is the result of a mistranslation of the word *ecclesia* as "church" instead of "assembly." He says, "The proper

---

64. Mason, *History and Life Work*, 70.

65. Mason, *History and Life Work*, 70.

66. See this history in Isgrigg, *Pentecost in Tulsa*, 20–22. The Church of God of Apostolic Faith organized in Ozark, Arkansas, led by Edwin Buckles, which has continued in influence in the Tulsa area. They integrated "church of God" with "apostolic faith" as the differentiator.

67. Kuykendall, "A. S. Worrell's *New Testament*," 254–80.

designation of a company of believers, answering to the New Testament ideal, is 'The assembly of God,' or 'The assembly of Christ,' at such and such place."[68] Worrell believed the assembly should be a free and cooperative independent gathering of believers, not an ecclesiastical consolidation of power by denominational bodies. This very argument was used by both B. F. Lawrence and T. K. Leonard, who are credited with choosing the name "Assemblies of God" in the first General Council.[69]

It is also important to note that they were not abandoning the previous names by choosing the name. They organized under this banner as an umbrella term under which "all the Apostolic Faith, Pentecostal, and previously labeled Churches of God in Christ" could cooperate.[70] As Glenn Gohr notes, the use of such names continued even after the AG was formed in 1914.[71] In 1915, Bell responded to the question, "Have you dropped the Churches of God in Christ?" to which Bell replied, "No indeed." He says, "We distinctly recognize and mention the 'Churches of God in Christ' as in fellowship and co-operation with us and all other Apostolic Faith and Pentecostal people."[72] Although the AG was formed, white COGIC churches continued, at least in theory. In fact, when a name change was discussed in 1927, J. R. Flower noted that a wide range of names continued to be used among the churches; very few used "Assembly of God."[73] So those present, when the name was adopted, were not arguing for a new name to replace COGIC because of any cultural, racial, or organizational issues with Mason's group.

CONCLUSION

The evidence in this chapter suggests a couple of ways in which the origin of the AG can be understood in relation to the Church of God in Christ. First, it is clear that Goss, Bell, and Pinson were part of a group of new leaders that inherited Parham's network but wanted to adopt a new name to replace the "Apostolic Faith." In the process, they first chose the Church

68. Worrell, *New Testament*, appendix C, 3.

69. Lawrence, "Assembly of God," 5–6; "Twelfth General Council," 6; Brumback, *Like a River*, 18.

70. *GC Constitution and Bylaws* (April 2–12, 1914), 1.

71. Gohr, "Assemblies of God," 11–15.

72. Bell, "Churches in Christ," 2.

73. "Twelfth General Council," 6.

of God with permission from Tomlinson. But they soon added "in Christ" to become Church of God in Christ. Second, it appears that either Flower misconstrued the relationship between Goss and Mason or confused the stories. There is no evidence that Goss had a relationship with Mason or that he got permission to use the name. There is evidence, however, that Pinson got permission to use the name "Church of God" and used it. There is also new evidence from Bell not found in other studies as to why it was expanded to "Church of God in Christ." Neither had to do with Goss and Mason; rather, it was, from the beginning, a quest to choose a proper biblical name. Having already affirmed that this was the proper name for the body of Christ by his own revelation of the "biblical" name, Mason did not object for the same reason Tomlinson did not object to this group using the "Church of God."

This suggests that rather than leaving Mason's group, they were already a separate group that changed names from Apostolic Faith to Church of God in Christ and then to the Assemblies of God. The fact that the group was majority white is symptomatic of the cultural situation of Pentecostal groups in the South. While having fellowship with black Pentecostal groups, the AG organized primarily among white Pentecostals. It is a legacy of separation, privilege, and unfortunate cultural accommodation that was not soon remedied in the AG. However, for the situation surrounding the founding of the AG, the shift in names does not appear to be an overtly racist abandonment of the "parentage" of Mason or his COGIC fellowship since no evidence exists that this was the case. Instead, it was a group navigating to their own identity and choosing their own name at a time when Pentecostal groups were struggling to differentiate without becoming another denomination.

Chapter 3

Aspects of the Finished Work Stream

INTRODUCTION

ONE OF THE IMPORTANT developments in the subject of Pentecostal origins is the recognition that there are two streams of Pentecostalism. During the first decade of the Pentecostal Movement, the leadership of the various groups came from the Wesleyan Holiness tradition and held to the doctrine of sanctification as a "second work of grace." As Steven Land has argued, the Wesleyan-Holiness orientation expressed by the five-fold gospel produced a vibrant Pentecostal spirituality characterized by a passion for the kingdom.[1] Wesleyan-Holiness Pentecostals emphasized sanctification as a definite work of grace that was needed to receive Spirit baptism. This position was held by most early Pentecostals, including Charles Parham, William Seymour, C. H. Mason, J. H. King, and A. J. Tomlinson. Most of these leaders belonged to the holiness tradition before they became Pentecostals.[2]

However, it has also been argued that the AG is part of a separate stream, labeled the "Finished Work," that developed over a theological argument about sanctification. Blumhofer and Menzies both recognize that many of the theological antecedents of the AG were from non-Wesleyan, Baptist, or Reformed evangelical traditions influenced by the Keswick stream of the Holiness Movement. Key figures in this stream, such as William Durham, Howard Goss, M. M. Pinson, and F. F. Bosworth, each accepted the doctrine of sanctification as a second work of grace, only to later

---

1. Land, *Pentecostal Spirituality*, 174–75..
2. Land, *Pentecostal Spirituality*, 186.

abandon the position in favor of a finished work position.[3] The rejection of this important holiness doctrine eventually resulted in forming a new Pentecostal stream that did not hold to holiness views of sanctification.

This chapter will examine how the AG became the primary locus of Finished Work Pentecostalism. It will give historical insights into the controversy that created the stream and the theological consequences of this position. While most scholars note the presence of the two streams, they have yet to articulate how the finished work perspective works out in the various tenets of Pentecostal theology. The chapter will begin with tracing the origins of finished work theology in the Durham controversy. Next, it will give insights into why the AG was the primary fellowship for finished work Pentecostals. Finally, it will explore critical theological insights into finished work theology.

DURHAM AND THE FINISHED WORK

The controversy over the role of sanctification began within Pentecostal ranks when William Durham proclaimed the message of the finished work of Christ in 1910. Durham was a highly influential Pentecostal leader in the Midwest and a pastor in Chicago.[4] Chicago was no stranger to revivalist evangelical movements. During the late 1800s, it became an influential center of Keswick theology because of D. L. Moody, Moody Bible Institute, and Revell Press. Chicago was also the home of the controversial healing evangelist John Alexander Dowie. From 1907 to 1910, Chicago became a center for Pentecostalism in the Midwest because of William Durham's North Avenue Mission and the Stone Church pastored by William Piper.

Durham was converted in a Baptist church in 1889. In 1903, he began his ministry when he was ordained in the World's Missionary Faith Association (WMFA). While in the WMFA, Durham traveled with G. L. Morgan, an evangelist who preached about the "finished work of Christ" but did not teach the Holiness position of the second work of grace.[5] It was in this context, which was similar to the Christian and Missionary Alliance, that he came to understand the concept of the "finished work" of Christ.[6] At

---

3. Faupel, *Everlasting Gospel*, 260.
4. Jacobsen, *Thinking in the Spirit*, 139.
5. Blumhofer, "William H. Durham," 123–42.
6. Funk declares, "Many Christians are not living here and many are not comprehending their full privileges in Christ in the heavenlies. But that is our place, we have access

some unknown point, Durham had a powerful experience of sanctification that he believed to be the baptism in the Spirit.[7]

In 1907, Durham decided to visit the Azusa Street Mission after hearing testimonies from people baptized in the Spirit there. After several weeks of seeking, Durham experienced the baptism in the Spirit and testified that God "finished the work" when he spoke in tongues.[8] Following his baptism in the Spirit, Durham experienced a crisis of faith that began a three-year investigation into the doctrine of sanctification.[9] Durham had been taught in holiness circles that his experience of sanctification was the baptism in the Spirit described in Acts. But after he received the Pentecostal baptism in the Spirit, which he knew was true because he spoke in tongues, he concluded that the teaching of sanctification as a definite work was not scriptural.

Early in 1911, Durham went public about his views on sanctification.[10] He forcefully renounced the doctrine, calling it "one of the weakest and most unscriptural doctrines that is being taught in the Pentecostal movement, and therefore ought to be ruled out as damaging."[11] Durham's meetings in Chicago were used to promote his finished work doctrine. Durham was surprised by the backlash that followed, commenting that "it had never occurred to me that it would be made a test of fellowship."[12] Durham immediately went on the defensive and began to interpret the resistance as a battle for the truth of the gospel. In July 1910, Durham identified the battle for the finished work as the first "great crisis" of the Pentecostal

---

to it through Christ's finished work.... Now as we take our place, we have entrance into all the spiritual blessings. They are handed down to us in, if we may so call them, sealed packages through the finished work of Christ." Funk, "In the Heavenlies," 2–3.

7. Durham, "Chicago Evangelist's Pentecost," 4. Durham later contradicted this testimony, claiming, "I had never believed that sanctification and baptism in the Holy Spirit were one and the same thing." Durham, "What Is the Evidence." Durham, "Chicago Evangelist's Pentecost," 4.

8. Durham, "Chicago Evangelist's Pentecost," 4.

9. Faupel, *Everlasting Gospel*, 266–67.

10. The actual issue, *Pentecostal Testimony* 1.7 (Feb. 1911), where he announced his new doctrine is lost to historians. However, Durham, "Sanctification," 1, describes the article and the effect it had on the movement. See also Durham, "Great Battle of Nineteen Eleven," 6.

11. Durham, "Sanctification," 1.

12. Durham, "Great Battle of Nineteen Eleven," 6.

Movement.[13] Over the next two years, his rhetoric became more hostile toward holiness positions.

Durham's obsession eventually led him to target what he thought was the focal point of error: the Azusa Street Revival. In 1911, he left Chicago to preach in the Azusa Mission while Seymour was absent. Durham admonished Seymour's congregation to abandon the second work theology. After several months, Seymour returned to find him preaching against the second work and tried to regain control of the mission. Durham rallied support for his position from Carrie Judd Montgomery, Frank Bartleman, George Studd, Frank Ewart, and F. F. Bosworth. Durham's antagonistic attempts to persuade "second work" Pentecostals caused a regrettable rift in the movement and pitted these two theological streams against each other.[14]

Durham gave three primary objections to the teaching of sanctification as a second work of grace. The first objection was that although the Bible taught the doctrine of sanctification, it was unscriptural to teach that it is a definite work of grace. He commented, "To my unbounded astonishment, I found that there is not even one Scripture that teaches that it is received as a second, definite, instantaneous work of grace."[15] Durham claimed that if holiness ministers could present "even one scripture" that defended the doctrine, he would stop preaching against it. Instead, he noted that the only defense holiness advocates had was "experience" or the "teachings of men."[16]

Second, Durham believed the second work of grace denied the sufficiency of salvation. He questioned how holiness people could teach that salvation does not settle the issue of sin in conversion. If salvation does not cleanse the believer, then how can they be saved? He says, "I deny that a man who is converted or born again is outwardly washed and cleansed and his heart left unclean with enmity against God in it."[17] For Durham, sanctification was the result of the finished work of Jesus on the cross. It is a

---

13. Durham, "Editorial," 4.

14. Durham, "Work of God in Los Angeles," 11; Durham, "Great Crisis Number Two," 4.

15. Durham, "Great Battle of Nineteen Eleven," 7.

16. Durham says, "I can nowhere find where Wesley ever taught dogmatically that sanctification is and must be a second instantaneous work." Durham, "Sanctification," 1.

17. Durham, "Some Other Phases of Sanctification," 9.

Aspects of the Finished Work Stream

"continual work or operation of the free grace of God" rather than a second work of grace.[18]

Third, Durham believed that the primary reason people believed the doctrine was because the Holiness Movement misunderstood the true nature of the baptism in the Spirit.[19] Pentecostals rightly noted that sanctification is not the baptism in the Holy Spirit. But, he says, "The mistake of the age is misnaming the experience."[20] He believed when holiness Pentecostals argued for this position, they were ultimately taking a non-Pentecostal position. The whole purpose of the Pentecostal Movement was to bring to light the true nature of the biblical experience of baptism in the Spirit. The true problem with the second work of grace was that it was depending on the Acts narrative to explain both the baptism in the Spirit and the experience of sanctification. He argues, "While one instance after another of conversion and receiving the Holy Spirit is recorded, not one single case is recorded where anyone got sanctified as a second, instantaneous work of grace."[21] Durham believed that the Pentecostal baptism experience should replace the holiness experience of sanctification. He says, "It is a lamentable thing to see Pentecostal people adding another experience and urging people to seek for three definite experiences, when they should stand with the Word of God for the only two it teaches in any place, namely conversion and the baptism in the Holy Spirit."[22]

Durham's chief concern was not the doctrine of sanctification as much as it was to uphold what he believed to be a biblical doctrine of baptism in the Spirit. This is demonstrated in his absolute conviction about the finished work and tongues as evidence. He says, "Brethren, the 'Finished Work of Calvary' and the baptism in the Holy Spirit and the tongues as evidence of it are the living issues of this day."[23] The finished work view corrected Holiness views of salvation, and initial evidence clarified the doctrine of Spirit baptism. The two doctrines worked together.

> When he receives Christ, he receives a full salvation in Him. He is now ready for the next great experience of receiving the Holy Spirit. This is always a definite experience. It is invariably accompanied

---

18. Durham, "Some Other Phases of Sanctification," 9.
19. Durham, "Open Letter," 12.
20. Durham, "Great Revival at Azusa Street Mission," 7.
21. Durham, "Sanctification," 1.
22. Durham, "Great Revival at Azusa Street Mission," 7.
23. Durham, "Great Battle of Nineteen Eleven," 7.

by the speaking in other tongues, as the Spirit gives utterance, as in the case of the Apostles at Pentecost. When a man receives the Holy Spirit, he is sealed unto the day of redemption. The baptism in the Holy Spirit, then, is the seal of a finished salvation in Jesus Christ.[24]

At first, Durham did not accept the doctrine of tongues as evidence and even opposed it.[25] But after seeing people receive the baptism and seeing that tongues always followed when people received and careful examination of scripture, he became convinced that "no truth is better established that people speak in tongues when they are baptized in the Holy Spirit."[26] Many rejected tongues as evidence because they were confused about the nature of the experience.[27] Durham believed that when Pentecostals compromise on the doctrine of evidence, they remove the power from it. He says, "Wherever they cease in any place to teach that the tongues are the evidence the power of God lifts and they have very few baptisms anymore."[28] Thus, Durham's prioritization of the experience of Spirit-baptism and emphasis on the evidence of Speaking in tongues was carried into the Assemblies of God.

A NEW PENTECOSTAL STREAM

The controversy with Durham revealed a separate theological stream within Pentecostalism that eventually resulted in the creation of the AG. Between 1910 and 1914, the Pentecostal Movement in the Midwest experienced several shifts in leadership that allowed this finished work stream to come to the forefront. After Parham's demise, E. N. Bell and Howard Goss took over the leadership of the Apostolic Faith movement, especially in the South.[29] Meanwhile, Durham was becoming the leader of the Pentecostal

---

24. Durham, "Two Great Experiences," 5.
25. Durham, "What Is the Evidence," 4.
26. Durham, "What Is the Evidence," 5.
27. Durham, "Speaking in Tongues," 10. Durham believed this was confirmed when holiness people were baptized in the Spirit in his meetings. He says, "Those who had been confident that they received the Holy Spirit before, and thus opposed this teaching, knew two things: first that they never had the baptism before; second that the doctrine that the tongues is the evidence was true." Durham, "Speaking in Tongues," 10.
28. Durham, "Speaking in Tongues," 11. It is likely here that Durham has the Azusa mission in his mind. See also Durham "Great Revival at Azusa Street Mission," 3–4.
29. Bell, "Notice about Parham," 3.

Aspects of the Finished Work Stream

movement in Chicago, and his message of the finished work was becoming the dominant position of Pentecostals in the central states.[30]

When Durham died unexpectedly in July of 1912, Bell and Goss were perfectly positioned to step in after Durham's death and become the new leaders of this association because of their position as regional leaders and champions of Durham's theology. After Durham's death, Bell continued to promote Durham's position on the finished work but with a more generous tone.[31] Bell recognizes that Durham's position "has been held and preached by many evangelical preachers for hundreds of years such as Charles Haddon Spurgeon and others, which was given new prominence by Durham."[32] In 1913, M. M. Pinson championed Durham's mission by making his way to Los Angeles and convinced Pentecostals of the finished work.[33] In the meantime, Bell and Goss issued credentials to 352 ministers with the white Churches of God in Christ, which would become the bedrock of leadership for the future Assemblies of God.[34]

When the call came in 1913 for a meeting of the Apostolic Faith and Churches of God in Christ, it was signed by five prominent leaders promoting the finished work: Bell, Goss, Collins, Pinson, and D. C. O. Opperman.[35] At the first General Council, Pinson gave the keynote address on the "Finished Work."[36] The second General Council was held in Chicago at the Stone Church, the center of the finished work camp.[37] Pinson recounts how he was once a "stickler for the second work of grace" and taught it. But after reading the books on holiness, he studied his Bible and found

---

30. Minter, "Antecedents to the Assemblies of God," 207.

31. Bell, "Cleansing and Holiness," 2; Pinson, "Sanctified in Christ," 4; Bell, "Second Blessing," 2, all echo Durham that the teaching sanctification is unscriptural, that it is not the baptism in the Holy Spirit, and object that it is the most superior attainment.

32. Bell, "Finished Work," 2.

33. Pinson, "From Los Angeles," 1.

34. For a list of all the ministers ordained under the Churches of God in Christ prior to the first General Council, see *Word and Witness*, Dec. 20, 1913, 4.

35. Bell, "Cleansing and Holiness," 2; Pinson, "Sanctified in Christ," 4; Pinson, "From Los Angeles," 1; Bell, "Second Blessing," 2; Bell, "Finished Work," 2.

36. Pinson's address was reprinted in 1964 in the *Evangel* but does not appear in the original minutes. Pinson, "Finished Work of Calvary," 7, 26–27.

37. The centrality of Chicago as an influence on the AG is so strong that Minter wonders, "would the denomination (AG) have been established if the Azusa Street Revival had never occurred?" Minter, "Antecedents to the Assemblies of God," 22. Minter's broader point is that the finished work movement can conceivably stand on its own as a separate stream.

that sanctification came through the cross. Despite his differences with the doctrine, he believed Holiness Pentecostals to be "sweet people" and encouraged people not to disfellowship them.

Though most of the founding members of the AG were supporters of Durham's finished work doctrine, many did not agree with the divisiveness of Durham's efforts. Instead, they called for a "theological truce" to the controversy.[38] After the initial years, the AG paid little attention to the distinctions over sanctification. As Bruce Rosdahl notes, the Statement of Fundamental Truths adopted the language of the second work position but reflected the Alliance theology of identification with Christ.[39]

Although most leaders moved on from the controversy shortly after the AG formed, some Holiness Pentecostal leaders continued to discuss it. For example, J. H. King credited the origin of the finished work doctrine to J. N. Darby and the Brethren. He condemned it as a "damnable heresy" that is nothing more than "Antinomianism, Darbyism dressed up in Zinzindorfian [sic] garb."[40] Pentecostal Holiness apologist W. H. Turner also defended Holiness doctrine against the AG and other finished work groups in 1948. Turner remarked that the major sin this "Calvinistic doctrine" is that "thousands have been urged to tarry for the infilling of the Holy Ghost without having received heart purity and this has led to all sorts of errors."[41] Turner followed King in claiming the finished work doctrine originated with Count Zinzendorf and was taken up by the Plymouth Brethren, who coined the term "finished work."[42] Zinzendorf was noted for his pietistic Christocentrism and the Moravian revival in which people sought the outpouring of the Spirit. Frank Macchia notes that Zinzendorf believed in a "universal outpouring of the Holy Spirit" that was "poured out upon the earth through the wounds of the crucified Christ."[43] From the standpoint of finished work critics, this view of sanctification was Calvinistic because it discouraged the active pursuit of holiness in Wesleyan sanctification.[44]

38. Rosdahl, "Doctrine of Sanctification," 103–8. He notes that William Piper, E. N. Bell, J. R. Flower, D. W. Kerr, and A. P. Collins rejected Durham's divisiveness and sectarianism caused by the debate and emphasized unity and called for a theological truce.

39. Rosdahl, "Doctrine of Sanctification," 103–8.

40. King, *Passover to Pentecost*, 104–8.

41. Turner, *Finished Work of Calvary*, 34.

42. Turner, *Finished Work of Calvary*, 30.

43. Macchia, *Spirituality and Social Liberation*, 16.

44. Clayton correctly draws the parallels between Wesley's defense against Zinzendorf and the second work proponent's defense against Durham. He argues that the rift

FINISHED WORK THEOLOGY

The founding of the AG was a pivotal moment in the story of the Pentecostal movement. Durham's regrettable actions divided Holiness from non-Holiness Pentecostals. However, it also brought theological differences that were latent in the early years to the forefront. The result of this controversy was not just a division of the movement but also revealed two theological streams within Evangelicalism that were present before the Pentecostal movement began.[45] William Kay points out that John Wesley, John Fletcher, and Phoebe Palmer were the theological forebearers of Holiness Pentecostalism. Separately, Charles Finney, A. J. Gordon, and A. B. Simpson were the theological forebearers of the Keswick theology that became the Finished Work tradition.[46] Edith Blumhofer argues that much of what is distinctive about AG doctrine is Keswickian rather than Wesleyan.[47] Blumhofer even characterized the AG Statement of Fundamental Truths as "largely an expression of Reformed evangelical theology."[48] But, as Bruce Rosdahl has argued, by labeling the finished work stream as "reformed," many scholars fail to recognize the way in which Wesleyan theology informed Keswick theology.[49] Although salvation is "finished" on the cross, Durham held

---

was over the orientation of the movement and the tensions between the Christocentric and Pneumocentric orientations of early Pentecostalism. He believes the Holiness label of Zinzendorfian views is accurate. Clayton, "Significance of William Durham," 27–42. However, Rosdahl points out that Clayton makes a weak defense of this claim since there is little to suggest that Durham was influenced by Lutheranism. Rosdahl, "Doctrine of Sanctification," 14–17.

45. Jacobsen notes that the original movement was scattered, diverse, and fluid, yet was held together by an emphasis on unity. He argues that controversies of the finished work, New Issue, and initial evidence were more so the process of "differentiation" than fragmentation. Jacobsen, *Thinking in the Spirit*, 10–11. See also Rosdahl, "Doctrine of Sanctification," 32.

46. Kay, *Pentecostalism*, 32.

47. Waldvogel, "'Overcoming' Life" (1979), 7–19. See also Waldvogel, "'Overcoming Life'" (1977). First, she argues that non-Wesleyan evangelicals were strongly oriented toward doctrine. Second, she notes that evangelicals were highly committed to premillennialist eschatology. The Pentecostal orientation toward eschatology was supported by millennialist orientation that was particularly influential in Keswick theology. Third, non-Wesleyans focused on the Holy Spirit as enduement of power rather than second work sanctification. Keswick Pentecostals replaced the doctrine of sanctification with Spirit baptism. Finally, she notes that the Finished Work healing movement contributed to an emphasis of healing in the atonement.

48. Waldvogel, "'Overcoming' Life" (1979), 15.

49. Rosdahl argues that Durham's doctrine of sanctification "identifies with Wesleyan

Arminian views consistent with Wesley and a doctrine of sanctification similar to that of the Christian and Missionary Alliance in its emphasis on "identification' with Christ."[50] A. B. Simpson argued that his view was neither Wesleyan nor Keswick.[51] Rosdahl says, "The net result is that those Pentecostal views which are Wesleyan in most areas, except their rejection of eradicationism, get improperly labeled as Reformed or Baptistic."[52] Instead, Rosdahl concludes that Durham's position is better characterized as "Finished-Work Wesleyan."[53]

Accepting Rosdahl's correction here, this may be a better way to think of the streams. Considering that it was John Fletcher's Wesleyan crisis theology that became a key development in the Holiness theology of the second work of grace, both progressive and instantaneous sanctification is essentially Wesleyan.[54] It is true that Fletcher rejected the idea that justification, sanctification, and glorification were finished in any sense, as Zinzendorf had argued.[55] Yet, it was Fletcher who was responsible for anchoring sanctification as an event-oriented Spirit baptism derived from Luke-Acts.[56] Fletcher's emphasis on a pneumatological crisis event also led

---

ideals in every area save the need for a second work of grace." Rosdahl, "Doctrine of Sanctification," 67.

50. Rosdahl, "Doctrine of Sanctification," 53–67. Durham's doctrine of sanctification rejected eradicationism and the second work in favor of progressive sanctification that was a voluntaristic act of consecration and identification.

51. Van de Walle quotes Simpson, "We believe that the Alliance teaching on the subject is neither Wesleyan nor, strictly speaking, an echo of even the excellent teaching given at the meetings annually held at Keswick. . . . Yet we believe that the point of view from which the subject of personal holiness is regarded by the teachers and working in the Christian Alliance is what we might term the 'Christ Life' rather than the sanctified life." Van de Walle, *Heart of the Gospel*, 101. He also notes that Simpson emphasized the holy life over the empowering life but also emphasized that it is Christ who dwells within that is the source of holiness that is progressive rather than terminal.

52. Rosdahl, "Doctrine of Sanctification," 4–5.

53. Rosdahl, "Doctrine of Sanctification," 68.

54. Wood, *Meaning of Pentecost*, 147.

55. Fletcher, *Works of the Rev. John Fletcher*, 1:209. He says, "If salvation of the elect was *finished* upon the cross, then was their *justification* finished, their *sanctification* finished, their *glorification* finished?"

56. Fletcher, *Works of the Rev. John Fletcher*, 1:142, "Upon the whole, it is I think undeniable, from the four first chapters of Acts, that a peculiar power of the Spirit is bestowed upon believers under the gospel of Christ; that this power, through faith on our part, can operate the most sudden and surprising change in our souls; and . . . our faith shall fully embrace the promise of full sanctification, or of a complete 'circumcision of the heart of the Spirit.'"

to Phoebe Palmer's altar theology of "holiness by faith," which shifted entire sanctification from a teleological event to an inaugural event.[57] Further, Fletcher's pneumatological eschatology divided history into three dispensations with an expectation of a latter rain outpouring at the end of the "dispensation of the Spirit" that will be in preparation for the millennium. Each of these characteristics suggests that Fletcher may have contributed to the emergence of finished work theology that stayed true to the Wesleyan Arminian soteriology instead of Calvinistic or Reformed theology.[58]

Though controversial and paternalistic in his views—especially toward Seymour—Durham highlighted for Pentecostals an important rebuttal to the Holiness doctrine of sanctification as related to Spirit-baptism. Durham was essentially reinterpreting the pre-Pentecostal four-fold gospel in light of the Pentecostal baptism.[59] The Wesleyan-Holiness Movement preached a four-fold gospel that wedded the experience of sanctification with baptism in the Spirit (salvation, sanctification/Spirit-baptism, healing, and second coming).[60] Because of the holiness beginnings of the movement, Pentecostals expanded the four-fold gospel to become the five-fold gospel by separating sanctification from Spirit baptism as two distinct yet connected experiences (salvation, sanctification, Spirit-baptism, healing, and second coming). This was a problem for Durham because he believed the very purpose of the Pentecostal outpouring of the Spirit was to bring light to the true nature of the biblical experience of baptism in the Spirit.

Therefore, for Durham, the Pentecostal baptism in the Spirit should not have been added to the four-fold gospel (creating the five-fold); it should have replaced sanctification in that formula. Thus, in Durham's four-fold gospel, salvation and sanctification were connected instead of sanctification and Spirit baptism (salvation and sanctification, Spirit-baptism, healing, and the second coming). This four-fold gospel is the heart

---

57. White, *Beauty of Holiness*, 139–40.

58. Dayton, "Pentecostal Studies," 170–71, hints at this when he discusses Fletcher's role in the reversal on Wesleyan characteristics in Evangelicalism.

59. Land, *Pentecostal Spirituality*, 75, argues that Wesley's doctrine of salvation was more of a *via salutis* rather than an *ordo salutis* like the protestant tradition. It is fair to say that this could also suggest a difference in orientation between the *via* of Wesleyan Pentecostals and the *ordo* of Finished Work Pentecostals.

60. Land, *Pentecostal Spirituality*, 186, comments, "The Holiness movement had seen purity and power as two sides of the same coin; for them sanctification was Spirit baptism."

of finished work theology. McQueen argues that finished work soteriology has a "tighter articulation" of the four-fold gospel than the five-fold articulation of Wesleyan Pentecostals.[61] Finished work soteriology is Christologically grounded in the completed work on the cross in which each aspect of the *ordo salutis* is fully present and experienced by faith. This produces a spirituality that places a heavy empirical emphasis on immediate results and instant experiences. Macchia believes that Durham's emphasis on the finished work was not to undo holiness theology as much as it was to center Spirit-baptism in the cross. He comments:

> The cross was not an abstract event that reconciles God to humanity totally apart from us but rather an all sufficient power for regeneration, sanctification, healing, and the empowered (Spirit-baptized) witness in that it had the resurrection and Pentecostal as its horizon as a part of a seamless flow of events by which the Spirit is mediated.[62]

In finished work theology, salvation is rooted in the cross and is the point by which salvation flows into other experiences.[63]

For Holiness-Pentecostals, the Spirit leads the process of transformation in salvation, sanctification, healing, and future redemption.[64] Kimberly Alexander explains, "For Wesleyan-Pentecostals, the Spirit, like Wesley's concept of grace/power, is perpetually given and responded to. The Spirit leads the believer toward the end. As the Spirit is given and responded to, the believer is transformed."[65] In finished work theology, the Christological orientation in the *ordo salutis* subordinates the role of the Spirit to the work of Christ because the Spirit's role is to actualize the work already accomplished by Christ.[66] The cross is the place where the Spirit's work is

---

61. McQueen says, "The identity of Christ as Savior, Healer, Spirit Baptizer and Coming King is almost completely integrated." McQueen, *Toward a Pentecostal Eschatology*, 154.

62. Macchia, "Pentecost as the Power of the Cross," 3.

63. This is why the Oneness tradition fits into the finished work stream, because of the way they collapse all three experiences into the one experience of salvation. See Macchia, "Pentecost as the Power of the Cross," 2; McQueen, *Toward a Pentecostal Eschatology*, 187, 197; Alexander, *Pentecostal Healing*, 182–94.

64. Land, *Pentecostal Spirituality*, 183.

65. Alexander, *Pentecostal Healing*, 233.

66. Macchia notes that both Durham and Seymour were Christologically centered. He says, "The early Pentecostals could very well have placed the roots of Spirit baptism in regeneration as well. They would have done this if it were not for the influence of the

mediated by looking back to the cross. This leads Alexander to conclude, "There is little or no emphasis upon being led *forward* by the Spirit, but rather, the Spirit constantly drives the believer *backward* to the Cross."[67]

The finished nature of salvation clearly affects the orientation of all aspects of the four-fold gospel of early Pentecostalism. In the cross, salvation is obtained "by faith" in the finished work of Jesus, which was linked to sanctification through the Keswick teaching on "holiness by faith."[68] Spirit-baptism in this tradition is also conveyed in "finished" concepts, particularly in the idea of evidences. Durham testified, "After being under the power for three hours, He finished the work on my vocal organs, and spoke through me in unknown tongues."[69] E. N. Bell similarly testified, "I did not fight tongues. But when the work was finished, the Spirit bore witness Himself as to the personal intelligence within by speaking a language I knew not."[70] This may also be why "initial evidence" continued to hold a high priority because of the verification of completion.[71] The empowerment of the Spirit is seen as a terminal event obtained by faith and completed when evidenced by speaking in tongues.

Similarly, healing is a finished work grounded in the atonement and appropriated by faith.[72] The work of Jesus on the cross provided a double cure for both sin and the effects of sin, which are available through faith. Carrie Judd Montgomery used the finished work to argue for a doctrine of healing in the atonement that accepted healing by faith.[73] A. J. Gordon and A. B. Simpson also promoted healing in that atonement and emphasized that healing was obtained in the same way as forgiveness and salvation, which is by faith. Judd focused the *ordo salutis* on "lying hold by faith" in what she called "faith's reckoning." She says, "Very simple and plain is

---

Wesleyan *ordo salutis* that they embraced at some tension with their developing theology of the cross." Macchia, "Pentecost as the Power of the Cross," 3.

67. Alexander, *Pentecostal Healing*, 233.

68. Kay, *Pentecostalism*, 32.

69. Durham, "Chicago Evangelist's Pentecost," 4.

70. Bell, "Testimony of a Baptist Pastor," 9.

71. Friezen, *Norming the Abnormal*, 135, discusses the AG's distinctive doctrine of "initial evidence" and the AG's expansion of that doctrine to include the idea of the tongues as a "continuing evidence" of the Spirit-filled life.

72. See Alexander, *Pentecostal Healing*, 209–15; Kay, *Pentecostalism*, 45.

73. Montgomery is a good example of finished work theology prior to William Durham and is an important theological link to late nineteenth-century evangelical theology. Miskov, *Life on Wings*.

our part in the obtaining of God's promised blessings, and this laying hold of faith is much easier of accomplishment than most of us are willing to believe. Our part is simply to reckon our prayers as answers, and God's part is to make faith's reckonings real."[74] Applied to salvation, faith is assurance above feeling. She says, "It is not necessary to feel some particular emotion in our hearts, but to act as though we believe what we profess to believe."[75] The particular emphasis on faith over feelings was an aspect of differentiation between Wesleyan-Holiness and Finished Work experiences.

How does finished work theology influence AG eschatology? Larry McQueen found that classical dispensationalism was the only model articulated in the finished work tradition in the first five years.[76] This would make sense for the AG, because of the way in which future prophetic events are often considered "history written in advance." For example, E. N. Bell comments, "The plan of the ages will roll on exactly as God has predetermined, and nothing can thwart the eternal ends which God has set out to accomplish."[77] The uniform eschatological position is reflective of the soteriological model of the finished work stream. In the same way that salvation, sanctification, Spirit-baptism, and healing are grounded in the finished work, the doctrine of the soon coming king is already "finished." As one AG writer puts it, "The translation of the saints will be as complete as the work on Calvary when he cried, 'It is Finished.'"[78] This emphasizes that in the same way the prophecies of Jesus' first coming were fulfilled to the letter, the prophecies concerning Jesus' second coming will only be accomplished when all the details come to pass. Even long after the finished work controversy settled and positions moderated, Stanley Frodsham comments:

> Christ is retained in heaven until the revival, the restitution, has come and has accomplished its work . . . Christ could not die on the cross until all that was written concerning His suffering was fulfilled and He Himself said, "It is finished." And he is being retained in heaven till the Father says, that all if fulfilled; that it is finished.[79]

---

74. Montgomery, "Faith's Reckonings," 1.
75. Montgomery, "Faith's Reckonings," 1.
76. McQueen, *Toward a Pentecostal Eschatology*, 198–99, 202.
77. Bell, "Questions and Answers," Mar. 22, 1919, 5.
78. "Soon Coming of Christ," 1.
79. Frodsham, "Coming Revival and the Coming Christ," 4.

Aspects of the Finished Work Stream

Therefore, McQueen concluded that finished work soteriology produces a theological orientation in which dispensationalism can be adopted as a "ready-made eschatology."[80] This is important because it gives further substantiation to Dayton's proposal of the great reversal.[81] Dayton argued that the changing commitments within the Holiness movement on the doctrine of sanctification had a correlating effect on eschatological orientation. Wesleyan view of progressive sanctification initially produced a postmillennial view of the future. However, Keswick theology introduced premillennialism into American culture, which eventually became the most popular position. Both Alexander and McQueen warn that the Finished Work emphasis on the finished nature of salvation can lead to an "over-realized" eschatology in which the full benefits are expected to be available in the now.[82] However, if that were true, AG eschatology would lead toward postmillennialism and realized eschatology, not futurism and premillennial dispensationalism.

While an emphasis on the "finished work" was one of the theological threads that created the AG, it was short lived as a primary emphasis. Yet, its orientation continues to be what makes the AG the primary fellowship in this stream of Pentecostalism. The doctrine of sanctification continues to be the most prominent of positions of difference, although in many ways even Wesleyan Pentecostals are having difficulty with its traditional view. Nevertheless, it was this break from Holiness teachings that created AG as a distinct body and the Oneness tradition a short time later.

---

80. McQueen, *Toward a Pentecostal Eschatology*, 179.

81. Dayton, "Pentecostal Studies," 171.

82. Alexander, *Pentecostal Healing*, 241; McQueen, *Toward a Pentecostal Eschatology*, 198.

Chapter 4

Aspects of Evangelical Identity

INTRODUCTION[1]

THE QUEST FOR ARTICULATING a uniquely Pentecostal theology has been a primary concern to Pentecostal scholars. As scholarship continues to mature, Pentecostals are seeking to orient all areas of theology through a Pentecostal lens. This pneumatological orientation has led some to question whether Pentecostal theology is more than simply evangelical theology plus a doctrine of the Spirit.[2] Further, some have suggested that the adoption of evangelical/fundamentalist approaches to theological inquiry and hermeneutics have in fact been detrimental to the development of Pentecostal theology. While some Pentecostals are seeking an alternative identity apart from Evangelicalism, a study of the periodical literature of the Assemblies of God reveals that evangelical identity was important from nearly the beginning. The AG saw itself as evangelical believers who also believed in the Pentecostal baptism with the Spirit and speaking in tongues. This evangelical identity was expressed in literature, Bible school courses, and even resulted an attempt to officially change the name of the Assemblies of God to "The Pentecostal Evangelical Church" in 1925.

---

1. This chapter is a revision of Isgrigg, "Pentecostal Evangelical Church."
2. Sterling, "Are Pentecostals Evangelicals?"; Archer, "Making of an Academic."

Aspects of Evangelical Identity

NINETEENTH-CENTURY EVANGELICALISM

In 1846, a broad coalition of Protestants in Britain formed the Evangelical Alliance with the goal of bringing unity to Protestants all over the world.[3] From this coalition, there emerged four common characteristics of evangelical identity: the atoning work of Christ on the Cross, the need for personal faith through conversion, the supreme value of the Bible, and the binding obligation of missionary activity.[4] When the Evangelical Alliance formed its American coalition in 1867, the main denominations that identified as evangelical included Anglicans, New School Presbyterians, Congregationalists, Baptists, and Methodists.[5] The Alliance succeeded in bringing together these various Protestant traditions in unity despite their diversity in theology, denomination, social characteristic, and geographical location.[6] Donald Dayton points out that Evangelicalism was formed as a trans-denominational corrective to protestant orthodoxy whose perfectionist tendencies to reform and revive the church were sometimes seen as "semi-heretical."[7] Evangelicalism reached its climax during the 1880s when Holiness revivalism and evangelical millenarianism expanded the earlier theological commitments to include an emphasis on divine healing and the sanctifying work of the Spirit. By the end of the nineteenth century, Evangelicalism, or what some have called radical Evangelicalism, became characterized by revivalism, restorationism, and Holiness theology. Essentially all evangelicals preached the four-fold gospel of Jesus as savior, sanctifier, healer, and coming king.[8]

---

3. Bebbington, *Dominance of Evangelicalism*, 21–23; Schaff and Schaff, "Doctrinal Basis of the Evangelical Alliance," 827–28.

4. Bebbington, *Dominance of Evangelicalism*, 23.

5. Bebbington, *Dominance of Evangelicalism*, 58.

6. Bebbington, *Dominance of Evangelicalism*, 52–71, points out that there were social layers to the movement in that Anglicans and Presbyterians enjoyed a higher social status of both clergy and adherents and consequently tended to be less revivalist. Other groups such as Baptist and Methodist had a lower form of church government, were comfortable with less traditional church settings, and tended to be more expressive and revivalist in their meetings.

7. Dayton, "Re-Thinking Evangelicalism," 257–60, mentions that Evangelicalism had three levels: Pentecostals at the bottom, Holiness movement in the middle, and Keswick (moderate middle-class) at the top.

8. Van De Walle, *Heart of the Gospel*. See also Dayton, *Theological Roots of Pentecostalism*, 21–22.

Prior to 1900, Evangelicalism breathed new life into protestant orthodoxy. After 1900, Evangelicalism intellectually shifted back toward orthodoxy in what would eventually become Fundamentalism.[9] Fundamentalism was both an intellectual reaction to modernistic liberalism as well as a shift away from the more revivalistic character of the late nineteenth century.[10] Whereas late nineteenth-century Evangelicalism was highly influenced by Holiness movement, Fundamentalism was attractive to the middle and upper class conservative denominations like Presbyterians and Baptists.[11] The heart of fundamentalist theology is expressed in the five doctrinal pillars: inerrancy of Scripture, virgin birth, substitutionary atonement, physical resurrection of Jesus, and physical return of Christ.[12] Though initially a reaction to Modernism, Fundamentalism narrowed the boundaries of accepted biblical orthodoxy to the point that by the 1920s the Holiness and Pentecostal Movements became targets of their critiques.[13] With the rise of the fundamentalist movement, Evangelicalism shifted away from the pneumatological orientation of Holiness theology toward a growing cessationist position. In the same way Evangelicalism was a Holiness corrective to Protestantism, many early Pentecostals saw themselves as a corrective to both Modernism and Fundamentalism's return to rigid orthodoxy.[14]

PENTECOSTALISM AND EVANGELICALISM

Are Pentecostals just evangelicals who are Spirit-baptized? In recent years, this topic has found its way into scholarly conversations about the nature of Pentecostal theology.[15] It is generally agreed that the Pentecostal Movement "was first and foremost a product of the spiritual milieu of America's Holiness movement."[16] As most histories highlight the holiness origins, Edith

9. Sandeen, *Roots of Fundamentalism*.

10. Dayton, *Discovering an Evangelical Heritage*, 130–31.

11. Sandeen, *Roots of Fundamentalism*, 164; Dayton, *Discovering an Evangelical Heritage*, 128–29.

12. Sandeen, *Roots of Fundamentalism*, xiv. These five key doctrines originated in 1910 from the General Assembly of the Presbyterian Church.

13. Spittler, "Are Pentecostals and Charismatics Fundamentalists?," 108–10.

14. Flower, "Present Position of Pentecost," 8; Sisson, "Coming Glory," 2. Both Flower and Sisson placed Pentecostals in a "middle ground" between modernists who denied the truth in the Bible and fundamentalists who held to the truth but denied the supernatural.

15. Sterling, "Are Pentecostals Evangelicals?"; Archer, "Making of an Academic."

16. Synan, *Holiness-Pentecostal Tradition*, 143.

Aspects of Evangelical Identity

Waldvogel Blumhofer emphasizes the ways in which much of Pentecostal doctrine is "evangelical" and attributes its roots as originating outside of Wesleyan-Holiness Movement.[17] She argues that the strong orientation toward doctrine, commitment to dispensational premillennialism, emphasis on the Holy Spirit for purity and power, and finished work views of healing were all characteristic of late nineteenth-century Evangelicalism, chiefly the non-Wesleyan streams. In particular, she believes that the "conservative evangelical doctrinal framework has a direct correlation to the doctrines that would later characterize the Assemblies of God."[18]

For Dayton, much of the debate over the holiness verses the evangelical influence in Pentecostalism is simply a matter of semantics. He believes that when Blumhofer and others use the term *evangelical* to denote non-Wesleyan influences on Pentecostalism, they fail to recognize the extent to which holiness theology influenced late nineteenth-century Evangelicalism. Holiness revivalism had a profound influence on evangelicals with its emphasis on crisis-centered experiences of salvation, sanctification, and healing. Because of this, Dayton argues for the use of a broader definition of Evangelicalism that includes both Keswick holiness and Wesleyan holiness.[19] By Dayton's definition, all late nineteenth-century evangelicals should be considered part of the Holiness Movement. Therefore, all Pentecostals, as originating from the Holiness Movement, should also be considered, at least to some degree, evangelicals.

Dayton has also established that Pentecostalism is best articulated by the four-/five-fold gospel of Jesus as savior, sanctifier, Spirit-baptizer, healer, and coming king.[20] But it is important to recognize that the five-fold gospel formula itself predates the Pentecostal Movement. Many evangelicals broadly promoted the four-fold gospel, originally articulated by Christian and Missionary Alliance founder A. B. Simpson. As Bernie Van De Walle points out, "To understand Simpson's theology is to understand late nineteenth-century American evangelical theology. Simpson's Gospel was not something peculiar to himself or the C&MA. Rather, in the late nineteenth

---

17. Waldvogel, "'Overcoming' Life" (1979), 7–19.
18. Waldvogel, "'Overcoming' Life" (1979), 9.
19. Dayton, "Pentecostal Studies," 156–57.
20. Dayton has argued, "Though the five-fold pattern was historically prior and thus has certain claims for our attention, the four-fold pattern expresses more clearly and cleanly the logic of Pentecostal theology." Dayton, *Theological Roots of Pentecostalism*, 21–22.

century, it was the heart of the gospel."[21] Early Pentecostals adopted the four-fold gospel rubric but added the distinctive of Spirit-baptism to the formula. Therefore, the "heart" of Pentecostal theology is also the "heart" of evangelical theology.

TRACING THE EVANGELICAL STREAM INTO THE AG

Tracing the evangelical identity within the AG begins with an analysis of the preamble of the AG's Constitution and Bylaws created in 1914 and the Statement of Fundamental Truths created in 1916. The founders had a vision for their movement that was remarkably similar to that of the Evangelical Alliance. While there is no direct historical evidence of a connection, there are several similarities between the founding concepts of the AG and the 1849 document ratified by the Evangelical Alliance (EA).

First, the AG has long used the concept of "voluntary cooperative fellowship" to describe itself in contrast to a denomination. The language of voluntary association was one of the central tenets of the EA as well. Note the parallel language in the EA documents: "It is simply a voluntary association of individual Christians for the promotion of Christian union and religious liberty." As a voluntary fellowship, they rejected sectarianism. "We have no intention or desire to give rise to a new denomination or sect . . . but simply to bring individual Christians into closer fellowship and cooperation."[22] This is similar to the language in the AG preamble that says, "[We] do not believe in identifying ourselves as or establishing ourselves into, a sect, that is a human organization that legislates or forms laws and articles of faith and has unscriptural jurisdiction over its members and creates unscriptural lines of fellowship and disfellowship."[23]

Like the EA that united various groups of like faith, the AG was intended to be a fellowship of various Pentecostal groups, as named in the preamble:

> We recognize ourselves as a General Council of Pentecostal (Spirit Baptized) saints from local Churches of God in Christ, Assemblies of God, and various Apostolic Faith Missions and Churches and Full Gospel Pentecostal Missions and Assemblies of like Faith

---

21. Van De Walle, *Heart of the Gospel*, 22–23.
22. Schaff and Schaff, "Doctrinal Basis of the Evangelical Alliance," 827.
23. *GC Constitution and Bylaws* (October 2–7, 1916), 3.

... whose purpose is neither to legislate laws of government, nor usurp authority over said various assemblies.[24]

The early fellowship was intended to be a council of various groups that could maintain their autonomy, not a denomination.

Second, there was a common rejection of creedalism. The EA declares it has "no authority to issue and enforce an ecclesiastical creed," rather its doctrinal statement intended only to "declare on what doctrinal basis it proposes to labor for its end."[25] Compare this to the Statement of Fundamental Truths that declares itself as "not intended as a creed for the Church, nor as a basis of fellowship among Christians, but only as a basis of unity for the ministry alone."[26] In both cases, doctrine was a basis for fellowship and cooperation, but was not an ecclesiastical creed that was forced on members of the body.

Additionally, they both saw the basic tenants of Christian doctrine as a basis of fellowship, not a creed that would bind the group together.[27] The core doctrines are (1) divine inspiration; (2) private interpretation of Scripture; (3) Trinity; (4) human depravity; (5) incarnation and atonement; (6) justification by faith alone; (7) the work of the Holy Spirit in conversion and sanctification; (8) immortality, resurrection, judgment, and eternal punishment; (9) ordinances of baptism and the Lord's Supper.[28] All of these parallel the AG Statement of Fundamental Truths with the exception of the Pentecostal distinctives of baptism in the Holy Spirit, healing, and ministry.

Third, the AG adopted the idea that a limited number of truths were essential to unity. The EA declares "the selection of certain tenets, with the omission of others, is not to be held as implying that the former constitute the whole body of important truth, or that the latter are unimportant."[29] Compare to SFT which declares, "No claim is made that it contains all truth in the Bible, only that it covers our present needs as to these fundamental matters."[30] The minimalist statement was important because of the way it fostered the unity of the Spirit. They did not intend to draw artificial lines

---

24. *GC Constitution and Bylaws* (October 2–7, 1916), 3.
25. Schaff and Schaff, "Doctrinal Basis of the Evangelical Alliance," 827.
26. *GC Constitution and Bylaws* (October 2–7, 1916), 10.
27. Schaff and Schaff, "Doctrinal Basis of the Evangelical Alliance," 827–28.
28. Schaff and Schaff, "Doctrinal Basis of the Evangelical Alliance," 827.
29. Schaff and Schaff, "Doctrinal Basis of the Evangelical Alliance," 827.
30. *GC Constitution and Bylaws* (October 2–7, 1916), 10.

that limited fellowship among believers. These statements were meant to state what is "essential to a full Gospel ministry" among a cooperative body.

The Evangelical Alliance and the AG share a common vision of being cooperative fellowship of ministers bound by a limited doctrinal framework. Both share a commitment to limited authority structures that avoids sectarianism and denominationalism. This suggests that the AG could have modeled their fellowship after this evangelical model. While this evidence is somewhat circumstantial, the real support is the self-identity expressed by ministers themselves.

EVANGELICAL "PLUS"

In the early days, the impetus for evangelical identification was primarily a result of AG leaders who kept a close eye on the modernist controversy.[31] When E. N. Bell was asked in 1919 where AG churches stood on modernist issues, he argued that all Assemblies are "opposed to all radical Higher Criticism of the Bible and against all modernism or infidelity in the church . . . They believe in all the real Bible truths held by all real Evangelical churches."[32] In Bell's mind, AG churches were "real evangelical churches" because they opposed Modernism. Stanley Frodsham believed the Pentecostal movement was a vehicle whereby evangelicals of all denominational varieties could be unified around a core of fundamental truths. He says:

> What a glorious fellowship I came into. I found Episcopalians, Baptist, Methodist, Presbyterians, people from people from undenominational missions, holiness people, and Christian and Missionary Alliance people by the hundreds had alike received this same baptism in the Spirit, and when we compared notes, we found that we all believed the same thing. To a man we stood for the infallibility and verbal inspiration of the Bible. We all believed in the virgin birth, the resurrection and miracles of our Lord that are being denied on every hand by modern churches. We all made

---

31. For example, in 1916, they were encouraged by the Presbyterian Church's commitment to "get back to fundamentals" and support of the "Fundamentals of the Faith." A few years later, in 1919, the *Evangel* published the doctrinal statement from the World Conference on Christian Fundamentals that affirmed the doctrines of inerrancy, the Trinity, virgin birth, sin, substitutionary atonement, premillennial return of Christ and bodily resurrection. The WCCF was the conference from which the adherents, became known as "fundamentalists." See "Back to Fundamentals," 7; Bell, "Doctrinal Statement," 8.

32. Bell, "Questions and Answers," Dec. 27, 1919, 5.

much of the atoning blood of Christ that cleanseth from all sin. We are all looking for the near and premillennial coming of the Lord Jesus Christ.[33]

Despite the growing number of evangelical critiques of Pentecostals, AG leaders answered their critiques by showing that the Pentecostal experience was biblical and not outside the bounds of the fundamentals of the faith.[34] In 1922, R. E. McAlister described the Pentecostal movement as "scriptural, dispensational, evangelical, missionary, aggressive, spiritual, pre-millennial, safe and sane."[35] The *Pentecostal Evangel* even periodically described itself as an "Evangelical, Pentecostal, and Missionary" publication.[36] The AG believed they shared an evangelical identity because of their mutual rejection of Modernism, their affirmation of basic evangelical doctrine, and their commitment to biblical Christian living. McAlister explains, "Where we differ from evangelical churches in the present day is in the belief that Pentecost can be repeated."[37]

FUNDAMENTALIST "PLUS"

Concurrent with the first decade of the fellowship, Evangelicalism gradually morphed into Fundamentalism, and the AG naturally shifted its language to adopt the label.[38] The AG did not adopt Fundamentalism as something foreign to their early character. It demonstrated a further identification with their doctrinal identity as evangelicals. Blumhofer says, "The question

---

33. Frodsham, "Why We Know," 4–5.

34. For example, Stanley Frodsham seeks to answer the critiques of R. A. Torrey, whom he considers "friends" and whom he holds in "high esteem" as a teacher of the fundamentals of the faith. Frodsham, "Why We Know," 4–5.

35. McAlister, "Pentecostal Movement," 5.

36. This label was used in several editions in 1917. *Weekly Evangel*, November 10, 1917, 9; *Weekly Evangel*, November 17, 1917, 8. The label of "Evangelical and Missionary Paper" reappeared in 1926 but omitted "Pentecostal" and disappeared again in 1928. See *Pentecostal Evangel*, May 5, 1926, 3; *Pentecostal Evangel*, March 24, 1928, 5, on the Consortium of Pentecostal Archives site.

37. McAlister, "Pentecostal Movement," 5.

38. I also recommend Zachary Tackett's research on the occurrences of the fundamentalist label in the periodical literature. Although many of the quotes I also found during my own research, I discovered after the fact that he documented these occurrences with similar conclusions earlier than I was for this study. See Tackett, "More Than Fundamentalists."

of whether they were fundamentalist did not preoccupy early Assemblies of God leaders; they simply assumed they were."[39] Russell Spittler notes that even though they were often adversaries, their approaches to the Bible, commitment to doctrine and opposition to Modernism were virtually identical. He therefore concludes, "Pentecostals... decidedly think and act like fundamentalists. Pentecostals are fundamentalistic, even if they were not classical fundamentalists."[40]

The first recorded mention of the fundamentalist label used to describe the AG came during a 1924 General Presbyters meeting in which Asst. General Superintendent David McDowell boldly proclaimed that Pentecostals were fundamentalists. This label resonated so deeply with Stanley Frodsham that he published McDowell's comments in the *Pentecostal Evangel*.[41] McDowell testified, "Praise God that I am a Fundamentalist, and that I am a Pentecostal Fundamentalist," to which Frodsham added, "That is what we all are."[42] Frodsham further used the label to appeal to *Pentecostal Evangel* readers for support for the paper, which stands "one hundred percent towards 'Pentecostal Fundamentalism.'"[43] McDowell's fundamentalist label grew in usage over the next few years, expressed through several other important leaders. In 1925, J. R. Flower addressed the students at Central Bible College on the present state of Pentecostalism. He commented:

> At this present time we have Modernism on the one hand and Fundamentalism on the other.... We can say like Paul, "I am a Fundamentalist of the Fundamentalists, of the strictest sect of the Fundamentalists am I one." But that is not enough.... We are Fundamentalists, but we are more than that.[44]

Similarly, in 1927, the *Pentecostal Evangel* advertised a correspondence course on Pentecostal doctrine by D. W. Kerr called "Fundamentals of the Faith 'Plus.'"[45] Kerr remarks, "We, as a General Council, are Fundamentalists, but Fundamentalists 'plus,' in that, while we stand with all true

---

39. Blumhofer, *Restoring the Faith*, 159.
40. Spittler, "Are Pentecostals and Charismatics Fundamentalists?," 114.
41. Frodsham, "Fundamentalist Plus," 4.
42. Frodsham, "Letter to Readers," 15.
43. Frodsham, "Letter to Readers," 15. Frodsham boasted that 50,000 copies of the *Evangel* were sent out every week, which amounted to 41,600,000 pages of "Pentecostal Fundamentalist literature yearly."
44. Flower, "Present Position of Pentecost," 8.
45. "Bible Study Course by Correspondence," 15.

believers for the 'faith once delivered to the saints,' we believe that this faith also includes . . . the Baptism of the Holy Spirit with signs following."[46] In the minds of these leaders, Fundamentalism fit perfectly within the core message of early Pentecostals because of its commitment to the belief in premillennial eschatology, the authority of Scripture, the deity of Christ, bodily resurrection, and vicarious atonement.[47]

Although the AG claimed to be fundamentalists, in 1928, fundamentalists declared Pentecostalism to be a "menace" to the church because of their view of tongues and healing.[48] Frodsham lamented the decision to "disfellowship" Pentecostals but vowed to continue to love the fundamentalists.[49] They were convinced they could win over their critics by demonstrating that they believed in the same fundamental truths.[50] M. M. McGraw comments, "Because a few Fundamentalists have declared the Pentecostal movement not of God, let us not worry. . . . If there be any doubt about God's looking upon us as God-sent Fundamentalists, the way to get that doubt removed is to persist in preaching on sin being cleansed from the heart and life."[51] The real pain caused by the fundamentalist rejection was not that they did not accept their identity as Pentecostals; it was that they were not willing to accept them as fundamentalists.[52]

THE PENTECOSTAL EVANGELICAL CHURCH

The most apparent move to identify the AG with Evangelicalism came in the 1927 General Council when a committee presented a full constitution

46. Kerr, "Fundamentals of the Faith 'Plus.'"

47. Menzies, *Anointed to Serve*, 27. See also Menzies, "Non-Wesleyan Pentecostalism," 199–211.

48. Frodsham, "Disfellowshipped," 7. For a thorough history of the relationship between Pentecostalism and Fundamentalism see King, *Disfellowshipped*.

49. Frodsham, "Disfellowshipped," 7.

50. Frodsham comments, "I do not know of a Pentecostal person anywhere who questions the inerrancy of the Scriptures, or one who doubts the virgin birth, the miracles, the physical resurrection, the Deity, or the efficacy of the blood atonement of our Lord Jesus Christ, nor one who has the slightest sympathy for the unproved theories of the evolutionists that are being propounded everywhere by the 'learned ignoramuses' of the earth today." Frodsham, "Letter to Readers," 15.

51. "Fundamentalism," 3–5.

52. Eventually the hostility exhibited by fundamentalists resulted in the fundamentalist label falling out of use by AG leaders after 1928; instead, they reverted to evangelical labels, especially leading up to the formation of the NAE.

and revision of the Statement of Fundamental Truths for consideration.[53] The biggest surprise contained in the committee's proposal was a proposed name change from The Assemblies of God to "The Pentecostal Evangelical Church."[54] J. Narver Gortner, the committee chairman, argued that there was "widespread dissatisfaction" with the name of the fellowship. He commented, "When the Revision Committee was looking for a name, we wanted to find one that would indicate what we are, one in harmony with our real character. And we all agreed that we are Pentecostal people. Then we are evangelical too, we believe in evangelization."[55] Many others from the council membership also added their support of the name. Noel Perkin recalls, "The new name suggested was considered descriptive of what we are; namely, a Pentecostal church both evangelical in doctrine and evangelistic in spirit."[56] Harold Moss commented, "We as a people are evangelical, that is, we have a world-wide evangelical program. . . . But that name is not sufficient as there are other evangelical churches, so we need another name to draw a clear line of demarcation—Pentecostal Evangelical Church."[57] E. S. Williams commented, "I wish we could change our name and adopt a title which would cause the remainder of the religious world to feel that we are part of the evangelical bodies of Christendom."[58] Evangelical identity was so commonly accepted in those days that F. E. Shelby added, "Whether we call ourselves 'Pentecostal Evangelical Church' or not, we are that anyway."[59] After much debate, the constitution was passed, but the name change measure was tabled and deleted from the final approved minutes.[60]

53. Although the preamble of the AG constitution was adopted in 1914, the full constitution was not created until a committee was given the task at the 1925 General Council. The committee returned to the 1927 General Council with a full constitution and revision the Statement of Fundamental Truths for consideration.

54. "Final Report of Revision Committee on Essential Resolutions," *GC Constitution and Bylaws* (September 16–22, 1927); "Twelfth General Council," 2–10.

55. "Twelfth General Council," 6. Members of the committee included J. N. Gortner, E. S. Williams, A. G. Ward, S. A. Jamieson, F. M. Boyd.

56. Perkin, "I Remember," 9.

57. "Twelfth General Council," 6.

58. "Twelfth General Council," 7.

59. "Twelfth General Council," 6.

60. "Twelfth General Council," 10. J. R. Flower later pointed out that the change proposed in 1927 would have involved a change in the original charter of the council that would have affected the assemblies who were incorporated in that name. It would have officially made the AG a denomination that would result in the abandoning of the original principles of independent and associated churches and was "repudiated" on

The proposed name change clearly reveals they were comfortable with an evangelical identity even as a Pentecostal fellowship.

THE NEW EVANGELICAL HOPE

In 1914, the AG organized intending to create a fellowship that facilitated cooperation toward unity within the body of Christ. However, the AG experienced a gradual separation from the rest of the evangelical world over the next two decades.[61] The Holiness Movement had separated from Pentecostals over the doctrine of tongues by the end of the first decade. Rejection by the Christian Missionary Alliance over speaking in tongues alienated many AG leaders from the family where they had received their Pentecostal experience.[62] The finished work controversy over the doctrine of sanctification in the mid-1910s caused a self-imposed isolation in the AG from other Holiness Pentecostal groups. As we have seen, in the 1920s, the AG sought a shared identity with the fundamentalists, only to be disfellowshipped over their stance on Pentecostal distinctives. The original vision of bringing unity to the Pentecostal movement and the body of Christ was all but lost. The AG had become what they hoped to avoid: a sect.

After two decades of isolation, a new hope for cooperation and identification was born as a moderate group of fundamentalist evangelicals sought to revive their association with evangelical denominations, including Pentecostals. After being rejected by the American Council of Churches and because of opposition to the liberalism of the Federal Council of Churches, the National Association of Evangelicals represented an opportunity for the AG to receive formal acceptance into the broader evangelical community.[63] In 1943, the General Council approved a resolution to join the NAE as a way to "identify ourselves with other Fundamental Evangelical groups without jeopardizing our denominational identity."[64] Leading the charge was Flower, who often advocated for the new association in the

---

such grounds. See *GC Constitution and Bylaws* (August 23–29, 1961), 29.

61. Menzies, *Anointed to Serve*, 177–82; Blumhofer, *Restoring the Faith*, 158. Blumhofer believes that the AG was intentionally isolated because of a rejection of other groups based on doctrinal superiority.

62. King, "Pentecostal Roots," 12–16; Menzies, "Non-Wesleyan Pentecostalism," 226–38.

63. Flower, "Why We Joined the NAE," 12.

64. *GC Constitution and Bylaws* (September 2–7, 1943), 8.

Pentecostal Evangel and letters to AG ministers. At least for Flower, the NAE had familiar goals that reminded him of the early days of the fellowship.[65]

Stanley Frodsham also compared the unity of the NAE to that of the vision of the first General Council. He says:

> At the first Council of the Assemblies of God held at Hot Springs, Ark., in 1914, the ministers who attended all came with one mind, determined to oppose the raising of walls that would separate us as a Pentecostal people from other children of God . . . Brother Flower, who was one of the company . . . recently in Council called us back to this vision, and read to us that original constitution in which this was so clearly set forth.
>
> When the National Association of Evangelicals came into being five years ago, those who called the convention did what no other group of Fundamentalist believers had done, invited the brethren of both the Holiness and the Pentecostal groups. They recognized us as a people outstandingly aggressive in evangelism and missionary vision, and acknowledged that our coming together with others who are true to the fundamentals of the faith could mean mutual blessing.[66]

Frodsham assured AG ministers that joining would not "compromise one iota" their Pentecostal testimony. Instead, joining it opened new understanding between Pentecostals and fundamentalists.

> One good Fundamentalist minister, who edits a well known magazine and who was decidedly opposed to Pentecost, now reads the *Pentecostal Evangel* and wrote to us a short while ago: "As I read your paper, I see we are not very far apart after all."[67]

The NAE represented a new chapter in the AG quest for evangelical identity. The AG finally had a home in the broader evangelical community, and for the next two decades, many leaders were elected to positions in the NAE.[68] That identity reached its climax in 1960 when AG General Superintendent Thomas F. Zimmerman was elected as president of the

---

65. Flower, "Basis Unity of Evangelical Christianity," 8.
66. Frodsham, "Fifth Annual Convention of the NAE," 6.
67. Frodsham, "Fifth Annual Convention of the NAE," 7.
68. AG leaders who held positions in the NAE include J. R. Flower, Ralph Harris, Thomas Zimmerman, Noel Perkin, E. S. Williams, Fred Vogler, and J. Phillip Hogan. See "Four A/G Officials Elected," 28–29.

Aspects of Evangelical Identity

NAE.[69] With Zimmerman's appointment, the Pentecostal Movement had officially emerged from marginalization and isolation to the top of the most prominent evangelical association in the world. Shortly after joining the NAE, fellowship opportunities opened with Pentecostal groups through the Pentecostal Fellowship of North America and the Pentecostal World Conference. The Assemblies of God had not only revived the vision of cooperation and fellowship but also led from the front.[70]

The identification of the Assemblies of God with Evangelicalism and Fundamentalism goes back nearly to the denomination's beginning. But how important is that identity today? Margaret Poloma's study of identity among AG ministers demonstrates that the AG has consistently defined itself primarily as "Evangelical Pentecostalism."[71] In her survey, Poloma found that "two-thirds of the pastors responding to the survey self-identified as being Evangelical."[72] She also suggests that a greater identification within the AG with the label "evangelical" has caused "seeds of ambiguity" that are symptomatic of a loss of Pentecostal identity.[73] However, she also notes that although AG ministers identified as evangelicals, that identity did not supersede their Pentecostal and AG identity.[74] I would argue that because the AG self-identifies as "more than evangelical," her statistics are reflective of this integrated identity.

DISFELLOWSHIPPING EVANGELICALISM

In the early twentieth century, evangelicals and fundamentalists "disfellowshipped" Pentecostals like an embarrassing relative from the larger evangelical family. A century later, a number of Pentecostal scholars are attempting to distance themselves from an evangelical identity. Attempts to cast Pentecostal theology as evangelical theology "plus" have been characterized as

---

69. "Assemblies Superintendent Named NAE Head," 14.
70. Blumhofer, *Restoring the Faith*, 197.
71. Poloma, "Future of American Pentecostal Identity," 153.
72. Poloma, "Future of American Pentecostal Identity," 160.
73. Poloma, "Future of American Pentecostal Identity," 164.
74. Poloma, "Future of American Pentecostal Identity," 158. She notes that 85 percent of AG pastors said that an AG identity was very important or extremely important, 69 percent said the identity as "evangelical" was very important or extremely important, and 88 percent said that the identity "Pentecostal" was very important or extremely important.

a "selling of a birthright for evangelical respectability."[75] The AG's quest to court evangelical acceptance is believed to have led to a "colonization" of Pentecostal ethos.[76] William Faupel warned that the Pentecostal movement was at a "crossroads" where two competing visions were present. The first is to see the movement as a subgroup of Evangelicalism, which he believes will only lead to the movement becoming "rationalistic and stale."[77] The alternative vision is to see the movement as distinct from Evangelicalism, with its own mission, hermeneutic, and theological agenda, because of its pneumatological orientation. Pentecostal scholars are offering constructive pneumatological contributions to the various disciplines within systematic theology. Kenneth Archer believes that casting Pentecostal theology as evangelical theology "plus" is no longer sufficient. He says, "To subsume Pentecostalism into the category Evangelicalism is to exclude aspects of Pentecostalism that are essential to its identity and undermine its capability to present an authentic Pentecostal theology."[78]

The dual concern of being co-opted by Evangelicalism and the desire for Pentecostalism to be recognized as a distinct tradition is warranted. As Archer notes, the differences are not primarily doctrinal; they are found in the manner and method by which they do theology.[79] First, Pentecostals have a doxological approach to theology, which is reflected in the way that propositional theology is subordinated to experience, testimony, song, and pneumatic expressions.[80] Secondly, Pentecostals don't just read the Scriptures; they experience the Scriptures through the Spirit. This is in contrast to traditional Protestant hermeneutics, particularly the hermeneutics of Fundamentalism. As Yong notes, Pentecostals read the word in conversation with the Spirit and the community.[81] Finally, whereas evangelicals are

---

75. Johns, "Adolescence of Pentecostalism," 3–17.

76. Jacobsen explains, "Mainstream evangelicals and Pentecostals were not cultural equals in America, and in this unequal situation, Pentecostals (the culturally weaker partners) could not help but be, in a sense, colonized by the stronger. Mainstream evangelicals' theological ideas, attitudes, and methods were soon being imported wholesale into the Pentecostal world, and a new evangelical paradigm of Pentecostal theology quickly began to replace the waning hegemony of Pentecostal scholasticism." Jacobsen, "Knowing the Doctrines of Pentecostals," 100.

77. Faupel, "Whither Pentecostalism?," 27.

78. Archer, "Pentecostal Way of Doing Theology," 304–5.

79. Archer, "Pentecostal Way of Doing Theology," 301–14.

80. Hollenweger, "Pentecostal Elites and the Pentecostal Poor," 201.

81. Yong, *Spirit-Word-Community*.

Aspects of Evangelical Identity

grounded in a modernistic historical-critical methodology, Pentecostals utilize more postmodern and post-critical methods in their contextual and narrative readings of Scripture.[82] These differences in the manner and method, among other concerns, suggest that evangelical approaches are insufficient to develop an authentic Pentecostal theology.[83] Archer therefore believes, "Pentecostalism should be appreciated for what it is—an authentically new living Christian spirituality with distinct theological view of reality."[84]

At the same time, historians struggle to accept the idea that Pentecostals are not evangelicals given the historical antecedents that led to the movement. Walter Hollenweger argued the Pentecostal Movement inherited a multiplicity of theological traditions: an African spirituality (oral root),[85] a Wesleyan holiness character (pietistic root),[86] and evangelical doctrine (Biblicism root).[87] Even though these three roots have affected the Pentecostal Movement, different streams find themselves influenced to varying degrees by these theological identities. The AG has historically been more comfortable with an evangelical identity than other groups and consequently more closely mirrors that tradition.

IMPLICATIONS

Considering the suggestions made by Pentecostal scholars about the theological, hermeneutical, and methodological challenges created by

---

82. Archer, *Pentecostal Hermeneutic*, 172–211.

83. Other concerns for Pentecostals found in their critique of evangelical identity include the exclusion of women, reversal on passivism, and social quietism.

84. See Archer, "Pentecostal Way of Doing Theology," 301–14.

85. Hollenweger, *Pentecostalism*, 18–19, argues Pentecostalism inherited from African spirituality the characteristics of orality in liturgy, narrative theology, testimony, and participatory worship. See also Hollenweger, "Black Roots of Pentecostalism," 33–44; Alexander, *Black Fire*.

86. Hollenweger, *Pentecostalism*, 144–52, notes Wesley's emphasis on free will and active sanctification was rooted in Catholic "free will" spirituality. Although the theology behind perfection was the catalyst, it was his emphasis on a three-stage *ordo salutis* that leaves a theological footprint on Pentecostalism.

87. Hollenweger, *Pentecostalism*, 181–200, notes the higher life evangelical theology of Oberlin and its theological successors, Charles Finney, Asa Mahan, William Boardman, and Robert and Hannah Whitall Smith, most influenced Pentecostalism. The characteristics of an emphasis on doctrinal orthodoxy, Biblicism, and premillennialism found their way into the Pentecostal ethos through this root.

evangelical approaches and the presence of the AG's clear identification with evangelical identity, a number of considerations should be made that help nuance this tension in Pentecostal theology. First, although the AG did not officially change its name to "The Pentecostal Evangelical Church," it is clear to me that they have always self-identified as such. This challenges the idea that the AG was "co-opted" by Evangelicalism or Fundamentalism or that it adopted an identity contrary to its original Pentecostal identity. They saw themselves as a subset of a larger evangelical family that also believed in the baptism in the Holy Spirit. Finished work streams demonstrate more evangelical characteristics and are more comfortable with an evangelical identity.

Second, these early AG leaders would disagree with the premise that their evangelical orientation was harmful to their Pentecostal theology. They believed that Pentecostals and turn-of-the-century evangelicals shared a common theological emphasis on salvation, healing, Spirit-baptism, sanctification, and the premillennial return of Christ. Even after being rejected by evangelicals/fundamentalists because of Pentecostal distinctive in the late 1920s, the AG warmly embraced the broader tradition and sought to express the ways in which they were similar despite the differences in the doctrine of Spirit baptism.

The AG's consistent identification with Evangelicalism confirms Hollenwegger's assertion that the Pentecostal Movement inherited a multiplicity of theological traditions, including the evangelical root.[88] This quest for evangelical identity, in this light, should not be seen as foreign to the Pentecostal identity. As Jacobsen points out, each root depends upon, confirms, and mutually criticizes each other in an effort to build a coherent whole.[89] Considering the way in which the AG has identified as both Pentecostal and evangelical, I think Gary McGee says it best. "The greatest hurdle in its path into the twenty-first century, therefore, stands in how successfully it recaptures what it means to be 'more than evangelical.'"[90]

---

88. Hollenweger, *Pentecostalism*, 181–200.

89. Jacobsen argues, "All the diverse versions of Pentecostalism stand to some degree on their own, mutually criticizing each other and confirming each other in complex ways. They are held together by overlapping (but not necessarily identical) concerns, practices and experiences, which, as each separate Pentecostal sub-tradition illustrates, can explained in a number of relatively coherent and consistent ways." Jacobsen, *Thinking in the Spirit*, 12.

90. McGee, "More Than Evangelical," 289–300.

Chapter 5

Aspects of Eschatological Influences

INTRODUCTION

THIS CHAPTER EXAMINES THE theological influences that shaped the eschatology of the Assemblies of God. Identifying the theological antecedents can be particularly challenging for a movement that claims no roots.[1] Many early Pentecostals believed that their theology originated directly from Scripture, not from ideas inherited from developments in church history. At the same time, Pentecostal papers regularly featured evangelical books of previous generations. These sources provided perspectives that were assimilated into the doctrines that were eventually codified into denominational beliefs.[2] This is particularly true in that most first-generation Pentecostals entered the movement from various denominational backgrounds, including Methodist, Holiness, Baptist, Presbyterian, and Christian & Missionary Alliance. With that, the prevailing eschatological positions at the turn of the century were premillennial and dispensational in nature. The task of the historiographer is to identify the theological and cultural influences on a movement and craft a historical account of influences that shaped the subject.

William Menzies pointed out there were several theological streams that influenced the AG's premillennial and dispensational eschatology.[3] He recognizes the high priority of eschatology in the early years in that four

1. Lawrence, *Apostolic Faith Restored*, 12.
2. Kay, "Three Generations On," 58–70.
3. Menzies, *Anointed to Serve*, 27–28.

of the sixteen fundamental truths focused on premillennial eschatology.[4] Because the AG developed at the same time Fundamentalism, he believed it was an "easy exercise" for early leaders to adopt evangelical and dispensational understandings of dispensational eschatology, even though they had to "modify" it in ways that managed the problematic elements for Pentecostal theology.[5] AG leaders were willing to overlook the tensions in dispensationalism by simply giving it a "proper Pentecostal baptism."[6]

Edith Blumhofer also notes that influence but is less positive about the effects upon the AG. She argues that during the decades of the 1920s–1930s the AG gradually left its restorationist roots and adopted fundamentalist positions (including eschatology) as it sought to gain acceptance into the broader evangelical world. She believed that this shift made the AG no more than "fundamentalism with a difference."[7] Concerns about this turn have led some to question the ability of dispensational premillennialism to reflect Pentecostal commitments. In fact, Gerald Sheppard noted that the "uneasy" tensions in dispensationalism are highly problematic for the AG but also argued that AG positions do not necessarily commit the AG to dispensationalism.[8] Yet, Margaret Poloma and John Green noted that 94 percent of AG ministers agree or strongly agree that the Bible clearly teaches a "premillennial" view of the future, and 98 percent reported believing in the immanent "rapture" of the church.[9] However, only "58 percent reported accepting a dispensationalist interpretation of Scripture, 42 percent rejected this approach."[10] Therefore, it seems that the current mood of the AG is to prioritize premillennialism, but they are not overly committed to dispensationalism as the primary emphasis.

If dispensational premillennialism had this tension, then how did these frameworks make their way into the AG? This chapter attempts to answer that question by looking at the influential materials that Pentecostals were reading in which these views were communicated. It will begin by looking briefly at the origins of dispensationalism and how it influenced the eschatology of the AG. Next, it will discuss some of the evangelical works

---

4. Menzies, *Anointed to Serve*, 77–78.
5. Menzies, *Anointed to Serve*, 329.
6. Menzies, *Anointed to Serve*, 27.
7. Blumhofer, *Restoring the Faith*, 137.
8. Sheppard, "Pentecostals and the Hermeneutics," 5–33.
9. Poloma and Green, *Assemblies of God*, 82.
10. Poloma and Green, *Assemblies of God*, 82.

that influenced early AG leaders and how those ideas were promoted. Finally, it will look at some of the earliest works by Pentecostals that were promoted but that have not been widely recognized by previous studies.

ADOPTING DISPENSATIONALISM

Dispensational premillennialism is a particular eschatological framework developed in the 1800s that affirms the historical divisions of history, the separation of the church and Israel, the rapture of the church, the tribulation, and the premillennial coming of Christ. In *Imagining the Future*, Isgrigg documented some of the popular expressions of dispensational paradigms by AG ministers in the *Pentecostal Evangel*, where most AG ministers modified dispensationalism to cultivate a robust pneumatological eschatology. When one evaluates AG eschatology simply by comparing the script and order of events, there is little difference from fundamentalist expressions of dispensationalism premillennialism. However, it is noted that the order of events was not the determining factor of what made their eschatology Pentecostal or non-Pentecostal; it was whether the Spirit was the foundational orientation and the primary sign of the last days as either end-times signs or end-time "sighs" of the Spirit. While views of the rapture and tribulation varied, some sort of dispensational approach, primarily rooted in the latter rain narrative, existed in most formulaic expressions.[11]

When most historians trace dispensationalism into history, they often begin with John Nelson Darby. However, this approach is incomplete because it fails to recognize the charismatic origins of the dispensational framework that was developed in the 1820s prophecy movement in Great Britain, particularly at Henry Drummond's Albury Conferences.[12] Interest in the subject of biblical prophecy developed as postmillennial cultural optimism was slowly shifting to premillennial pessimism as the industrial age was challenging cultural institutions.[13] The prophecy discussions at the Albury Conferences led to two key developments in how premillennialism was expressed. First, they came to a consensus that the present age would get worse and worse, which would terminate in a time of judgment before the coming of Christ and the millennial kingdom.[14] Second, Edward Ir-

11. Isgrigg, *Imagining the Future*, ch. 11.
12. Isgrigg, "Charismatic Origins of the Rapture."
13. Prosser, *Dispensationalist Eschatology*, 116; Kay, *Pentecostalism*, 38.
14. Drummond, *Defense of the Students*, 124–25. See also Prosser, *Dispensational Eschatology*, 137.

ving introduced the concept of a "the latter rain" outpouring of the Spirit that would take place before Christ's coming, which would be an end-time sign that God was restoring the gifts of the Spirit, including speaking in tongues.[15] John Nelson Darby, a disgruntled Anglican priest in Dublin, attended these conferences and adopted three concepts that became the hallmarks of his dispensational teachings about premillennialism.[16] First was the belief that history could be divided into various "dispensations" terminated by a period of judgment. The second was the belief that national Israel would be restored in anticipation of the second coming of Jesus to reign on earth from Jerusalem. The third and most notable is that there will be two phases of the coming of Christ: a secret rapture before the tribulation and the glorious appearance of Christ when he returns to earth.[17]

Although Darby's writings were not a direct influence on the AG, the works of other prominent evangelicals who used similar frameworks were all sources for the development of AG eschatology. The concept of the rapture of the Spirit-filled bride was popularized in the 1860s and 1870s by Joseph Seiss in the *Prophetic Times*.[18] Dispensational views were further disseminated by the Niagara Conference on Prophecy, started by James Brookes, and the Northfield Prophecy Conference, started by D. L. Moody in the 1880s.[19] Further, dispensational frameworks for premillennialism were mainstreamed in William E. Blackstone's popular work *Jesus Is Coming* in 1878 and later *The Scofield Reference Bible* in 1910.[20] As Pentecostalism emerged at the beginning of the twentieth century, Pentecostals adopted the latter rain dispensational framework as one of their primary rationales for the restoration of tongues.[21]

ESCHATOLOGICAL INFLUENCES ON THE AG

In the first decade of the Pentecostal Movement, there were very few books on eschatology by Pentecostals in print. Therefore, when AG leaders

---

15. Isgrigg, "Latter Rain Revisited," 439–57.
16. Crutchfield, *Origins of Dispensationalism*.
17. Wilkinson, *For Zion's Sake*, 179–80; Prosser, *Dispensational Eschatology*, 137.
18. Hummel, *Rise and Fall of Dispensationalism*, 51–66.
19. Faupel, *Everlasting Gospel*, 99.
20. Wilkinson, *For Zion's Sake*, 252–57.
21. Isgrigg, "Latter Rain Revisited," 439–57.

wanted to recommend eschatology books to their readers, they naturally drew from books on the topic by respected evangelical leaders. In 1917, the AG published its first list of recommended resources on eschatology, which included *Lectures on Revelation* by William Lincoln and *The Revelation* by Arno Gaebelein.[22] In 1919, the list of recommended eschatology books was expanded to include *Jesus Is Coming* by W. E. Blackstone, *Prophecy and the Lord's Return* by James Gray, and *What Do the Prophets Say?* by C. I. Scofield.[23] Other prophecy books by prominent evangelical authors continued to be promoted throughout the 1920s and 1930s.[24] Three of the most influential non-Pentecostal resources were *Lectures on The Apocalypse* by J. A. Seiss, *Jesus Is Coming* by W. E. Blackstone, and the *Scofield Reference Bible*.

J. A. Seiss

Joseph Seiss was a respected Lutheran pastor and scholar whose *Lectures on the Apocalypse* was one of the few books on Revelation that was promoted early by the AG.[25] Seiss's books and teachings were a popular source for many Pentecostal periodicals.[26] In 1919, when asked what commentary on Revelation they recommended, the editors of the *Pentecostal Evangel* comment, "We know of nothing better than the 'Lectures on the Apocalypse' by Joseph Seiss."[27] E. N. Bell often quoted from Seiss in his answers to questions about eschatology.[28] Seiss's *Apocalypse* was also a regular part of the General Council Reading course for ministers and laypeople.[29] In addition, the *Voices of Babylon*, a commentary on Daniel, was also featured regularly

---

22. "Book of Revelation," Feb. 3, 1917, 15; "Important Books on the Book of Revelation," 3.

23. "Evangel Book Shelf," 16.

24. See "Prophecy," 15; "Second Coming and Prophecy," 15; "Books on Prophecy and the Lord's Return," 16; "Therefore Ye Also Be Ready," 16.

25. Seiss, *Lectures on the Apocalypse*, 6.

26. McQueen, *Toward a Pentecostal Eschatology*, 78–81, 129, 164, 205, notes that both Elizabeth Sexton of the *Bridegroom's Messenger* and G. F. Taylor of the *Pentecostal Holiness Advocate* used Seiss's *Apocalypse* as their primary source on prophecy.

27. Bell, "Few Questions about Books," 12.

28. Bell, "Questions and Answers," Feb. 8, 1919, 5; Bell, "Questions and Answers," June 25, 1921, 2.

29. "General Council Reading Course," Jan. 5, 1924, 8; "General Council Reading Course," Feb. 14, 1931, 15; "General Council Reading Course," Feb. 17, 1934, 16.

in the *Pentecostal Evangel*.[30] Seiss's books were popular, but it was his role as editor of the *Prophetic Times* that he was most influential in disseminating millennial views to a broad audience of evangelical traditions.[31] His "Prophetic Creed," published in the *Prophetic Times*, denounced postmillennialism and summarized the tenets of dispensation eschatology.[32] Articles from his popular paper were regularly included in the *Pentecostal Evangel*.

One of Seiss's main contributions that influenced the Holiness and Pentecostal Movement was the concept of the Spirit-filled bride. Seiss's teaching on the parable of the ten virgins laid the groundwork for the Pentecostal understanding of Spirit-baptism as the minimum requirement for the rapture.[33] But for Seiss, the same pneumatological orientation is applied to his concept of the literal 144,000 from Israel who will receive the seal of the Spirit.[34] Like the seal on the bride, the seal that is applied to their forehead is the baptism in the Holy Spirit. Seiss believed that during the tribulation, the outpouring of the Spirit promised in Joel would come upon Israel. He says, "The Pentecostal Baptism from heaven shall be renewed in them with its original vigor. All the fruits and manifestations of the Holy Ghost, which characterized the apostles and early Christians at the beginning, shall reappear in them, perhaps with augmented power."[35] The seal of the Spirit empowers this company of Jews to be preserved, assured, and to minister in power much as the early apostles experienced. Pentecostals drew from Seiss because of the way his eschatology was so closely wedded to his pneumatology.

W. E. Blackstone

Perhaps the most popular prophecy book of the late nineteenth-century evangelicals was W. E. Blackstone's *Jesus Is Coming*. Blackstone was a

30. "Further List of Helpful Books," 32.

31. Faupel, *Everlasting Gospel*, 99.

32. Prosser, *Dispensational Eschatology*, 207–8. It is interesting to note that the Prophetic Creed held that Christ's return "will not be to depopulate, annihilate, or destroy the earth, but to renovated it by judicial administrations." It further claimed that the earth and heavens will be "renovated" into the new heavens and new earth.

33. Seiss, *Parable of the Ten Virgins*, 24.

34. Seiss says, "They are Jews of a particular class, singled out from the Israelitish populations on account of spiritual attainments and character not found in the rest." Seiss, *Lectures on the Apocalypse*, 409.

35. Seiss, *Lectures on the Apocalypse*, 420.

Aspects of Eschatological Influences

Methodist Episcopal minister and prophecy enthusiast who frequented the prophecy conferences. First published in 1878, *Jesus Is Coming* became popular because of its straightforward explanation of dispensationalist premillennialism. Several of the prophecy movement's most famous leaders claim that his book shaped their own understanding.[36] This book was highly recommended by the AG and was included in the list of prophecy books in the *Evangel* on a regular basis. Bell notes, "'Jesus is Coming' has received wide circulation and has probably done more to awaken a sleeping church to this great truth than any other agency."[37] When the General Council began a "Reading Course" for *Pentecostal Evangel* readers in 1924, *Jesus Is Coming* was selected as the Bible prophecy text.[38] P. C. Nelson recommended Blackstone's book in *Bible Doctrines* as a source for those who want to "go deeper" on the topic of prophecy.[39]

Blackstone's dispensational approach is seen clearly in his seven ages (*aions*) of Bible history: Innocence, Antediluvian, Government, Patriarchal, Mosaic, Christian, and Millennial Age, to be followed by the eternal age of the New Heavens and New Earth.[40] C. Norman Krause notes that Scofield heavily relied upon Blackstone's seven ages more so than Darby's dispensations.[41] Blackstone outlines many of the standard doctrines of dispensationalism, but he also includes chapters where he offers rebuttals to objections to dispensational teaching. One of the objections he notes is that his dispensational understanding "disparages the work of the Holy Spirit," to which he responds, "Not so!"[42] For Blackstone, the Holy Spirit is active throughout this dispensation in teaching, guiding, and comforting

---

36. R. A. Torrey testifies that it was the "first book that made the coming of Jesus Christ a living reality to me." Wilbur Chapman, a prophecy enthusiast himself, comments that this book "revolutionized my thinking." A. T. Pierson calls it the "best brief compendium I have seen on the Lord's coming." Revell Publishing and Moody Bible Institute sent this 1916 "presentation copy" free of charge to missionaries, ministers, and theological students. Blackstone, *Jesus Is Coming*, 1, 246.

37. Blackstone, "Times of the Gentiles," 6. See also advertisements in *Pentecostal Evangel*, May 31, 1919, 16; *Pentecostal Evangel*, Nov. 11, 1922, 23; *Pentecostal Evangel*, May 10, 1924, 16; *Pentecostal Evangel*, Mar. 9, 1935, 16; *Pentecostal Evangel*, Sept. 18, 1937, 16.

38. "General Council Reading Course," Jan. 5, 1924, 8; *GC Constitution and Bylaws* (September 2–7, 1943), 23.

39. Nelson, *Bible Doctrines*, 153.

40. Blackstone, *Jesus Is Coming*, 222–23.

41. Kraus, *Dispensationalism in America*, 34–35.

42. Blackstone, *Jesus Is Coming*, 129.

believers. But the primary role of the Holy Spirit is to seek out and prepare a bride for Jesus, which will be the true church among the visible churches.[43] When Christ returns, the Spirit's work will be finished for a time, but he will ultimately have "a part in the glory and triumph of the millennial dispensation."[44] For Pentecostals, there was an appreciation that Blackstone's dispensational emphasis did not rule out the Holy Spirit.

The Scofield Reference Bible

One of the most influential resources on eschatology was the popular *Scofield Reference Bible*, which first appeared in the *Evangel* in 1914.[45] Cyrus I. Scofield published his Bible in 1909 in consultation with fellow evangelical editors James Gray, William Eerdman, Arno Gaebelein, and A. T. Pierson.[46] Scofield's Bible was groundbreaking because of its helpful notes and cross-references. Though *The Scofield Reference Bible* is often associated with popularizing Darby's dispensational model, it should be better understood as an amalgamation of popular teachings from that era. Scofield himself "disclaimed originality" when it came to the content of his Bible; instead, he engaged in "summarizing, arranging, and condensing" everything he had gained from the evangelical community in both Europe and America.[47]

The *Pentecostal Evangel* highly recommended *The Scofield Reference Bible* to the AG constituency, calling it "a wonderful Bible" that has "gained universal favor with Pentecostal people."[48] The paper also regularly promoted the Bible, often with full-page ads.[49] However, the growing tension with fundamentalists over the doctrine of the Holy Spirit made some in the AG nervous about the AG's promotion. From 1917 to 1918, the Bible received pushback from AG ministers because of fears it was anti-Pentecostal.[50] But the editors, E. N. Bell and J. R. Flower, defended the Bible and highlighted its usefulness on many evangelical truths. E. N. Bell commented:

43. Blackstone, *Jesus Is Coming*, 95.
44. Blackstone, *Jesus Is Coming*, 129–30.
45. *Christian Evangel*, Aug. 8, 1914, 3.
46. Scofield, *Scofield Reference Bible*.
47. Scofield, *Scofield Reference Bible*, introduction.
48. "Scofield Reference Bibles," 16.
49. "Scofield Reference Bible," 16.
50. Isgrigg, *Imagining the Future*, 71–75.

Our Pentecostal people are so well taught on these lines of the Baptism with the Spirit, surely none of them would follow Scofield's wrong conclusions on this matter. Rather, take the many good things in his Bible, and pass these mistakes up to his ignorance of full Pentecostal light.[51]

As editors, the loss of revenue from selling the Bible may have given them added incentive not to see it dropped from the paper.

The Scofield Reference Bible continued to be advertised and used among Pentecostals. But a few years later, the growing tensions with Fundamentalism led to renewed concern from readers. In 1924, the AG Executive Presbytery removed the Bible from their advertisements over objections to his views of the Holy Spirit, such as the dispensational views of the Sermon on the Mount, the postponed kingdom, and Spirit-baptism.[52] The ban continued until 1926 when leaders decided the overall value of the dispensational framework in the Bible was of such great importance that they overlooked what they considered as minor points of difference on the Holy Spirit, the kingdom, and ecclesiology.[53] The Executive Presbyters concluded that *The Scofield Reference Bible* was "perfectly sound" and would once again sell the Bible as long as it was accompanied by the list of issues of disagreement.[54]

PENTECOSTAL INFLUENCES

Since the AG organized and codified its doctrine a decade after Azusa began, one might assume that early Pentecostal leaders, such as Charles Parham, William Seymour, G. F. Taylor, or William Durham, impacted the development of the AG's eschatological doctrine. However, Parham's eschatology was so unique that few of his views were adopted by the AG, or by any other Pentecostal groups for that matter. In fact, his view of the bride, the tribulation, and his doctrine of hell were all "disapproved" by the General Council

---

51. Bell, "Notes on Modern Bibles," 5.

52. McGee, "Historical Background," 22. There is no record of official action to remove the *Scofield Reference Bible* from circulation in the *Pentecostal Evangel*.

53. It is interesting to note that Scofield had very limited notes on 1 Thess 4 not at all referring to this event as the rapture nor explaining its connection to the dispensation that would follow. The word *rapture* does not regularly occur in the Bible's notes and is not included in the topical index. *Scofield Reference Bible*, 1269.

54. "Great Move Forward," 3.

within the first decade.[55] William Seymour certainly emphasized the soon-coming return of Jesus and bridal theology. But eschatological doctrine was not central to the statement of faith in the *Apostolic Faith*, and his book, *Doctrines and Disciplines*, is "absolutely silent" on eschatology.[56] Similarly, William Durham's preoccupation with the finished work doctrine meant he spent little time on eschatology. The only testimony of his eschatological beliefs comes from a few brief mentions in passing in the *Pentecostal Testimony*.[57] Finally, and surprisingly, G. F. Taylor's 1907 book, *The Spirit and the Bride*, was never recommended in the *Pentecostal Evangel*, despite its place as the earliest Pentecostal book on eschatology. These early Pentecostal leaders had little demonstrable influence on the AG's eschatology,

Therefore, the book recommendations in the *Pentecostal Evangel* provide the best perspective on who may have influenced the early AG ministers. From 1914 to 1916, the *Pentecostal Evangel* did not promote any resources on Revelation or Bible prophecy.[58] However, as world events escalated and interest in prophecy increased, the AG thought it was important to recommend books on the subject by Pentecostals.[59] They chose three books by Pentecostals that were in circulation at the time: *The New Testament* by A. S. Worrell, *Outlines Studies in Revelation* by C. M. Turner, and *The Latter Rain Covenant* by D. W. Myland. These three works represent the only Pentecostal eschatology books made available to the AG ministers prior to the move to publish their own doctrinal books in 1925.[60]

A. S. Worrell

One of the earliest Bibles recommended in the *Pentecostal Evangel* was A. S. Worrell's translation of the New Testament, which was published in 1904. Worrell was a well-known Baptist, Greek scholar, educator, college

---

55. *GC Constitution and Bylaws* (September 16–22, 1927), 31; the council disapproved of the post-tribulation position. The doctrine of eternal punishment was affirmed in the 1916 Statement of Fundamental Truths.

56. Synan and Fox, *William J. Seymour*, 52–58. Jacobsen, *Thinking in the Spirit*, 81, concludes that this absence demonstrates that eschatology was not the core message.

57. Durham, "Our Pentecostal Book," 16. Durham had plans to produce a book, but it was never written.

58. Frodsham, "Things Which Must Shortly Come," 6.

59. The first book list appeared in *Weekly Evangel*, Feb. 10, 1917, 16. The first prophecy or Revelation books were promoted in "Important Books," 3.

60. See "Our Pentecostal Books," 16.

president, and editor of several periodicals.[61] Worrell published several books around 1900 that described the basics of the "Full Gospel," which focused on living the Spirit-filled life.[62] Worrell testifies that he was a Christian for over forty years before he was filled with the Spirit in 1891.[63] After hearing about the Pentecostal movement, he visited Azusa Street and spent several weeks there seeking the baptism for himself.[64] Believing that the movement was indeed the manifestation of the latter rain outpouring of the Spirit he wrote a defense for the movement that was carried in several Pentecostal papers.[65] Worrell's status as an educated Baptist scholar and his endorsement of the Pentecostal movement made it natural for Pentecostals to endorse his NT translation.[66]

Worrell's NT provided several important emphases that were influential to AG. First, as a Baptist scholar, Worrell was well known and trusted by AG founders E. N. Bell and A. P. Collins. Bell attended seminary in Louisville, Kentucky, where Worrell lived and published his paper *The Gospel Witness*. Bell often recommended Worrell's NT and quoted from it in his articles.[67] It was Worrell who convinced Collins to seek the baptism in the Spirit and who also prayed for Collins's wife, which resulted in her healing.[68] When Worrell died in 1908, J. W. Welch was named executor for the estate giving him the rights to republish his NT through GPH.[69]

---

61. Kuykendall, "A.S. Worrell's *New Testament*," 270; Blumhofer, *Assemblies of God*, 1:103.

62. Worrell, *Full Gospel Teachings*, 114. Worrell's "full gospel" consisted of redemption, full consecration by yielding to God, the Spirit-filled life, divine healing, and the premillennial advent of Christ. Worrell did not believe that the gifts of the Spirit were relegated to the apostolic age (*Full Gospel Teachings*, 38–54).

63. Worrell, *Full Gospel Teachings*, 53–54, "Formerly, I had, on many occasions, had the Spirit mightily on me and blessed with me; but on the occasion referred to, the Spirit was far more mightily and blessedly in me; and I realized, at that time, the opening up of the well of living water in me, whose blissful flow has never subsided."

64. "Signs Shall Follow," 2.

65. Worrell, "Wonderful Times Coming," 2; *Christian Evangel*, Sept. 18, 1914, 1–2; *Word and Witness*, Sept. 1914, 1.

66. It is worth noting that William Durham used Worrell's translation and advertised for it in *Pentecostal Testimony* 2.8 (July 1910) 16.

67. Bell, "Seventh Day Trouble," 9.

68. Lawrence, "Works of God," 4.

69. "Worrell's New Testament," 7. Worrell's NT was revised and republished in 1957. See *Pentecostal Evangel*, Feb. 3, 1957, 13; *Pentecostal Evangel*, Dec. 29, 1957, 30.

Second, Worrell's Pentecostal experience allowed him to express dispensational eschatology with a Pentecostal framework of the exclusive rapture of the Spirit-filled church.[70] In the same way that "the assembly" is the only true church, Spirit-filled believers are the only true believers who are ready for the rapture. Worrell argued that a true Christian is "fully consecrated, Spirit-filled, watching, expecting and waiting with a deep desire for His coming."[71] Worrell also used the latter rain to argue for the restoration of the full gospel and the fullness of the Spirit. He believed that a "small class of *Spirit-filled, Christ-indwelt*, people" was a sure sign that Christ's coming was near.[72] He says:

> The truly consecrated, Spirit-filled ones, who are "*watching*" (Luke 21:36), "*waiting*" (1 Thess. 1:10), and "*ready*" (Matt. 24:44), will be among those who are caught up without seeing death. The unconverted and the unconsecrated Christians are not *ready* to meet the Bridegroom; and, like foolish virgins, they will be left behind, to go into the *tribulation*.[73]

Worrell's emphasis on the empowerment aspects of Spirit-baptism demonstrates the way in which the concept of the bride was easily modified by Pentecostals.

C. M. Turner

The first commentary on the Book of Revelation that was recommended to the *Pentecostal Evangel* readership was *Outline Studies in the Book of Revelation* by C. M. Turner in 1916.[74] Turner was an evangelist from Ohio

---

70. Kuykendall, "A. S. Worrell's *New Testament*," 278.
71. Worrell, *Full Gospel Teachings*, 128.
72. Worrell, *Full Gospel Teachings*, 123.
73. Worrell, *Full Gospel Teachings*, 115 (emphasis original).
74. Turner, *Outline Studies*. Stanley Frodsham says, "The *Evangel* office has been slow to recommend any special writing on this great theme, although there has been an endorsement in general of the writings of Myland, Seiss and others; but the *Evangel* is now in possession of a quantity of the lately published writings of C. W. M. Turner. . . . This is an excellent book which makes the Book of Revelation easy to understand. We recommend it to our readers." Frodsham, "Things Which Must Shortly Come," 6. Turner's book was also advertised in evangelical sources such as D. L. Moody's *Christian Workers Magazine*. See *Christian Workers Magazine* 17 (Sept. 1916) 213 on the Consortium of Pentecostal Archives site.

who attended the October 1916 General Council in St. Louis.⁷⁵ Turner's relationship with the Pentecostal Movement in Ohio made his work a favorite for the editors, who called his book a "valuable book on prophecy which sets forth the Book of Revelation from the standpoint of one of the best scholars in the Pentecostal movement."⁷⁶ It was so popular in the AG that within three months, the *Evangel* was sold out of copies, and Turner appealed to the readership to help him fund the second edition.⁷⁷

The title *Outlines Studies* is a good description of this work. Rather than going verse by verse, Turner uses each section of the book as a way of thematically talking about the biblical teaching on eschatological events. Turner believed that reading the book of Revelation would place a burden on believers that would convince them of their need for baptism in the Holy Spirit. He even notes a man who, after reading Revelation, went to the woods to pray and was overcome with weeping until he received the baptism in the Spirit.⁷⁸ The closeness of Christ's return convinced Turner that believers should earnestly seek "to be endued with power from on high" to overcome the perils of apostasy taking place as the age comes to a close. He says, "It is only the Baptism of the Holy Ghost that will make us full overcomers in these perilous times." In response to the deteriorating conditions in the world, he believed God was sending the "latter rain outpouring of the Spirit" that is spoken of by the prophet Joel.⁷⁹ This outpouring of the Spirit is one of the "marked signs of the imminence of the Lord's return."

As a Pentecostal, Turner pays particular attention to the passages in Revelation that discuss the Holy Spirit. For example, Turner interprets the seven-fold Spirit in the opening chapters as the seven activities of the Holy Spirit. Turner also connects this seven-fold spirit to the image of the Lamb in Rev 5:6. He interprets the seven horns of the Lamb as Christ's "kingly

75. "Council Roll," 11.

76. "Outlines Studies of the Book of Revelation," 11. This ad includes recommendations from Charles Blanchard, president of Wheaton College, and fellow Ohio Pentecostal D. W. Kerr.

77. "Book of Revelation," Feb. 3, 1917, 15; "Book of Revelation," Mar. 24, 1917, 12; "Outlines Studies of the Book of Revelation," 11. Turner's book continued to be recommended until 1920 when newer fundamentalist resources and later AG works took prominence. The fact that Turner had to request help from *Evangel* readers to print the second edition could suggest that the book fell out of use due to the costs associated with printing further editions.

78. Turner, *Outline Studies*, 59.

79. Turner, *Outline Studies*, 21. Turner references a tract he wrote called "Latter Rain Outpouring of the Holy Spirit."

power" and the seven eyes as the "complete Baptism of the Holy Spirit," which vocationally qualifies Jesus for his coronation as King.[80] He also sees the baptism in the Spirit as the "sealing" of the 144,000, although it is interpreted as a literal number of Jewish believers in literal fulfillment of Joel's prophecy.[81] This mighty outpouring of the Spirit upon Israel during the tribulation will result in gentile believers from every tribe and nation being saved during the tribulation. Similarly, the two witnesses receive a mighty baptism of the Holy Ghost that equips them to be witnesses.

Despite his Pentecostal orientation, his interpretation of events followed the primary interpretations by Scofield and others as to the dispensational script.[82] He argues that the present church dispensation is a "parenthesis" in God's plan in which he is actively drawing out a gentile people to fulfill his plans. The gentile dispensation will end with the rapture of the church, which will be the point at which God resumes his plan for Israel during the final seven years of the dispensation called the Tribulation. The millennium will begin when Christ returns with his bride from heaven and sets up his rule in the New Jerusalem. At that time, the promises concerning Israel will be fulfilled, and Christ will reign in righteousness on earth for one thousand years.[83] During the millennium, humanity will experience a "special outpouring of the Holy Spirit," and Israel will bless the nations of the earth with the gospel.[84] Under the reign of Christ, all of creation will undergo a transformation that reverses the curse of Eden. For Turner, the creation will be purified but not annihilated. Out of the purification of the millennium will emerge the new heavens and new earth, which will be the eternal dwelling for humanity and God.

Turner's attempt to interpret prophecy and the book of Revelation in light of his Pentecostal experience is key to understanding early AG eschatology. On the one hand, Turner interprets the symbols of the Holy Spirit in light of his experience of the baptism in the Holy Spirit. On the other hand, Turner's Pentecostal hermeneutic does not allow that experience to change the way in which he understands the order of events or the script in general. For information on understanding the events, he draws on evangelical

---

80. Turner, *Outline Studies*, 27–28.
81. Turner, *Outline Studies*, 44.
82. Turner, *Outline Studies*, 64.
83. Turner, *Outline Studies*, 155.
84. Turner, *Outline Studies*, 156–57.

sources by J. A. Seiss and C. I. Scofield. Turner's tendency toward connection without integration is a pattern that AG writers will follow.

D. W. Myland

David Wesley Myland was a popular Pentecostal evangelist who was reared in the Christian and Missionary Alliance (C&MA). In 1909, Myland published a series of lectures on the "Latter Rain Covenant" in the *Latter Rain Evangel*.[85] Several years later, he also published a series of articles on the book of Revelation.[86] Both of these teachings were compiled and published as books by the *Latter Rain Evangel*'s publishing house,[87] and were highly recommended in the *Pentecostal Evangel*.[88] Although the concept of the latter rain was already present in evangelical circles, Myland gained notoriety as the one who "revealed" this truth to the Pentecostal Movement.[89] In 1912, he left the C&MA over their stance on the tongues and founded Gibeah Bible School in Plainfield, Indiana, with J. R. Flower. Though he never joined the AG, Myland was influential in Pentecostal circles, especially in Chicago and Ohio's Pentecostal C&MA community.

Myland's theology of Pentecost was fluid, and his approach to eschatology was pastoral and poetic.[90] Myland's eschatology and pneumatology are intimately intertwined and interdependent. In fact, it was during a time of sickness that Myland testified he was carried away in the Spirit

---

85. Myland, "Latter Rain Covenant" (June 1909), 15–22; Myland, "Latter Rain Covenant" (July 1909), 2–3, 15–22; Myland, "Latter Rain—Its Designs and Operations," 11–18; Myland, "Fifth Latter Rain Lecture," 13–19; Myland, "Literal and Spiritual Rain," 17–23.

86. Myland, "Book of the Revelation of Jesus Christ," 5–12; Myland, "Book of the Revelation of Jesus Christ" (Feb. 1911), 2–6; Myland, "Book of the Revelation of Jesus Christ" (Mar. 1911), 2–6; Myland, "Book of the Revelation of Jesus Christ" (Apr. 1911), 3–7; Myland, "Book of Revelation" (May 1911), 13–17; Myland, "Book of Revelation" (June 1911), 4–9; Myland, "Book of Revelation" (July 1911) ,6–10; Myland, "Book of Revelation" (Aug. 1911), 5–13; Myland, "Book of Revelation" (Sept. 1911), 14–19; Myland, "Revelation of Jesus Christ," 19–22.

87. Myland, *Latter Rain Covenant*; Myland, *Revelation of Jesus Christ*. For this study I chose to use the *Latter Rain Evangel* articles over the books because they were the original sources for the book.

88. "Important Books," 3.

89. Isgrigg, "Latter Rain Revisited," 439–57.

90. Jacobsen refers to Myland's eschatology as "irenic," "pastoral," and "practical" rather than developed and technical. Jacobsen, *Thinking in the Spirit*, 120–22.

while speaking in tongues and received the revelation of the latter rain covenant.[91] Myland believed that the existence of the Pentecostal movement could only be explained as a sovereign act of the Spirit of God intended to move history toward the return of Christ.[92] Myland's popularization of the "latter rain" concept helped shape the theological orientation and self-understanding of the Pentecostal movement. While many give Myland credit for its origin, as noted earlier, the concept of the latter rain was not new.[93] What was unique was the covenantal application of the latter rain promise of Pentecost in which the literal covenant with Israel also applies to "spiritual Israel," which is the church.[94] By tracing the rainfall in Palestine from 1860 to 1908, Myland draws a parallel between the physical rainfall and the spiritual rainfall in the concept of the latter rain. He says, "For just as the literal early and latter rain was poured out on Palestine, so upon the church of the First Century was poured out the spiritual early rain, and upon us today is being poured out the spiritual latter rain."[95] Myland linked the promise of the Pentecostal outpouring of the Spirit in Acts 2 and the covenantal promise of the latter rain in Deut 11. Through this metaphorical connection, Myland parallels the spiritual fulfillment of the promise of the latter rain on the church with the literal fulfillment in Palestine.[96] Therefore, the literal rainfall in Palestine was a confirmation of the eschatological rainfall throughout the world, in which the Spirit established the "days of heaven on earth."[97]

---

91. Myland, "Latter Rain Covenant" (June 1909), 15; Myland, "Latter Rain Covenant" (July 1909), 15; Myland, "Latter Rain—Its Designs and Operations," 13–14. However, Myland is disingenuous to claim such, as Myland's version was little more than an application of the concept of the literal and spiritual aspects of the latter rain popularized by mid and late eighteenth-century evangelicals. See Isgrigg, "Latter Rain Revisited," 454–56.

92. Myland believed the prayers of those prior to the movement during the previous decades were being answered by the outpouring of the Spirit. He says, "The church was only praying for rain, ordinary rain, and God sent the latter rain for it was time." Myland, "Latter Rain Covenant" (July 1909), 18, 21.

93. Myland, *Latter Rain Covenant*, preface. In Myland, "Literal and Spiritual Rain," 17, Piper comments, "The Latter Rain Covenant! Who ever heard of it before? . . . In our study of theology we have found nothing which in uniqueness and originality equals these expositions in the blessed latter rain truths."

94. Althouse, *Spirit of the Last Days*, 18.

95. Myland, "Latter Rain Covenant" (June 1909), 15.

96. Myland, "Literal and Spiritual Rain," 19.

97. Myland, "Latter Rain Covenant" (July 1909), 4.

A unique feature of his dispensational framework is a three-fold interpretive approach to Scripture.[98] The first layer of meaning in a text is a literal historical fulfillment in which there is a physical fulfillment through the early and latter rains being restored to Palestine. The second meaning is a spiritual and personal fulfillment through the latter rain experience of the baptism in the Spirit. The third meaning is the "prophetical" or "dispensational" application, in which the Spirit will be poured out on Israel in preparation for the coming millennial age.[99] He says, "Now we are in the Gentile Pentecost; the first Pentecost *started* the church, the body of Christ, and this, the second Pentecost, unites and perfects the church unto the coming of the Lord. While we are busy getting ready for His return, the Jew is busy getting ready to return to the land of his people."[100] Through his "dispensational" approach, he is able to separate and yet correlate Israel and the church.[101] Just as the literal rain is falling on literal Israel, who is the "terrestrial bride," the Pentecostal outpouring of the Spirit is preparing the "celestial bride," who is spiritual Israel.[102] At the rapture, Jesus will come for his "spiritual bride." At the appearing, he will return with the church, his spiritual bride, and be embraced by Israel, his earthly bride.

For Myland, bridal requirements are somewhat fluid and, despite his emphasis on the latter rain, are not necessarily pneumatologically centered. He often uses the concepts of bride, church, and body interchangeably. Those who are born again are "born into the kingdom," but those who are baptized in the Holy Spirit are baptized "into the Body."[103] On the one hand, he reflects his C&MA heritage, in that the bride will be those who are "saved and sanctified."[104] On the other hand, he gives significance to the Pente-

---

98. Myland, "Latter Rain Covenant" (July 1909), 15. Myland says, "There are many scriptures that are not only double-barreled, but triple barreled; they are literal, typical and prophetical; or putting it in other words, historical, spiritual and dispensational."

99. Myland, "Latter Rain Covenant" (June 1909), 21.

100. Myland, "Fifth Latter Rain Lecture," 14.

101. Myland, "Fifth Latter Rain Lecture," 14.

102. He says, "Spiritually the latter rain is coming to the church of God at the same time it is coming literally upon the land, and it will never be taken away from her, but it will be upon her to unite and empower her, to cause her to aid in God's last work for this dispensation, to bring about the unity of the body, the consummation of the age, and the catching away of spiritual Israel, the Bride of Christ." Myland, "Fifth Latter Rain Lecture," 13. See also Myland, "Literal and Spiritual Rain," 18.

103. Myland, "Book of the Revelation of Jesus Christ" (Feb. 1911), 11.

104. Myland, "Fifth Latter Rain Lecture," 15.

costal experience for admission into the bride. He says, "The paramount and essential significance of this Pentecostal movement, beyond all tongues and interpretation, is the transfiguring power of the vision of the glorified Lord on the soul of man, preparatory to the transfiguration of the Bride."[105] Though missions is of primary importance, the true purpose of the gentile dispensation is not to convert the nations; it is to prepare a bride for the bridegroom.[106] However, after the rapture, God will form another bride, the Jewish bride consisting of 144,000 Jewish people who will be sealed and protected throughout the tribulation.[107]

Myland offers a unique approach to Revelation where he outlines four schools of interpretation: Preterist, Presentist/Historical, Futurist, and the "harmonic school."[108] To Myland, the harmonic school is the most important because it recognizes that there is truth in each of these approaches. For Myland, all Scripture, especially the book of Revelation, can only be understood through prayer and the illumination of the Holy Spirit.[109] His pneumatic approach is evident in the way he recognizes various thematic elements such as the seven consummations, beatitudes, and songs.[110] But the overall purpose of the book of Revelation is to "reveal Jesus Christ to the churches" in his resurrected, manifest, perpetual, and victorious life.[111]

Another important aspect of Myland's eschatology was his multiple rapture theory. Myland's covenantal approach separates the rapture companies based on their identity as Jews and gentiles.[112] The first company to be raptured is the bride, who is ready at the beginning of the tribulation. Second, during the tribulation, God will seal the Jewish bride (144,000) and will take them to heaven about halfway through. After that, the tribulation saints who are martyred for their testimony of the Lamb and believers who endure the second half of the tribulation will be raptured toward the end of the tribulation, when they will be sealed and protected until the end of the tribulation when they receive their resurrection and translation in order

---

105. Myland, "Book of the Revelation of Jesus Christ" (Jan. 1911), 11.

106. Myland, "Book of the Revelation of Jesus Christ" (Feb. 1911), 10–11.

107. Myland, "Book of Revelation" (Aug. 1911). 8–9.

108. Myland, "Book of Revelation" (Dec. 1910), 2–4.

109. Myland, "Book of Revelation" (Dec. 1910), 7.

110. Myland, "Book of the Revelation of Jesus Christ" (Jan. 1911), 5–12.

111. Myland, "Book of the Revelation of Jesus Christ" (Jan. 1911), 11–12.

112. Myland, "Book of Revelation" (Sept. 1911), 14–15. This scenario, though covered throughout his commentary, is best expressed in this section.

to meet Jesus and his bride as they descend to earth to establish the kingdom.[113] All in all, Myland identifies seven distinct groups in Revelation.[114]

Myland's covenantal approach does place a value on the destiny of creation, which he believes will be renewed, not destroyed. Because God promised Noah he would never destroy the world, only a portion of the Earth will be affected by the judgments of the tribulation.[115] During the millennium, the Earth will be renewed and restored physically, healing of the cosmic realm, spiritually in the worship of the Messiah, and ethically in the restoration of the kingdom of God.[116] The new creation will be a "renewed heaven and renewed earth; not the old heaven and old earth taken away entirely. God gave you a new heart, but you are still Mrs. Smith. So this earth is going to be regenerated just like men."[117] The separation of church and Israel becomes permanent in the New Jerusalem where the earthly people (Israel) will rule Jerusalem, while the heavenly people (church) will rule everything outside the city.[118]

Myland's approach to eschatology is complex and filled with typologies. His multi-dimensional hermeneutical approach is Spirit-oriented and is open to levels of interpretation. Although he is convinced of his harmonic approach, "Time will decide all details of the various shades of truth, and as we get nearer to the *parousia* of the Lord, we shall come nearer together."[119] Despite that, he takes the details in Revelation quite literally, even to the number of saved who will rule during the millennium. In the end, the Spirit plays a role in restoring the latter rain before the eschaton but does not enable any sort of pneumatological understanding of the end. Like Turner, this mechanistic approach connects the Spirit with the script but does not allow the two concepts to integrate to any great degree.

---

113. Myland, "Book of Revelation" (Sept. 1911), 15.

114. Myland says, "Now in this survey we have seven ranks or classes; the perfect and complete number. (1) the four living creatures; (2) the twenty-four elders; (3) the Bride; (4) the first section of the tribulation saints; (5) the 144,000; (6) the second section of tribulation saints; and (7) all the rest of the saved. Seven classes." Myland, "Book of Revelation" (Mar. 1912), 14.

115. Myland, "Book of Revelation" (May 1911), 14.

116. Myland, "Book of Revelation" (Feb. 1912), 11. Myland identifies seven conditions of the Millennium: liberty of conscience, renewal of the earth, righteousness, perfect cosmic conditions, perfect health, long life, and perfect peace.

117. Myland, "Latter Rain Covenant" (July 1910), 19.

118. Myland, "Book of Revelation" (Mar. 1912), 14.

119. Myland, "Latter Rain Covenant" (Dec. 1910), 3.

CONCLUSION

Several conclusions can be made from these early eschatological influences. First, the AG relied heavily on evangelical works that were standards for that era. They endorsed these resources and adopted the basic dispensational frameworks they employed. One of the key features was the emphasis on the Spirit in preparing the bride for his coming. This was a common idea in evangelical eschatology that fit perfectly within the Pentecostal dispensational framework of the latter rain. Second, the Pentecostal resources had a wide variety of positions on the rapture, primarily due to the concept of the Spirit-filled bride and the classification of people based on their acceptance of the Pentecostal experience. Seiss's concept of the exclusive Spirit-filled rapture continued in Worrell, Turner, and Myland and prompted each author to hold to multiple rapture positions. Although later the AG took a stance on a general rapture doctrine and rejected the Spirit-filled exclusive rapture, in these early days, a variety of views were present.[120] The editors of the *Pentecostal Evangel* were certainly comfortable with these varieties and endorsed such works for the young fellowship.

Finally, a variety of hermeneutical frameworks are presented in these works. While Blackstone and Scofield took rather conventional dispensational interpretations, you see multiple hermeneutical approaches in these Pentecostal authors. Turner paid particular attention to interpreting Revelation through a pneumatological lens. His interpretation of images like horns and eyes as the Holy Spirit shows that he did not hold to literalist interpretations. Instead, his figurative approach gave the Spirit freedom to interpret the text pneumatologically. Even more characteristic of this fluid approach is Myland's four-fold interpretive framework. His literal, spiritual, prophetic, and dispensational layers are unique and eschew the flat reading of Scripture often found in literalist approaches to the Scripture. Furthermore, his "harmonic" approach to the text allowed readers to find truth in each approach, allowing the Spirit to provide layers of meaning to Scripture.

---

120. Isgrigg, *Imagining the Future*, 69–71.

Chapter 6

Aspects of Eschatological Variety

SEVERAL IMPORTANT DEVELOPMENTS WERE documented in my 2021 study of AG eschatology.[1] One of the most surprising was the variety of positions on various eschatological tenets within the premillennial framework. While dispensational frameworks were often utilized, there were definite modifications to allow for Pentecostal distinctives. There was also some variety in emphasis, tribulation positions, and rapture theories alluded to in the study. Because this work was limited to analyzing eschatology in the *Pentecostal Evangel*, doctrinal books were excluded from the analysis. Yet, these doctrinal sources are essential and provide another layer of insight into some of the variety in the AG in eschatological positions. This chapter will explore some of those nuances captured in early expressions by AG leaders. It will also draw other insights from early leaders that help to frame how eschatological variety was not only common but may explain why the Statement of Fundamental Truths was broad enough to accommodate those positions.

PNEUMATOLOGICAL APPROACHES

The first task is to explore the eschatology of some of the early works published before and after the founding of the Gospel Publishing House. During the first decade of the AG, there were no books published by GPH on eschatology until they began a series of their doctrinal books in 1925 called

---

1. See Isgrigg, *Imagining the Future*, ch. 11.

the Pulpit and Pew Series. Before this, two eschatological works by AG ministers were published apart from the AG: Elizabeth Sisson's *Foregleams of Glory* (1912) and A. P. Collins's *The Sign of Son of Man* (1919). When the GPH did publish its works in 1925, there was a mix of theological approaches and Bible prophecy approaches.[2] This section will focus on the various works of this first generation. What is unique about these works is that they present a pneumatologically based eschatology rather than concentrating on prophetic events. While each one is different, they offer a glimpse into the eschatological orientation of these early authors.

Elizabeth Sisson

Elizabeth Sisson is a lesser-known early AG minister.[3] Sisson had a long and varied career as an evangelist, missionary to India, and editor, and was a close friend of Carrie Judd Montgomery and Maria Woodworth-Etter. In 1871, before leaving for India as a missionary, Sisson attended a holiness convention led by William Boardman. She testified, "God met me again, baptizing me with His Spirit, and taking me into closest relation with Himself."[4] In the early 1880s, Sisson returned from India to recover from an illness, and she settled into a healing house in Bethshan, London. In 1885, she attended the Keswick convention and spoke during many sessions.[5] In 1887, equipped with the baptism in the Spirit, she returned to the US to minister with Carrie Jude Montgomery, and for a short time, she co-edited *Triumphs of Faith*.[6] She also regularly spoke at meetings in the early Sun-

2. Beginning in 1925, GPH began publishing a series of eschatology books by AG authors. The first books included *Little Flock in the Last Days* by Alice Luce, *Things Which Must Shortly Come to Pass* by Stanley Frodsham, and *Are the Saints Scheduled to Go through the Tribulation?* by J. Narver Gortner. See "Our Pentecostal Books," 16. The publishing of the Pulpit and Pew series marked a significant moment in the AG's organizational development. With the revision of the Statement of Fundamental Truths in 1927, new emphasis was placed on publishing materials for the next generation of AG ministers.

3. A. G. Ward called Sisson "a rare Christian character, a woman deeply taught of God, and of wide Christian experience. Her articles are worthy of a place in the writings of the church." Sisson, *Faith Reminiscences*, 5.

4. Sisson, *Foregleams of Glory*, 126; Sisson, "Holy Ghost and Fire," 6–10.

5. *Record of the International Conference*, 74–75, 161–62. Sisson attended the 1885 Keswick Convention where she was exposed to Boardman and the latter rain teaching on the Baptism in the Holy Spirit.

6. Sisson, *Foregleams of Glory*, 195–98.

derland Pentecostal conventions of A. A. Boddy.[7] Prior to the organizing of the AG, she spent time ministering with F. F. Bosworth and S. A. Jamieson in Pentecostal Meetings in Texas.[8] Sisson was also a regular guest at the Stone Church in Chicago.[9]

Sisson was the first woman to speak at a General Council when she gave the keynote address at the 1917 Council in St. Louis.[10] Later that year, she officially joined the AG at the age of seventy-four, despite her insistence that she did not need ordination "from man."[11] Sisson held no official office, but she holds the distinction of the only woman to speak at a General Council in the early years. Sisson also became the first AG woman to have a doctrinal book published when GPH published her *Faith Reminiscences* as a part of the first series of books called The Pulpit and Pew Full Gospel Series that were offered in 1925.[12] She was a frequent contributor in Pentecostal magazines on eschatological topics including the *Confidence*, *Triumphs of Faith*, *Pentecostal Evangel*, and *Latter Rain Evangel*.

In 1912, Sisson published *Foregleams of Glory*, the earliest book on eschatology by an AG author. The book contains a collection of essays on eschatological topics, particularly the resurrection.[13] Sisson's eschatology is permeated with the pneumatological concept of the latter rain. For her, the Pentecostal Movement is not simply another revival; it was an answer to decades of prayer for God to send the "latter rain" upon the church in the last days.[14] She says, "God has poured out the latter rain to *ripen* the harvest,

7. Boddy, "Preliminary Meetings," 4–6.

8. Sisson, "Man Born Blind," 109–10.

9. The *Latter Rain Evangel* published over seventy of her sermons and articles, many of which she delivered at the Stone Church Pentecostal conventions.

10. *GC Constitution and Bylaws* (September 9, 1917), 5. Sisson also spoke in response to a sermon by A. P. Collins on the Second Coming of the Lord, where she remarked that she "left a letter at home directing what to do in case she should be caught up whilst away on her present trip" (20).

11. In Sisson's application for ordination, when asked whom she is ordained by, she replies, "By the Lord." Sisson, "Application for Ordination."

12. Sisson, *Faith Reminiscences*.

13. Sisson, *Foregleams of Glory*, 9–88, This book was a collection of sermons and articles published in the *Latter Rain Evangel* from 1909 to 1912.

14. Sisson, *Foregleams of Glory*, 126–27. Sisson, "End Not Yet," 6–9. Sisson's involvement in the Keswick conventions where the latter rain was a common theme was most likely the reason this motif was so important to her. Sisson, "These Wars! Why?," 17, comments, "Little did we think when earlier we cried for the rain of the Spirit, that our prayers would loose the fateful lightning."

for the double work of fruitage and of judgment."[15] The time of outpouring is the signal that the age of the gentiles that began with power is coming to a close with power to produce the harvest of souls.[16]

For the most part, Sisson follows the common premillennial dispensational script for the events of the last days.[17] However, her dispensational eschatology is pneumatically centered on the church age as the age of the Spirit. The goal of this dispensation is not simply the salvation of the gentiles; it is the bride's preparation through baptism in the Spirit. The Pentecostal Movement itself is a sign of the dispensational plan unfolding. Those who experience the baptism and Pentecostal manifestations serve as signs to the nations that the age of the Spirit is ending. She says, "Pentecost with all its demonstrations of the Spirit is a sign. A mighty sign. And the Pentecostallers when yielded to the Holy Spirit are a sign people."[18] The restoration of the experience of the baptism of the Holy Spirit was a sign of the end and served to announce the nearness of the coming of the Lord.

A second important eschatological concept is the priority of the resurrection. In *Foregleams of Glory*, she lays out a detailed understanding of the doctrine of resurrection, a doctrine she considers "most practical, though by most believers little understood."[19] She rejects the common affinity with heaven as the ultimate goal for the believer. She says, "The popular notion that at the death of the body each saint comes into full bliss and the full powers of the eternal life, is nowhere taught in the Word."[20] In her mind, heaven and the expectation of being caught up to heaven was but a shadow of the glory that would be found in the resurrection. She places such great importance on the doctrine of resurrection that she refrains from using the term *rapture* in her writing. Her treatise on resurrection identifies how the doctrine of resurrection is vital to God's dispensational plan. She notes two separate resurrections described in Rev 20: one before the millennium and one after. The first resurrection is reserved for those who have exhibited a martyr's "character" either through death or "through faithfulness to His

15. Sisson, "These Wars! Why?," 17.

16. Sisson, "Coming Glory," 3.

17. She says, "We are taught by this book after Christ's coming ensues 'The Tribulation, the Great' (thus the Greek gives it) and after the tribulation, the millennium, and after the millennium the Great White Throne Judgment, and after this the New Heavens and New Earth." Sisson, *Foregleams of Glory*, 39.

18. Sisson, "Sign People," 2–3.

19. Sisson, *Foregleams of Glory*, 50.

20. Sisson, *Foregleams of Glory*, 50.

Aspects of Eschatological Variety

truth, yet for such loyalty they bore a martyr-life."[21] Those who are counted in the first resurrection will receive the occupation of restoring the earth during the millennium. She says:

> Now we know that in every government there are the ruled-over-ones and the ruling ones. So in the Kingdom of God, there are the blessedly ruled-over-ones, and those whose joy it is to sit with Jesus in His throne, and bring in all gladness of regeneration of this earth in the Millennium Age.[22]

Therefore, the millennial reign serves as a reward for mature believers who give a martyr witness in this life. Like the apostle Paul, the character of the first resurrectionists "know Christ in deepest intimacy and the power of the His resurrection—that is, the power of the Holy Ghost, the full and deepening power of Pentecost."[23] The occupation of the first-resurrectionists will be the "restoration of this sinful earth" and "for the release of a groaning creation."[24] God's purpose during the gentile/Holy Spirit dispensation is to develop and mature the bride for the coming bridegroom through the baptism in the Spirit. For Sisson, the millennium is reserved for Spirit-filled believers. The rest of the believers will be resurrected after the millennium.

Here, Sisson's unique theology of the Spirit-filled bride is connected to the millennium rather than the rapture.[25] The Pentecostal experience prepares the bride for the return of Jesus. She says:

> A large part of the host of God in each generation have not known the baptism with the Holy Spirit and fire, though they have experienced the operations of the spirit in conviction, conversion, and something of the keeping power of salvation-lived below their dispensation; never came into its privileges and its power, and thus will never come up in its resurrection.[26]

Therefore, there are two types of believers: Spirit-baptized who are the bride, and those without the baptism who are the church.[27]

---

21. Sisson, *Foregleams of Glory*, 12.
22. Sisson, *Foregleams of Glory*, 13.
23. Sisson, *Foregleams of Glory*, 16–17, 58–59.
24. Sisson, *Foregleams of Glory*, 16–17.
25. Sisson, *Foregleams of Glory*, 34.
26. Sisson, *Foregleams of Glory*, 32.
27. Sisson, *Foregleams of Glory*, 34–35.

Another significant aspect of Sisson's eschatology was the resurrection's relationship to creation and Rom 8:19–20. Just as she de-emphasized heaven as the home of believers, she had great hope for the present creation and its importance in God's plan. She recognizes that the world is "groaningly anticipating a release from bondage" and that "with resurrection is somehow involved the liberation of all creation."[28] The creation, which was subject to sin and frustration, shares the fate of the human beings God created. The resurrection of believers "ends creation's wait, and begins creation's deliverance from the bondage of sin into the liberty of the resurrection."[29] The process of sanctification is the preparation of the body and the soul for resurrection. Sanctification is a type of pneumatological groaning within believers for the resurrection that is mirrored in creation.[30] Through the Holy Spirit, "this new nature, yearning, stretching, reaching and groaning in them" and awaiting their glorification in resurrection.[31] The Spirit prepares the bride for the task of renewal of the whole creation by the Spirit. Resurrection is not the destruction of the old in favor of the new. It is a pneumatological process of renewal through the power of the Spirit.

Another significant eschatological nuance is Sisson's understanding of tribulation as redemptive and a gift of God's love. Reading Revelation in a literal sense, the tribulation is indeed an awful period, but it is not empty of purpose. The tribulation period is a useful time of purging for the church, Israel, and the nations. The coming judgment in the tribulation is not an act of vengeance; it is an act of his grace and love. She says, "A new expression of his love! Judgment is His second remedy when His first has proved ineffectual."[32] The idea of judgment as a remedy is an essential concept. She comments, "Because of these judgments, these death-dealing blows of the Almighty are not only punitive, but remedial. Great Tribulation events deal first with the church, then with the Jews, then with the world. In each instance, it is a punishment unto a remedy."[33] As the latter rain outpouring prepares the bride, the church who rejects this move of the Holy Spirit is being prepared for tribulation. This process is not punitive but is a "holy remedy" for their purification and testing which forces them

---

28. Sisson, *Foregleams of Glory*, 9.
29. Sisson, *Foregleams of Glory*, 50–51.
30. Sisson, "May We Tarry," 6.
31. Sisson, *Foregleams of Glory*, 66.
32. Sisson, "These Wars! Why?," 16.
33. Sisson, "Three Aspects of the Great Tribulation," 16–17.

to fully commit themselves under threat of martyrdom. It is also a gift to the Jews who have for two thousand years been "destroyed and preserved" for this moment of redemption.[34] Tribulation is also a purification of the nations of the world. She says:

> The Great Tribulation is proven as God's clearing house for the church, Israel and the world. Punitive but remedial, have been His measures in their threefold aspect. Solemn work! Awful work! Holy work! Blessed work! The work of the Great Tribulation![35]

The redemptive nature of tribulation reflects her latter rain understanding of the healing, sanctifying, and redemptive work of the Spirit. The same Spirit that baptizes with power also baptizes with sanctifying fire. Sisson's eschatology presents a unique Pentecostal eschatological outlook on the return of Christ. The Spirit is empowering, sanctifying, and preparing God's people, the nations of the world, the Jewish people, and the creation itself.

A. P. Collins

Archibald P. Collins published the *Sign of the Son of Man: Sermons on the Second Coming of Christ* in 1919.[36] Collins, a former Baptist minister from Fort Worth, Texas, began teaching school at age nineteen and taught for ten years before being called to ministry. At the age of thirty, Collins gave up teaching to pursue training for ministry at Baylor University until he heard about the Pentecostal Movement in 1907.[37] After being baptized in the Spirit in 1908, Collins left the Baptist pastorate and became a pastor and evangelist in Texas and Arkansas.

Collins was a close friend of E. N. Bell and Howard Goss and one of the earliest leaders of the white Churches of God in Christ. He was present at the first General Council in 1914 and served as the second chairman of the Council for one year (1914–15).[38] Collins was a loving man who be-

---

34. Sisson, "These Wars! Why?," 16.

35. Sisson, "Great Tribulation," 2; Sisson, "Three Aspects of the Great Tribulation," 18.

36. Collins, *Sign of the Son of Man*.

37. Collins, "Baptized Baptist Preacher," 1.

38. *General Council Constitution and Bylaws* (November 15–29, 1914), 8. Collins failed to show up for the November 1915 Council despite the fact he was the acting chairman. The October 1915 Council in St. Louis was called because of the growing

lieved there was no place for division among the body of Christ, but he was also considered a defender of the faith.[39] Collins wrote a couple of articles on the signs of the times in the *Pentecostal Evangel*. Collins admits to not having an interest in cemetery plots and life insurance because he is expecting the Lord in his lifetime.[40] In 1915, he was one of the first to articulate a statement of faith in the *Pentecostal Evangel*.[41]

Collins believes there is a "dispensational line of thought that runs through the Bible," yet he expresses it in two unique ways.[42] First, his understanding of dispensations is tripartite in nature. He divides history into three periods of two thousand years. The first two dispensations consist of two thousand years before Noah's flood and two thousand years after the flood until the first coming of Jesus (Old Testament).[43] The third period of two thousand years is from the time of Jesus until today.[44] He says, "I am expecting that the near the end of the two thousand years, He will come again."[45] Collins views the closing of the dispensation as the reason for the outpouring of the Holy Spirit. He says, "It seems in these last days the Lord is letting us have a good time by pouring out His Holy Spirit and putting hallelujahs in our souls."[46] The final thousand-year period is the millennium, which is to be a Sabbath of the Earth, "a time of rest for the creation when it will be delivered from corruption."[47] During the millennium, the Earth will be "restored to her pristine beauty" and put on "her garment of

---

controversy on baptismal formulas, but Collins, who was Bell's friend and current chairman, did not participate because he was opposed to any sort of centralization on doctrine. J. W. Welch was elected in his place. See *GC Constitution and Bylaws* (October 1–10, 1915), 3; Brumback, *Like a River*, 51; Blumhofer, *Restoring the Faith*, 132.

39. McCafferty, "My Pastor," 4.
40. Collins, *Sign of the Son of Man*, 69, 72.
41. Isgrigg, *Imagining the Future*, 44.
42. Collins, *Sign of the Son of Man*, 70.

43. It is implied in this section that the antediluvian period is two thousand years like the others, but Collins does not state it specifically. I am inferring this conclusion from his recognition that the other two are both two thousand years. Traditional linages of Adam to Noah would put the death of Noah at the age of 950 some two thousand years after creation.

44. Collins does not use the dispensational language of "church age" or the "age of the Spirit." He simply describes this period as the time before he will come again.

45. Collins, *Sign of the Son of Man*, 70.
46. Collins, *Sign of the Son of Man*, 70.
47. Collins, *Sign of the Son of Man*, 71.

salvation."[48] All of nature will be redeemed as nations will be ruled, beasts will change their nature, and wars will cease in the reign of Jesus.

Much of Collin's assessment of the world in his day makes it easy for him to believe in the nearness of the return of Christ. The sermons compiled in this book were preached as WWI ended and movement toward the League of Nations was considered. He summarizes:

> All signs portend the soon coming of our Lord Jesus Christ. Politically, there is perplexity and great distress of nations. Financially, the clash between capital and labor seems inevitable. Socially, there is an alarming decline in morals—lovers of pleasure more than lovers of God. Industrially, the world is right up to the spirit of the world on two lines: locomotion and communication. The wireless telephone and the airship. Religiously, the awful apostasy of Christendom is evident to the faithful in Christ. The denial of the deity of Christ and the inspiration of His word, the repudiation of fundamental doctrine of the atonement are conditions that only judgment can correct.[49]

For Collins, the "signs of the Son of Man" are upon his generation. The Spirit is essential to Collins but not in the same way as other early Pentecostals. Believers should be ready for the imminent coming of the bridegroom, but Collins does not emphasize the Spirit in connection with the bride. The baptism in the Holy Spirit is the "normal condition for every child of God" in a continuationist sense.[50] But it is also a "last days" outpouring preparing for the end of the dispensation. Collins shows how early Pentecostalism modified dispensationalism to explain a Pentecostal understanding of the world.

E. N. Bell

E. N. Bell is one of the best-known founders of the AG. Bell impacted so many of the critical issues of the early years of the fellowship. He was one of the more educated AG founders, with degrees from Southern Baptist Seminary and the University of Chicago. Bell spent seventeen years with the Southern Convention of the Baptist Church. Bell was baptized in the Spirit at Durham's Chicago Mission in 1908. He served as the first chairman and

---

48. Collins, *Sign of the Son of Man*, 90.
49. Collins, *Sign of the Son of Man*, 111.
50. Collins, *Sign of the Son of Man*, 108.

the primary voice of the fellowship as editor of the *Pentecostal Evangel*. As Bell went, so the fellowship went. As editor of the paper, Bell began publishing a sampling of the questions he received in a regular column called "Questions and Answers."[51] The Gospel Publishing House compiled these responses into Bell's only book, *Questions and Answers*, in 1923.[52] Bell served the fellowship faithfully until he died in 1927.

Bell was highly influential in developing the AG's positions in the Statement of Fundamental Truths, especially as the primary architect of the four eschatological fundamental truths.[53] It was clear that Bell believed that the time was coming for the return of Christ and the "soon catching away" of the saints.[54] This is followed by the return of Christ and the saints and the setting up of the millennial kingdom or one thousand years. He identifies the return of Christ as the "end of the age of gentiles." The millennium is a time to "subdue the nations." Bell's writings are full of information on the pattern of the rapture, the antichrist ruling during the tribulation, the return of Jesus with his saints, the millennial kingdom, and the final victory over Satan.

Bell's approach to the bride's identity is perhaps different than some of the early Pentecostal interpretations. He hesitates to hold to the threads of the exclusive Spirit-filled bride teaching common in early Pentecostalism. Instead, he notes, "the scriptures nowhere so accurately and definitively define who are the bride that we can dogmatically say just so and so constitute it and no more."[55] Instead, he held to the view that all Christians will be raptured. That said, Bell's view of the bride in Rev 21 is less literal than most would view. He notes that the angel offers to show John the bride, but what John sees is an actual city coming down from heaven. Bell recognizes that though some take this as a literal city, he sees it more symbolically. He says, "even if a real city, with literally golden streets, (the Holy City) would

---

51. Bell "What Is the Bride?," 1. Beginning in January 1916, Bell had a regular segment of the paper designated for answering people's questions in *Pentecostal Evangel*.

52. Bell, *Questions and Answers*.

53. This is demonstrated in Isgrigg, *Imagining the Future*, 46–48. Bell's early doctrinal formulations was likely what shaped the eschatological truths, not D. W. Kerr as is most often argued. Bell said the following: "We believe in the pre-millennial coming of the Lord Jesus to reign with the saints 1000 years, Rev. chapters 19 and 20. In the new heaven and new earth as here promised." Bell, "For Strangers. Who Are We?," 1–2.

54. Bell, "Second Coming Near," 1.

55. Bell, "What Is the Bride?," 1.

amount to nothing except as inhabited by the people of God."[56] So for Bell, both the city and the bride are symbols depicting believers, rather than a literal reality. He says, "The main thing is to be sure we are a child of God, fully and absolutely surrendered to His will and walking joyfully and gladly in all light of his word, filled with His Spirit, working for the salvation of souls, keeping your lamps trimmed and burning, looking for the return of the Bridegroom. I feel for sure that those who do this will be among the Bride."[57] Later, when asked if one needs to be Spirit-filled to be part of the bride, he says, "Every child of God asleep in Christ, who has walked in the light he has, will go up in the rapture."[58]

Another unique feature of Bell's eschatology is his ambiguous position on including Christians in the tribulation. In bridal theology, only the spirit-filled bride will be raptured, but the other not-ready Christians will go through the tribulation. By rejecting this view, the nature of the relationship with the tribulation muddies. He says the Great Tribulation is "a period of about three and one half years, such as not yet been."[59] He says, "It is 'generally agreed' among us, though not unanimously, that the saints go up about the beginning of the great tribulation mentioned in Rev. 3:10 . . . and in Rev. 7:14 which begins proper with the last three years and a half."[60] Is Bell a mid-tribulationist since the Great Tribulation is only half of the entire seven years? It appears he leaned that way. In one question about when the "saints go up," he gives two options: before the seven-year tribulation or in the middle of the seven-year tribulation. Bell says, "This editor is inclined to the latter."[61] While later authors took strong positions that argued for pre-tribulation,[62] Bell is an example of some of the uncertainty of that interpretation in this era.

S. A. Jamieson

Samuel A. Jamieson was a successful Presbyterian pastor for twenty-five years before joining the AG. Jamieson was a well-educated minister who

56. Bell, "What Is the Bride?," 1.
57. Bell, "What Is the Bride?," 1.
58. Bell, *Questions and Answers*, 30.
59. Bell, *Questions and Answers*, 72.
60. Bell, "Questions and Answers," Feb. 8, 1919, 5.
61. Bell, "Questions and Answers," Mar. 30, 1918, 9.
62. Gortner, *Are the Saints Scheduled*.

graduated from Wabash College and Lane Theological Seminary. He pastored several large churches and was superintendent of the Presbyterian Church in Minnesota before resigning to seek the Pentecostal experience.[63] He received the baptism in the Spirit under the ministry of Maria Woodworth-Etter in Texas in 1908.[64] Jamieson's prior leadership ability, theological training, and passion for Pentecostal truths made him a logical choice for early leadership in the AG. He was elected as an executive presbyter in 1914 and pastored in Tulsa, Oklahoma, where he eventually became the Oklahoma district superintendent.[65] In 1920, Jamieson was given the responsibility of starting the first General Council Bible School in Auburn, Nebraska.[66] After it failed, he took up a pastorate in Chicago and became the Illinois district superintendent. Jamieson published the first doctrinal book from GPH in 1926 with his *Pillars of Truth*.[67] Jamieson was a member of the committee that crafted the Statement of Fundamental Truths in 1916 and a member of the committee tasked in 1927 to revise the SFT, adopt the constitution, and propose the name change to Pentecostal Evangelical Church.[68] His presence in both the writing and revising of the SFT, coupled with his academic background, demonstrates his doctrinal influence.[69]

Jamieson's *Pillars of Truth* contains teachings on twelve doctrinal and discipleship topics such as the Trinity, the Bible, tithing, the blood, the bride, and the resurrection. Although this book does not deal with the whole of eschatology, he deals with two important topics that give insight into his eschatology: the bride and the resurrection. Jamieson's writing style shows both his maturity as a minister and his level of education. He often quotes his sources, such as Presbyterian ministers James McCosh and Archibald

---

63. Jamieson, "How a Presbyterian Received," 2; Blumhofer, *Assemblies of God* 1:144–45.

64. Glenn Gohr notes that Jamieson received the baptism in the Spirit in 1912; however this contradicts Jamieson's own testimony, which cites 1908. Gohr, "Early A/G Leader," 9–10; Jamieson, "How a Presbyterian Received," 2.

65. Gohr, "Early A/G Leader," 9–10.

66. The Mid-West Bible School never made it off the ground. In 1921, the Executive Presbytery chose to try again with a school in Springfield with D. W. Kerr at the helm. Blumhofer, *Assemblies of God* 1:316–17; Brumback, *Like a River*, 85–86; Menzies, *Anointed to Serve*, 141.

67. Jamieson, *Pillars of Truth*.

68. "Final Report of Revision Committee on Essential Resolutions," *GC Constitution and Bylaws* (1927), 3.

69. Brumback, *Like a River*, 134.

Hodge, as well as evangelical leaders A. T. Pierson, William Boardman, and Andrew Murray. He makes several references to church history and is very aware of the modernist controversy and higher criticism.[70] His thoughtful and reflective engagements with theological issues demonstrate the intellectual, educational, and writing ability present in many early AG leaders. Jamieson also wrote several articles on eschatology for the *Pentecostal Evangel*.[71]

The first concept Jamieson covers in *Pillars of Truth* is the bride of Christ. The bride is the "mystical body of Christ" that is a "small select company" of believers.[72] Jamieson does not attempt to "dogmatize" who will be in the bride. Next, he asks when the bridegroom will come, to which he answers, "How long depends on us."[73] When the bridegroom does come for his bride, he will "rejoice when he sees the Holy Ghost coming up into the heavens with His mystical body."[74] Jamieson's mention of the Holy Ghost ascending with the bride reflects the view that after the rapture, the Spirit will return to the Father with the bride. He does not mention the Holy Spirit's role in the bride selection since he is not willing to speculate on the criteria. He says, "God has not commissioned the church the special mission of gathering together the bride; that position already pre-empted. It has been already given to the blessed Holy Spirit, and you are not on the job."[75]

The second eschatological topic Jamieson discusses is the resurrection. He begins with a defense of the importance of Christ's resurrection, perhaps because of its significance in the defense against Modernism. The

---

70. Jamieson says, "Higher Criticism has done its very best to discredit God's Word. It has gone through the Bible, denied parts, recast other portions and rejected still others entirely, until those who have followed the teachings of these Higher Critics have nothing left that is worthy of faith. I do not know what terrible judgment will fall upon Charles Foster Kent, Professor of Biblical Literature in Yale University, for producing the shorter Bible; God only know. . . . May God have mercy on the Modernistic teachers of today who are dissecting the Word of God." Jamieson, *Pillars of Truth*, 12.

71. Jamieson, "Second Coming of Christ," 6; Jamieson, "Five Judgments," 7; Jamieson, "New Heaven and New Earth," 6; Jamieson, "His Coming Draweth Nigh," 10–11; Jamieson, "Seven Fears and Seven Cheers," 2; Jamieson, "Who Are the Departed Dead," 8–9; Jamieson, "Sign of the Times" (Apr. 4, 1931), 1–2; Jamieson, "Sign of the Times" (Apr. 11, 1931), 6–7.

72. Jamieson, *Pillars of Truth*, 78.

73. Jamieson, *Pillars of Truth*, 84.

74. Jamieson, *Pillars of Truth*, 84.

75. Jamieson, *Pillars of Truth*, 79. Quote not cited.

resurrection of Christ fulfills prophecy, proves his deity, completes our justification, gives the church a living head, and establishes his office of high priest.[76] Next, he turns his attention to the resurrection of the saints. He says, "Christ's resurrection secures ours, because His resurrection seals and completes His redemptive power; and the redemption of our persons involves the redemption of our bodies (Rom. 8:23)."[77] Just as Christ's natural body is raised in resurrection, so too at the "rapture," his "mystical body" is also raised. The nature of the resurrection body will not be "the substitution of a new body, but the transformation of the old body."[78] The resurrection of the body will come before the millennial kingdom. He does not adequately explain the details of resurrection as applied to those who are not the bride, the special called out ones. He only mentions that the wicked dead will rise at the end of the millennium.

Jamieson's most significant contribution to eschatology is in a 1922 article on "The New Heavens and New Earth."[79] This article is the only article in this era that explains this doctrine at any length.[80] He says, "Some are under the impression that this earth and the heaven about us are going to be entirely destroyed, but that is not the case. The planet on which we live is by no means to be annihilated. We have to reason to believe that any atom of matter that God brought into existence will ever be entirely destroyed."[81] Quoting 2 Pet 3:11, where it says the Earth will dissolve, he argues that a better translation is "to loose" and "the word therefore means deliverance, release and emergence into a new condition."[82] He concludes, "It is to be transformed, renewed, glorified and be made a fit place for the habitation of God's redeemed people."[83] Jamieson's transformational eschatology is an important insight into the doctrine of the new heavens and new earth found in the Statement of Fundamental Truths. Creation is not discarded in favor of a new version. Rooted in the concept of resurrection and regeneration, the Earth's renewal shares the same destiny as the body.

76. Jamieson, *Pillars of Truth*, 99–100.
77. Jamieson, *Pillars of Truth*, 101.
78. Jamieson, *Pillars of Truth*, 103.
79. Jamieson, "New Heaven and New Earth," 6.
80. Isgrigg, *Imagining the Future*, 256–59.
81. Jamieson, "New Heaven and New Earth," 6.
82. Jamieson, "New Heaven and New Earth," 6. Jamieson appears to be using J. A. Seiss as the source for this definition and quotes him directly following.
83. Jamieson, "New Heaven and New Earth," 6.

He says, "'ALL THINGS NEW.' A new creature in Christ Jesus, a new body, 'like unto his glorious body,' a new earth and a new heaven, all of grace divine."[84] In hope, the future creation will be loosed from its bondage of sin and will share in the transformation and sanctification of the Spirit found in the resurrection.

D. W. Kerr

Daniel Warren Kerr was one of the senior members of the Executive Presbytery and one of the five members commissioned to write the Statement of Fundamental Truths in 1916. Kerr began his ministry in the Evangelical Church, where he pastored for five years before joining the Christian and Missionary Alliance.[85] Kerr was the founding pastor of Alliance Tabernacle in Dayton, Ohio. Ohio was a hotbed of C&MA influence, and Kerr, along with his friend and colleague D. W. Myland, traveled with A. B. Simpson in a famous Ohio Quartet. Kerr's diligence and acumen for writing must have impressed Simpson, as he was the author of several articles in *Living Truths*, the weekly magazine produced by Simpson.[86]

Kerr had other influences as well. In 1896, at a convention in Ohio, Kerr was involved in baptizing a minister from the Defenseless Mennonite Church named J. E. Ramseyer. Ramseyer left the Mennonite brethren and began an independent organization of ministers called the Missionary Church Association.[87] D. W. Kerr is listed as one of the key founding members. The group was encouraged to join the C&MA, but leaders insisted that the group remain undenominational. Initially resistant to the Pentecostal experience, the Pentecostal outpouring in the Alliance brought the Kerrs face to face with it. In 1907, Kerr witnessed an outpouring of the Holy Spirit at Beulah Park, Ohio, where many in the Alliance had received the baptism in the Holy Spirit. Though cautious at first, Mr. and Mrs. Kerr entered a prayer room one night and came out filled with the Spirit and speaking in tongues.[88]

---

84. Jamieson, "New Heaven and New Earth," 6; emphasis original.
85. Wilson, "Kerr-Pierce Role in A/G Education," 6.
86. Kerr, "Ministry of Christ," 3.
87. Bixler, "Founding Issues," 18.
88. M. Kerr, "All May," 8–9.

Kerr's influence on early AG doctrine is substantial.[89] Kerr was an intelligent, stately man. Though he went to college, he was not formally trained in theology. Kerr was knowledgeable in Greek. He was a "better-trained man than the average Pentecostal man of his day."[90] His theological and educational passion led him to help found three Assemblies of God Bible colleges, including Central Bible Institute. According to William Menzies, Kerr contributed the most significant language to the fundamental truths.[91] Despite his theological acumen, Kerr only wrote one book, *Waters in the Desert*, in 1927.[92] This book takes a pneumatological approach using the metaphor of water to address issues of unity, the Trinity, theology, tongues, and the new heavens and earth.

Featured prominently is a chapter exploring the eschatological waters from the throne as an analogy in the believer's journey with God. Kerr's understanding of the importance of the new heavens and earth is centered on the identity of the bride. The bride and bridegroom are images of the expectation of a future reality. This expectation contains images of an imagined future when Christ begins a new life with his people, redeemed from the whole earth. He says, "With the full revelation by the Spirit of the cosmopolitan character of the finished product, and the elimination of all racial, social and sexual distinction from the composite body of believer which will constitute the new order of things in the new heavens and the new earth."[93] The new earth is the long-awaited "finished product" consisting of a glorified earth and a glorified bride to enjoy relationship forever. Kerr recognizes that heaven is not the destiny of believers. Only in the new heavens and earth can the true kingdom of God be established with "its social, religious, and governmental activities after the power of an endless life."[94] This culmination is the goal of history and the "true destiny of man." In Kerr's mind, this act of restoration is the fulfillment of God's original plan to have people called out from every nation. That which was not accomplished in Israel and was attempted in the church will be realized when the body is fully unified in the bride of Christ.[95]

---

89. Menzies, "Tongues as 'The Initial Physical Sign,'" 175–89.
90. Menzies, *Anointed to Serve*, 119.
91. Menzies, *Anointed to Serve*, 119.
92. Kerr, *Waters in the Desert*.
93. Kerr, *Waters in the Desert*, 138.
94. Kerr, *Waters in the Desert*, 139.
95. See Kerr, "Twofold Aspect of Church Life," 3.

Aspects of Eschatological Variety

While Kerr's eschatology is not clearly defined in his book, two other sources give insights into some of his eschatological diversity. First is an article from the *Latter Rain Evangel* in October 1919 called "The Two-Fold Aspect of Church Life: Will the Church Go through the Tribulation?"[96] The second half of this "two-fold" message on the church in relation to the tribulation never made it to print. The second source of Kerr's eschatology is a manual on the Ages published with his son-in-law, Willard C. Peirce. This document called "Outline Studies in the Chart of the Ages" was crafted in order to provide "the accurate understanding of which is absolutely essential to a correct interpretation of Scripture."[97] This treatment contains the most information on his eschatological scheme, though there is little explanation or summary of his beliefs.

Kerr's eschatological diversity is well documented by Glen Menzies and Gordon Anderson.[98] They point out that Kerr was an example of the variety of positions that existed within Pentecostal views of premillennialism. They comment, "While he believed in the rather unorthodox theory of at least two Raptures separated in time by 7 years, he did not divide the church by promoting this view."[99] Key to Kerr's three-fold formula includes the division of people in Rev 12: the man-child, the Woman, and the overcomers. The man-child is the portion of the church that is not "effeminate" in living out the gospel. They will be taken at the pre-tribulation rapture. The woman, on the other hand, is not ready but is kept from temptation. She must spend time in the wilderness before she is taken.[100] This second rapture is halfway through the tribulation, before the Great Tribulation. The third portion of the church is the Remnant. They endure the tribulation and are saved at the third rapture of the church before the millennium. Kerr says, "Not all will reach the goal at the same moment of time, but at different intervals and in different sections."[101] It is pretty remarkable that this three-fold rapture view was given to the General Council on September 26, 1919. Similarly, Kerr's 1924 dispensational study that he and Willard Peirce taught at CBC contains a chart with both a pre-tribulation rapture and a

---

96. Kerr "Two-Fold Aspect of Church Life," 2.
97. Kerr and Peirce, "Outlines Studies in the Chart," 1.
98. Menzies and Anderson, "D. W. Kerr and Eschatological Diversity," 16.
99. Menzies and Anderson, "D. W. Kerr and Eschatological Diversity," 16.
100. It appears that Kerr is judging the lack of leadership and biblical fortitude by calling the church "effeminate."
101. Kerr, "Two-Fold Aspect of Church Life," 6.

post-tribulation rapture. At some level, these ideas were promoted in these early AG circles. Kerr's unique views show the diversity of beliefs about the rapture and tribulation present in the early years.

Alice Luce

Alice Eveline Luce was a missionary to India and church-planting pioneer who entered the Pentecostal movement in 1910.[102] She was born in England in 1873, and at age twenty-two, she became a missionary with the Anglican Church Missionary Society. While in India, word of the Pentecostal movement had reached her in 1910, and she sought out the baptism in the Spirit for herself. She became ill shortly after and returned to England in 1912 to recover. In 1915, she moved to Texas to become a missionary to Mexico and was ordained in the AG by M. M. Pinson. In 1926, she helped found the Spanish-speaking Berean Bible School in San Diego with veteran missionary to Mexico H. C. Ball. Alice Luce was known in the AG as a missionary strategist, Bible school educator, and Hispanic missionary. She wrote three books that the GPH published: *The Messenger and His Message* (1925), *The Little Flock and the Last Days* (1927), and *Pictures of Pentecost*.

Luce's *Little Flock and the Last Days* is a significant work because it is the only book on eschatology book by a woman that GPH published. While she did not intend the book to be an "exposition on prophecy, nor a study of social or international conditions in the twentieth century," she wanted to bring light to the topic of Christ's return and encourage believers to be prepared for his coming.[103] She does not spend much time dealing with the timing of events or specific teaching on end-time themes. However, her latter rain understanding of the Pentecostal movement orients her pneumatic eschatology. The events may not deviate from the dispensational scheme, but the purposes and the causes are certainly pneumatically oriented. She often includes extensive quotes from other authors, including several English Brethren writers such as G. E. Pember.

Luce identifies seven purposes of Christ's coming that outline the basic understanding of her eschatology. First, Jesus must come to receive his own, the bride of Christ. She notes that although she is not dogmatic, she believes the "watching ones" will be taken in the rapture of the bride.[104] Sec-

---

102. Isgrigg, "Luce, Alice Eveline." Also see McGee, "Luce, Alice Eveline," 543–44.
103. Luce, *Little Flock and the Last Days*, v.
104. Luce, *Little Flock and the Last Days*, 38.

Aspects of Eschatological Variety

ond, Jesus is coming to release the body of believers from sin and its effects. The salvation of the soul is only the beginning of God's redemption. Jesus is coming to resurrect believers to rule and reign in the millennium. Third, Jesus must come to fulfill the prophecies about the restoration of Israel. She says, "If we believe that God's Word says what it means and means what it says, we must expect Jesus to come as a literal king and reign over Israel on a literal throne in Jerusalem."[105] This coming is after the time of tribulation and the antichrist's rule and defeat at Armageddon.

During the millennium, the Spirit will pour out on Israel in fulfillment of Joel 2, and the gospel will reach the nations through redeemed Israel. The fourth purpose for the return of Jesus is to readjust the nations. The fifth purpose is to judge the nations during the reign of the antichrist and judge the wicked in the final great white throne judgment. Sixth, Jesus must come reign as King of kings to put an end to man's dominion once and for all. She says, "No one but Jesus can ever put things right, no one nation can ever be strong enough to maintain the balance of power, to prevent racial hate, jealousy, suspicion, and warfare among the races. But Jesus can do it, glory to His Name!"[106] Finally, Jesus must come to restore nature. She sees the promise in Rom 8:20–22 as a promise of the fulfillment of millennial prophesies. Jesus will institute peace, reverse natural disasters, extend the ability of the Earth to produce and sustain people, and reverse the curse on animals and nature. She says:

> The suffering and groaning of nature in this time of the dominion of sin, is not a hopeless mourning over something irrevocably lost. On the contrary, it is a suffering in hope, a death which is only the gateway of entrance into new life . . . the whole creation, though it suffered with him in this fall, will ultimately be redeemed and restored to greater beauty and fertility than ever.[107]

What is most significant about Luce's eschatology is her emphasis on sign-based eschatology. She identifies the signs of wars, famines, pestilences, and earthquakes as "characteristic of the whole of this church age, the dispensation of grace."[108] These signs are the significant signals of the end;

---

105. Luce, *Little Flock and the Last Days*, 40–41.
106. Luce, *Little Flock and the Last Days*, 44–45.
107. Luce, *Little Flock and the Last Days*, 47–48.
108. Luce, *Little Flock and the Last Days*, 32–37. Like many in this era, Luce provides her readers with brief detailed information on examples of these phenomena.

they are common to the whole church age but have increased in frequency during the twentieth century.

The first of the significant signs of the end is the budding of the fig tree, which is the restoration of the Jewish nation.[109] The fig tree (Israel) did not produce fruit when the nation rejected Jesus at his first coming. However, this tree will once again bud in anticipation of the return of Jesus. In the meantime, God has divided all people into three classes: the Jews, the nations, and the church. Each of these three classes of people is a sign of this gentile dispensation. The miraculous preservation of the Jews for the day of their restoration is not only a sign of God's election but also a signal of the dispensational plan of God. Through the tribulation, Israel will experience both physical rebirth as a nation and spiritual rebirth under the Messiah. She says, "The whole nation will have a change of heart and will be truly converted to God."[110] After that, a great outpouring of the Spirit as the latter rain upon Israel, prophesied in Joel 2, "and the whole nation—contrite, cleansed, and clothed with the Spirit of God—will be ready to fulfill their mission to all the nations of the earth."[111] The reign of Jesus is not limited to the millennium. She says, "We often speak of His reign of a thousand years in the millennium, but this does not imply that he will not continue to reign there after that period is over; for the Scripture clearly states that his reign will be eternal."[112] Therefore, believers are to pray for the peace of Jerusalem and offer prayers to "hasten the return of the Lord" who is bring these things to pass.

The second significant sign of the near return of Christ is what she calls the "signs of summer in all the trees." Taken from Jesus' prophecy in Luke 21, the fig tree and "all the trees" show signs that "summer is nigh."[113] Just as the fig tree (Israel) is being prepared for the coming reign of Jesus, the nations are also being prepared and re-aligned. She points to the political realignment of nations following WWI and the awakening of smaller nations as the fulfillment of the prophecy in Dan 2 of the iron and clay being shattered into smaller pieces. She says, "Compare the map of Europe to-day with what it was before the war, to see how all the trees have begun

---

109. Luce, *Little Flock and the Last Days*, 49–72.
110. Luce, *Little Flock and the Last Days*, 70.
111. Luce, *Little Flock and the Last Days*, 70–71.
112. Luce, *Little Flock and the Last Days*, 67.
113. Luce, *Little Flock and the Last Days*, 73.

Aspects of Eschatological Variety

to shoot forth."[114] The scale of national realignment, the introduction of scientific and technological advancement, and the rise of self-rule and social degradation serve as definite signs of the fulfillment of God's plan for the nations. The time of the rule of the gentiles is coming to a close, and the nations are preparing for a new government of the rule of Christ.

The third significant sign of the soon return of Christ is the latter rain outpouring of the Spirit.[115] She sees the latter rain prophecy of Joel to be twofold in its purpose. The early rain is the rain of the first Pentecost. But the latter rain of fulfillment is both for the church and for the future outpouring upon Israel. On the one hand, the Pentecostal Movement has been raised up to reverse the "havoc which modernism has wrought" and to restore fruitfulness to the church.[116] On the other hand, the latter rain ultimately fulfills the promises to pour out his Spirit on Israel. She says, "This is one of the marvelous pictures of Pentecost in the Old Testament; and we see here not only what the fullness of the Spirit will do for us in our own souls, but also in our ministry for God. These promises will all be fulfilled literally to the Jews after the Second Coming of Jesus, but there is also a spiritual application of them in this church age to every believer who will seek the Latter Rain."[117] The benefits of the Joel outpouring are correlated to the Pentecostal benefits of the baptism of the Spirit. The symbols of provision, oil, victory, and favor of God are all pictures of the Spirit-filled life. But the promise of rain is of particular importance. She says, "The Former Rain was given copiously on and after the Day of Pentecost, when the disciples all lived in the love and power of the Spirit, and mighty signs and wonders were done in Jesus' name. There is no reason why similar or even greater signs should not mark these days of the Latter Rain if only the church would be faithful in her ministry of intercession."[118] However, Joel's prophecy of the latter rain also included a prophecy of judgment. She says, "We find Pentecost connected with the last days, with the repentance of God's people and with the Day of the Lord, including his judgments, the Battle of Armageddon, the Lord's deliverance, prosperity in the land and His presence abiding there."[119]

---

114. Luce, *Little Flock and the Last Days*, 77.
115. Luce, *Little Flock and the Last Days*, 89–107.
116. Luce, *Little Flock and the Last Days*, 92.
117. Luce, *Little Flock and the Last Days*, 93.
118. Luce, *Little Flock and the Last Days*, 100.
119. Luce, *Little Flock and the Last Days*, 192.

Luce contributes several important concepts to Pentecostal eschatology. First, she sees the latter rain as the foundational eschatological concept for understanding the Pentecostal movement. The outpouring of the Holy Spirit is a last-day sign signaling the coming of Christ and anticipates the fulfillment of the prophecies of the Old Testament. Secondly, the latter rain has a dual fulfillment in the Pentecostal Movement and later in the restoration of Israel. The restoration of Israel is another sign of the latter rain as Israel buds both physically and spiritually. Therefore, she understands the Spirit as vital to the future salvation of Israel. During the tribulation period, the Spirit is actively blessing Israel and calling her to salvation by the Spirit. Dispensationalism separates the plan of God for Israel from that of the church, particularly concerning the tribulation where the Spirit is removed from the Earth. For Luce, not only is the Spirit present in the tribulation, but the work of the Spirit is an extension and culmination of the latter rain restoration of the Spirit that is bringing this dispensation to a close and will restore, save, and empower Israel in preparation of the coming reign of God on earth. That movement of the Spirit culminates in the ultimate renewal of all creation under the reign of Jesus and his saints.

SIGN-BASED APPROACHES

As the GPH began publishing more works, one genre that they regularly published was prophecy-based works that take a sign-based empirical approach to prophecy. This methodology attempts to prove the nearness of Christ's return by correlating the times' signs from Scripture with current events and phenomena. These books often give copious historical facts that are intended to inspire the reader to believe in the nearness of the Lord's return. Scripture takes a secondary role to empirical evidences such as the number of earthquakes, crime statistics, the amount of money spent on alcohol, political situations, divorce rates, war and death statistics, and other cultural indicators of moral and spiritual decay.[120] In this era, prior to Israel becoming a state, one of the surest signs was the developments in the rebirth of the nation and the return of the Jews to Palestine.[121] This section will look at two of these sign-based approaches.

---

120. Isgrigg, *Imagining the Future*, 181–83.

121. Empirically based arguments fall out of use around the 1960s in the *Pentecostal Evangel*. It could be that growing disappointment with eschatological delay coupled with Israel becoming the prominent sign of the end led to this approach falling out of use.

Frank Boyd

The *Budding Fig Tree* by Frank Boyd displays a typical sign-based approach. To make his case, he painstakingly assembles an "array of historical facts" about political and historical developments in the world for the coming of Christ.[122] For Boyd, prophecy is an empirical enterprise that validates faith and the word of God and gives surety of the future. Sign-based approaches often argue that prophecy constitutes the "objective side" of Christian faith that is verifiable outside the personal experience, therefore being surer.[123]

Although Boyd points out that there are "multiplied signs" in the world that the age is closing, he focuses this work on two particular signs: the return of the Lord in relation to the gentiles and the Jews.[124] He argues that when Israel rebelled against God, the "times of the Gentiles" began, in which Israel faded to the background of history. But as God prepares to renew his rule over his people in the coming Messianic reign, Israel is being stirred and drawn back to the land.[125] At the same time, the realignment of nations that resulted from WWI was the fulfillment of the prophecies about the gentiles.[126]

Boyd believes the culmination of the rule of the gentiles is expressed through the democratic rule of the people, which is "preparing the way for the deification of humanity in the final great superman, the Antichrist."[127] He laments the transition of "once proud monarchies" as they have fallen into "some form of republican government."[128] Boyd criticizes the cry for "freedom of thought and speech" in American discourse because he believes it replaces the voice of God. This suspicion of democratic forms of government was common in the first decade of Pentecostalism because of populism and the rise of socialism. Boyd notes that democratically elected leaders of European nation-states were set up to be the basis for the "ten

---

122. Boyd, *Budding Fig Tree*, 10. Boyd even goes so far as to give statistical probabilities of prophecies being fulfilled by chance. His sole goal is to prove the prophecies are true.

123. Boyd, *Budding Fig Tree*, 14–15.

124. Boyd, *Budding Fig Tree*, 22–23.

125. Boyd, *Budding Fig Tree*, 26–31.

126. Boyd, *Budding Fig Tree*, 38. Boyd believes Satan stirred Germany to begin the war in hopes of thwarting God's plan for realignment, particularly the European nations that were combining in the League of Nations.

127. Boyd, *Budding Fig Tree*, 32.

128. Boyd, *Budding Fig Tree*, 32.

kingdoms" rule of the beast of Revelation. Boyd gives meticulous social data to argue that the rising tide of lawlessness will result in society demanding a leader who will promise to bring peace, which will result in the antichrist coming to power.[129]

In the second half of the book, Boyd turns his attention to the "indestructible Jew." For Boyd, the "greatest proof of the inspiration of the Bible" is the Jewish people.[130] Boyd carefully charts the history of the Zionist movement and the miraculous details of the current state of the return to the land, including documentation of the populations, wealth, and agricultural developments that were taking place.[131] Despite the miraculous developments, Boyd notes, "The sad fact is that this is all being done in unbelief and reliance upon the arm of flesh entirely. The chastening hand of the Almighty will be upon them once more in the fires of the Great Tribulation."[132] The tribulation is seen as a time of testing and purging to bring Israel to a place where they will receive the Messiah when he is revealed from heaven. He says, "The earth will be ruled then, not as a monarch, nor as a great democracy, nor as an autocracy, but as a theocracy."[133] During the reign, Jerusalem will be rebuilt, a new temple will be built, and the ceremonies and sacrifices will be instituted as ceremonies that are reminders of Christ's sacrifice.[134] The millennium will also see the "complete fulfillment" of Joel 2 as the Spirit will pour out on the Jewish people. Boyd concludes his treatment with encouragement that Christ will reign with his saints, but few details about millennium are given.

---

129. Boyd comments, "The reaction from a state of anarchy, confusion and chaos is always expressed in the call for a strong leader or ruler, who is both wise and powerful enough to bring back harmony and order. The present break-up in society, for society is surely disintegrating, will doubtless end in this chaotic state. Then will be the call for the superman." Boyd, *Budding Fig Tree*, 75.

130. Boyd, *Budding Fig Tree*, 76.

131. Boyd, *Budding Fig Tree*, 89–110.

132. Boyd, *Budding Fig Tree*, 110.

133. Boyd, *Budding Fig Tree*, 112.

134. Boyd justifies this ideas with a quote from W. C. Stevens that says, "while at first thought unexpected, if not repugnant, to our idea that all sacrifices are forever past, may be viewed as retrospective; in both cases the value consists in seen through them the person of Jesus Christ in all aspects of His sacrifice for us." Boyd, *Budding Fig Tree*, 114.

Stanley Frodsham

Stanley H. Frodsham was one of the five-member committee appointed to prepare the Statement of Fundamental Truths. At his first General Council in 1916, he was elected as the general secretary and held the post for three years, from 1916 to 1919.[135] He also served as the editor of the *Pentecostal Evangel* from 1921 to 1948.

Frodsham's *Things Which Must Shortly Come to Pass* was published in 1928.[136] It is characteristic of the sign-based Bible prophecy approach in which current events are proof of Christ's near coming, such as disease rates, moral decline, denominational decline in conversions, economic figures, and critiques of modern warfare. He divides his work into twelve narratives of a coming reality. He calls the current decline in denominations and conversions "The Coming Apostasy" and refers to the political and economic woes in the world as the "Coming Sifting." Drawing on the imagery of the deliverance of God's people from the plagues of Egypt, he calls the catching away of the bride "The Coming Exodus" without the use of the term *rapture*. The fulfillment of God's plan to restore Israel, demonstrated by the Zionist events following the First World War, is proof of the "Coming Restoration." The hope of the millennium is expressed as the "Coming Kingdom," although he never uses the word *millennium*. Each of these images that are to come is rooted in copious amounts of current events yet tied to limited scriptural references.

The removal of the bride from the Earth is related to the "Coming Exodus," but the term *rapture* is not used. He says, "What will take place at his coming? A greater exodus, an exodus of all those who shelter beneath the saving blood of the Lamb of God."[137] In this imagery of exodus, he correlates the plagues of the exodus with the judgments to come. As he discusses images in Revelation, he cites the opinion of several "Historicists" and "Futurists" to buttress his argument for papal Rome as the fulfillment of Babylon. The concept of the millennium is better developed than the return of Christ. It is an expectation that "a time is coming when the Lord will come to earth, and the kingdom will be restored to Israel, a time when prophecy will be fulfilled."[138] Citing several OT prophetic scriptures,

---

135. Menzies, *Anointed to Serve*, 132–33.
136. Frodsham, *Things Which Must Shortly Come*.
137. Frodsham, *Things Which Must Shortly Come*, 69.
138. Frodsham, *Things Which Must Shortly Come*, 104.

Frodsham argues that the kingdom will be universal, peaceful, free from ferocity, free from sickness and the curse, and where men will know the Lord. This time of the kingdom is not called the millennium, nor is the length defined. While earthly judgment is described in many parts of this work, the final judgment is overlooked. The millennium, for Frodsham, is primarily centered on restoring the Jewish homeland. It fulfills the OT expectations of the kingdom of God and re-establishes the theocracy, where God rules through his son, Jesus Christ. It also re-establishes Jerusalem as the judicial capital of the whole earth.[139]

Like Boyd, Frodsham locates the fulfillment of Joel 2 in the restoration of Israel, when the promise of the Spirit being poured out on Israel is fulfilled. He says, "The Gentile nations will come under this mighty downpour of God's presence and will enjoy with God's restored people multiplied spiritual blessings."[140] Whereas early Pentecostals saw Joel's prophecy being double fulfilled on the Day of Pentecost and in the present Pentecostal revival, Frodsham locates the fullness of this prophecy in the millennium. He says, "Some may object, 'That was fulfilled on the Day of Pentecost.' But they did not exhaust God's resources that day. If reference is made to the prophecy in Joel, we see that this outpouring is connected with what we may expect in the last of the last days. . . . These things and the outpouring mentioned by Joel we are told to expect 'before the great and terrible day of the Lord come.'"[141]

In the "Coming Ages," Frodsham understands the culmination of the age is when Jesus puts down all his enemies, and God will be all in all (1 Cor 15). At that point, "the earth itself and all it contains will be subjected to the fires of judgment" and will receive a "complete purification."[142] The heavens, as the place where the devil rules, will be dissolved with fervent heat. While this burning of the present world happens, believers will be "far above all the scene of the coming great conflagration. From this place they will doubtless watch the final scene of Judgment."[143] He says that there will be a creation

---

139. Boyd, *Budding Fig Tree*, 113.

140. Boyd, *Budding Fig Tree*, 115.

141. Frodsham, *Things Which Must Shortly Come*, 108–9. Frank Boyd follows this same understanding of a triple fulfillment of Joel's prophecy. He says, "The promise of Joel 2:28,29, while partially fulfilled at Pentecost and again in thee later days, will have its complete fulfillment in the millennial age." Boyd, *Prophetic Light*, 92.

142. Frodsham, *Things Which Must Shortly Come*, 111–12.

143. Frodsham, *Things Which Must Shortly Come*, 112.

of the "new heavens and a new earth in which righteousness will dwell."[144] The New Jerusalem is described according to the literal dimensions in Revelation. Images of the first Eden are restored in the city to come.

BIBLE PROPHECY

The third type of eschatology books the GPH published in this era focused on explaining the complex concepts of Bible prophecy. The genre of prophetic studies concentrates on the nature of prophetic interpretation and dispensational studies more so than the theology of the Blessed Hope.[145] These books see prophecy as a discipline of study and discuss the nature of prophecy, the rationale for studying prophecy, the Old Testament prophecies fulfilled in Christ, and the importance of future prophecy. Ralph Riggs claims, "The whole Bible is God's word and therefore prophecy: a great part of it is His foretelling of future events."[146] Prophetic books often set forth a dispensational framework for prophecy as a philosophy of history. Frank Boyd says of dispensations, "As applied to the Bible itself it reveals the different classes of people God addresses in the Scripture, the various periods, or ages, marked off by the Lord for the accomplishing of his purposes."[147] However, other authors are careful to note that they are not bound by dispensational categories. Another element stressed in prophecy books is the way that prophecy validates the reliability of the Bible. The doctrine of inspiration and the study of prophecy are inexorably linked. Frank Boyd comments, "The Bible rests its whole claim to veracity and authority upon fulfilled prophecy."[148] Prophecy serves as an external verification of the Bible as truly God's word. As suggested by George Marsden, the concept

---

144. Frodsham, *Things Which Must Shortly Come*, 112. This phrase using the plural of "new heavens" is more reflective of the 16th Fundamental rather than the singular version used in Revelation.

145. The list of books in the genre include Ralph Riggs, *Path of Prophecy* (1937); Frank Boyd, *Introduction to Prophecy* (1948); Frank Boyd, *Ages and Dispensations* (1955); Frank Boyd, *Prophetic Light* (1968); Stanley Horton, *Bible Prophecy: Understanding Future Events* (1995).

146. Riggs, *Path of Prophecy*, 19.

147. Boyd, *Ages and Dispensations*, 3. Boyd follows Scofield's formula of seven dispensations: Innocence, Conscience, Human Government, Promise, Law, Grace, Millennium.

148. Boyd, *Introduction to Prophecy*, 13.

of biblical prophecy was one of the primary reasons for the origin of the doctrine of inerrancy.[149]

This section will look at two unique approaches to prophecy and prophetic books. The first is by Ralph Riggs, who looks at prophecy as a discipline of theological study. Though prophecy teaching often comes with a literalist interpretation, Riggs sees both historical and future fulfillment to prophecy, which balances understanding original author intent and Spirit-rooted future application. Similarly, Myer Pearlman presents a common futurist interpretations of Revelation with allegorical application. These two approaches show a variety of eschatological perspectives on prophecy.

Ralph Riggs

In 1937, Ralph M. Riggs was the first to write a comprehensive book on biblical prophecy called *The Path of Prophecy*.[150] This book does not claim to be a "dispensational study" (although arranged under dispensational headings) nor was it intended to be an in-depth study of Revelation and Daniel.[151] Riggs recognizes that prophecy interpretation is a source of contention and that he has no desire to become involved in any discussion of the "correctness of other interpretations." Instead, he takes a narrative approach to offer a "harmonious running story" of the future. As the divine author of the Scriptures, the Holy Spirit not only guided the truth revealed, but is also the interpreter of Scripture in the believer.[152] Those who study prophecy must do so with humility, diligence, and regard for teachers that the Holy Spirit has used to teach the subject. However, he rejects the idea that prophecy teaching is settled by one perspective. He says, "Differing viewpoints can be respectfully listened to, compared with various statements of the Divine body of Prophecy, spread before the Lord in prayer, and accepted to that degree to which they harmonize with the Scripture and received the witness of the Spirit."[153]

Riggs sets out his hermeneutical framework in the first chapter that guides his interpretation, including harmonizing texts, recognizing figures of speech, double references in some prophetic scriptures, and the

149. Marsden, *Fundamentalism and American Culture*, 56–62.
150. Riggs, *Path of Prophecy*.
151. Riggs, *Path of Prophecy*, v.
152. Riggs, *Path of Prophecy*, 24.
153. Riggs, *Path of Prophecy*, 26–28, 110–11.

overarching belief that all prophecy is "a study of the unveiling of Christ."[154] One of his hermeneutical rules is that the immediate context of interpretation must be primary. However, he argues that prophecy breaks this rule when "bursts of prophecy" are considered unrelated to the immediate historical context.[155] Riggs also notes that figures of speech should not be interpreted literally when not warranted by the text. While he prioritizes the "literal meaning," he warns against interpreting symbols literally.[156] Finally, the primary hermeneutical principle is "double reference," in which prophetic verses describe past and future fulfillments.

An example of the "double fulfillment" is the last days as a "Pentecostal visitation" prophesied in Joel. He believes that Joel's prophecy had a past (Day of Pentecost) and a future fulfillment, not in the Pentecostal movement, but during the tribulation. He says:

> It is true that Peter claimed that the visitation on the day of Pentecost . . . was in fulfillment of prophecy (Acts 2:4, 16), but the prophecy's close association with the tribulation events (Joel 2:30–31), would indicate that there would be a pouring out of the Spirit at the time of the great tribulation, too.[157]

The dual nature of this interpretation, though not new in Pentecostal circles, shows his recognition of historical and future fulfillment.

A glaring departure from the past/future interpretation is found in his interpretation of the destruction of Jerusalem in Matt 24, Mark 13, and Luke 19. Riggs points to twenty-five different prophecies given by Jesus that were all fulfilled in the Jewish-Roman war "during the lifetime of the generation to which he spoke."[158] Riggs does not seem to give room for the double fulfillment or future fulfillment of these passages. He says, "In the destruction of Jerusalem by Titus, the Roman general, in 70 A.D., every single one of the features of this prophecy was fulfilled."[159] He believes this is confirmed by the fact that the Gospel of John "does not contain this prophecy."[160] The rejection of Jesus as Messiah by the Jewish nation led to Jerusalem's destruction and thus began the church age.

154. Riggs, *Path of Prophecy*, 28–34.
155. Riggs, *Path of Prophecy*, 29.
156. Riggs, *Path of Prophecy*, 31, 110–11.
157. Riggs, *Path of Prophecy*, 113.
158. Riggs, *Path of Prophecy*, 101.
159. Riggs, *Path of Prophecy*, 102.
160. Riggs, *Path of Prophecy*, 101.

Riggs's treatment of Christ's return also has a somewhat fluid meaning. As he turns to the parable of the ten virgins, he draws from earlier concepts of only those being Spirit-filled as ready for the rapture. He comments, "He is coming in the capacity of a bridegroom and that the abundance of the Holy Spirit in one's life . . . is the right preparation for His coming."[161] But for Riggs, the rapture is not the only resurrection event. He says, "The second coming of Christ, then, is not a single event or appearance any more than His first coming was. . . . That is but the first of the series of His visits, seen and unseen, to this earth in His task of taking possession that which the little book gives Him."[162] Here, he also draws from the multiple rapture concept found in earlier interpreters.

His interpretation of Rev 12 also buttresses the multiple rapture concept. As he turns to various interpretations of the book of Revelation, Riggs discusses the identity of the dragon, woman, and man-child in Rev 12. He concludes, "The woman is the Virgin Mary and the man child is Christ."[163] The offspring is not limited to Christ, "Christ and His saints of the Old and New Testaments."[164] Riggs calls the rapture of the saints at the beginning of the tribulation the "out-resurrection" mentioned by Paul in 1 Cor 15. This special resurrection of the "advanced company" is something to be attained because they will receive a "better resurrection."[165] Those believers who are not part of that company will go through three and one-half years of tribulation (mid-trib), while those who are saved during the tribulation are "latecomers" and are raptured as the man-child resurrection at the end.[166] Riggs appears to support earlier Pentecostal expressions of the exclusive Spirit-filled rapture theology with a mid-tribulation theology for non-Spirit–filled Christians. He says that this explains Paul's teaching of the harvests in 1 Cor 15. He summarizes, "Christ is the sheaf; the company of twenty-four elder, the first fruits; the man-child company, the regular harvest; and a few latecomers as the gleanings?"[167] That said, his exegesis of Rev 4 related to the rapture is thinly supported internally and rather used intertextually with the parables of Jesus to support his futurist understanding

---

161. Riggs, *Path of Prophecy*, 122.
162. Riggs, *Path of Prophecy*, 163.
163. Riggs, *Path of Prophecy*, 157.
164. Riggs, *Path of Prophecy*, 159.
165. Riggs, *Path of Prophecy*, 161.
166. Riggs, *Path of Prophecy*, 162.
167. Riggs, *Path of Prophecy*, 162.

of the succeeding chapters of Revelation. These examples show Riggs struggles to maintain his historical-grammatical hermeneutic throughout his futurist interpretations.[168] That said, it is a clear example of variety in tribulation positions and hermeneutical approaches to prophecy.

Myer Pearlman

In 1941, Myer Pearlman published *Windows into the Future*, offering a "practical and devotional commentary" on the book of Revelation.[169] Although the title gives a glimpse of his futurist orientation to the book, Pearlman's primary objective is to provide practical teaching from the book rather than an explanation of the symbols and language of Revelation. Pearlman believes the value of the book of Revelation is that it sheds light on the last days. But it also comforts in times of trouble, inspires people to be courageous, and lifts believers above fear.[170] This wonderfully practical application is applied to every chapter of the book with his lightly treated perspectives on the future.

The first example of his practical interpretation is the vision of the 144,000 in Rev 7.[171] He uses a literal interpretation of this company as the tribes of Israel during the tribulation. Yet, his application to believers is applied spiritually to assure them that they are sealed and preserved by the Holy Spirit in life's tribulation. He says, "The seal is a symbol of the Holy Spirit, who is called holy because His chief work is sanctification of human nature."[172] He interprets the second company of the great multi-ethnic multitude to be those who are saved in the tribulation, saying, "These are the tribulation saints of the future."[173] But again, he devotionally interprets it differently. Pearlman says, "But is there not a sense in which we are all tribulation saints? . . . We are all called upon to bear the tribulation that comes in the path of daily duty."[174] All of the symbols are interpreted figuratively as symbols of the Christian life. Another example is Pearlman's commitment

---

168. Riggs, *Path of Prophecy*, 111.
169. Pearlman, *Windows into the Future*.
170. Pearlman, *Windows into the Future*, 9–13.
171. Pearlman, *Windows into the Future*, 67–71.
172. Pearlman, *Windows into the Future*, 71.
173. Pearlman, *Windows into the Future*, 94.
174. Pearlman, *Windows into the Future*, 76.

to a future time of great tribulation that will precede the coming of Christ.[175] Pearlman notes that "with the rejection of Christ and the destruction of Jerusalem the prophetic clock stopped . . . after the Church age, God begins dealing with Israel and the prophetic clock begins ticking."[176] However, when it comes to interpreting the identity of the woman and man-child in Rev 12, Pearlman chooses not to suppose any particular interpretation of the symbols. Instead, he seeks the "spiritual and practical truths" of the symbols.[177] Another example is his interpretation of the "little book" in Rev 10. He says, "Deviating somewhat from the literal meaning, we may think of the little book as suggestive of the Bible, which is meant to be an open book—open to all people."[178]

Pearlman also takes a devotional approach to Rev 4 and the calling of John to heaven. While others use this passage for the rapture, Pearlman does not mention this interpretation. Instead, he emphasizes that the intent was to inspire John to "see earth's events from heaven's viewpoint." Heaven is a place where not only does God rule, but the church is triumphant over the persecution and trouble of the world. He says, "When we view earth's affairs from heaven's viewpoint, pessimism gives way to optimism, faith, and hope, and we learn that despite appearances, God's in His heaven, and all shall be right with the world."[179]

Another interesting turn in interpretation is the Lion/Lamb of Rev 5. Pearlman notices that "John looked to see a lion," but what he saw was "a Lamb." Because he is not bound to literalist interpretations, Pearlman is able to see the symbolic reinterpretation of the lion image with the lamb. Pearlman notes, "Thus we learn that at the center of the universe, at the very seat of power and glory, is sacrificial love. The might of Christ is the power of love. . . . Only love has the right to power, for Love alone knows how to use it."[180]

A final example is his interpretation of the mark of the beast. He notes the common interpretation of 666 being historical, referring to Nero or the pope. But he argues the name is not important because "when the Antichrist

---

175. Pearlman, *Windows into the Future*, 93.
176. Pearlman, *Windows into the Future*, 94.
177. Pearlman, *Windows into the Future*, 99–104.
178. Pearlman, *Windows into the Future*, 88.
179. Pearlman, *Windows into the Future*, 46.
180. Pearlman, *Windows into the Future*, 54.

appears, we will know his name."[181] Instead, he suggests the number is not literal because "numbers are symbolical, that is they have a spiritual meaning."[182] So rather than rooting the "mark" in any contemporary issue, he argues that the number six represents man's failure to measure up to God's standards. He says, "We live in days of materialism when men are enlisting politics and economics in the effort to perfect man. Their theory seems to be: a good environment will make good men. . . . All human efforts to improve human nature amount to 6; the divine 7 that changes the heart, is needed to change man's habits and man's environment."[183]

Pearlman demonstrates how Revelation can be interpreted in more ways than simply a literalist or futurist approach. Whereas some prophetic teachers would shun such an approach, Pearlman demonstrates how rich understandings can be gained from utilizing symbolic and practical application approaches to Revelation. Focusing on the book's value to the present reader allowed the symbolic nature of Revelation to emerge more faithfully to the apocalyptic genre. This is, no doubt, a pneumatological approach that engages the imagination and focuses on transformational readings of the text.

CONCLUSION AND TIMELINE

Each of the books and contributions of AG authors provided a glimpse into some of the diversity of perspectives on eschatology. Many other books published by the AG may not be as creative or flexible. From sign-based approaches that read the newspaper alongside the Bible to prophecy books focusing on the biblical genre of fulfilled and unfulfilled prophecy to Revelation commentaries that range from literal to symbolic, together, these books demonstrate that there is a wide range of variety within a traditional premillennial framework.

While surveying only a few in this chapter, books on eschatology have been some of the most consistently published books from the GPH. The timeline below provides a comprehensive list demonstrating the rich history of AG publishing on eschatological topics. In this list, a few observations can be made. Thirty-four volumes on eschatology/prophecy were published by the GPH between 1925 and 2005. Twenty-three of the

---

181. Pearlman, *Windows into the Future*, 121.
182. Pearlman, *Windows into the Future*, 122.
183. Pearlman, *Windows into the Future*, 122.

thirty-nine volumes were by six key AG leaders. Stanley Horton published the most with seven, Frank Boyd published five, Ralph Riggs published four, J. N. Gortner published three, and Stanley Frodsham and Myer Pearlman published two. Two of the first four were published by women (Sisson and Luce), and there were no volumes published by women since.

GPH published all these books unless they have an (*), which were by AG authors but were published before GPH was printing books.

- 1912 – *Foregleams of Glory (Resurrection Papers)*—Elizabeth Sisson*
- 1919 – *Sign of the Son of Man*—A. P. Collins*
- 1925 – *The Budding Fig Tree*—Frank Boyd
- 1927 – *The Little Flock in the Last Days*—Alice Luce
- 1928 – *Things Which Must Shortly Come to Pass*—Stanley Frodsham
- 1928? – *Jesus Coming at Hand* (collection of articles)
- 1930 – *Are the Saints Scheduled to Go through the Tribulation?*—J. Narver Gortner
- 1934 – *Coming Crisis and Coming Christ*—Stanley Frodsham
- 1937 – *The Path of Prophecy*—Ralph M. Riggs
- 1938 – *What Will Happen Next? God's Forecast of the Future*—Harry J. Steil
- 1941 – *Windows into the Future*—Myer Pearlman
- 1943 – *Daniel Speaks Today*—Myer Pearlman
- 1948 – *Introduction to Prophecy*—Frank Boyd
- 194? – *Studies in Daniel*—J. Narver Gortner
- 1948 – *Studies in Revelation*—J. Narver Gortner
- 1950s – *Signs of the Times*—Frank Boyd
- 1950 – *Even So Come*—Hart R. Armstrong
- 1950 – *Those Who Are Left*—Hart R. Armstrong
- 1951 – *War against God*—Hart R. Armstrong
- 1955 – *Ages and Dispensations*—Frank Boyd
- 1959 – *Waiting . . .* —C. M. Ward
- 1962 – *God's Calendar of Coming Events*—Ralph Riggs

Aspects of Eschatological Variety

1963 – *Bible Prophecy*—Stanley Horton (teachers' manual)

1963 – *Dispensational Studies*—Ralph Riggs

1967 – *Promise of His Coming*—Stanley Horton

1967 – *Studies in the Revelation of Jesus Christ*—Frank Boyd (Berean)

1968 – *Prophetic Light*—Frank Boyd (revised 1988 Berean)

1968 – *The Story of the Future*—Ralph Riggs

1975 – *What You Should Know about Prophecy*—Stanley Horton

1975 – *What You Should Know about Prophecy*—C. M. Ward (adapted from Horton)*

1975 – *It's Getting Late*—Stanley Horton

1975 – *Preparing for the Storm*—Kenneth Barney

1977 – *God's Plan for This Planet*—Ian Macpherson

1979 – *Countdown: A Newsman's Look at the Rapture*—Dan Betzer

1981 – *What's Ahead? A Study of End-Times Events*—Charles Harris

1991 – *The Ultimate Victory*—Stanley Horton

1995 – *Bible Prophecy: Understanding Future Events*—Stanley Horton

1996 – *Our Destiny: Biblical Teachings on Last Things*—Stanley Horton

2005 – *Letters to the Seven Churches*—James K. Bridges

Chapter 7

Aspects of Theology and Education

INTRODUCTION

FROM THE BEGINNING, THE Pentecostal Movement had a complicated relationship with theology and the pursuit of education. Some early Pentecostals rejected the need for education because they believed the Holy Spirit and the power of God was a more significant validation of ministry. Elizabeth Sisson rejected the notion that she needed credentials, education, or degrees to validate her ministry.[1] She remarked:

> You might hold all the offices of the church, and append to your name all the letters of the alphabet bestowed by all the universities of Europe and America, but these things of the power and learning and intellect of man will not release the demon oppressed, will not heal the sick, etc. But praise God, through the simple believer, under the power of the Holy Ghost, these things are wrought.[2]

The problem with education was not the pursuit of knowledge; it was that pursuit at the expense of simple faith in Jesus and the Scriptures. The Pentecostal revival emphasized restoration of the heart over the knowledge of the head among the clergy of the church.

Though fellow critics of higher criticism, many early leaders did not consider themselves uneducated or anti-intellectual. The fact that

---

1. Sisson's application for credentials reveals this sentiment. When asked "have you been ordained and by whom?" on the application, Sisson responds, "By the Lord." Sisson, "Application for Ordination."

2. Sisson, "Coming Glory," 2.

Aspects of Theology and Education

Modernism was shaping higher education was the chief objection to traditional education. The development of Pentecostal Bible schools was a protest to Modernism's higher critical understanding of the Bible. In a sense, they believed they were restoring education to its purest form through the study of Scripture rather than formal theology.

This careful relationship with the academy has led to several mischaracterizations of Pentecostals. First, there is the characterization that Pentecostals are better doers than thinkers. This certainly was the sentiment expressed by Russell Spittler in 1975 when he declared, "Pentecostals have always been better at evangelism than writing theology. We are known more for foreign missions than for theological books."[3] This means that Pentecostalism valued missional action rather than writing about it. Over two and a half decades later, Frank Macchia echoed Spittler's sentiment to assert that Pentecostals had historically lacked "critical theological reflection."[4] While Spittler and Macchia both applaud this characteristic as vital to the movement's missional aspect, these assessments convey that Pentecostals were not particularly interested in theological training or expression. Roger Olsen similarly comments, "Endemic to Pentecostalism is a profoundly anti-intellectual ethos. It is manifested in a deep suspicion of scholars and educators and especially biblical scholars and theologians."[5] But Amos Yong and Dale Coulter argue they were more so anti-rationalists, rather than anti-intellectuals. They note, "Antirationalism, on this view, is simply a shorthand way of identifying a mode of intellectual activity outside of Baconian evidentialism."[6] Their experiences of the Spirit provided an alternative path toward moral refinement and enlightenment to that of external and social paths of education.

The characterization of Pentecostals as anti-intellectual is overstated when looking at AG leaders and their relationship to higher education, doctrine, and theology. This chapter will address these issues in light of the early origins of the AG. First, it will explore early sentiments toward education in AG ministers. Second, it will chart the development of attitudes toward doctrine and theology in the AG. Third, it will explore the

---

3. Spittler, "Theological Opportunity," 243.

4. Macchia, "Struggle for Global Witness," 8–9.

5. Olsen, "Pentecostalism's Dark Side," 27. See also Lewis, "Why Have Scholars Left," 69–86; Menzies, *Anointed to Serve*, 141.

6. Yong and Coulter, *Holy Spirit and Higher Education*, 139.

AG's various doctrine and theology books for the different methodological approaches of doing theology as Pentecostals.

THE AG AND HIGHER EDUCATION

Early Pentecostalism was filled with people from various theological streams who received the baptism in the Spirit. Whereas historians are correct that Pentecostalism appealed to the disinherited in society, many ministers within the movement came from established theological traditions. This was particularly true in the AG. Some of the AG's most prominent early leaders were educated in colleges and seminaries. E. N. Bell held a bachelor's degree from Stetson University and a seminary degree from Rochester Theological Seminary and spent three years at the University of Chicago. J. R. Flower was not trained in theology but spent two years preparing for a law career. S. A. Jamieson was a "scholarly" Presbyterian minister who spent nine years at Wabash College and Lane Theological Seminary.[7] Arch P. Collins did his ministry training at Baylor University. T. K. Leonard spent two years at Findlay College, a Church of God institution.[8] P. C. Nelson was trained at Denison University and later Rochester Theological Seminary, where he trained under Augustus H. Strong.[9] This core group of leaders understood the value of education and educational institutions.

The main concern over higher education was how seminaries were indoctrinating their clergy into higher criticism. This created suspicions that Modernism had taken over denominational seminaries, teaching anti-supernaturalism that undermined faithful Christian beliefs. For example, one Pentecostal mother laments, "We sent our only son to the University of Chicago, and he comes home an avowed infidel."[10] The problem with "modern theology" was that it had turned Christianity into "religion without an experiences, a theory without facts, a form of worship without power."[11]

Jonathan Perkins, a staunch critic of higher criticism, admits, "Education is needed, for it is the proper disciplining of the faculties of the mind

---

7. Jamieson, "How a Presbyterian Preacher Received," 2; Brumback, *Like a River*, 136.
8. Chapman, "Thomas King Leonard," 17.
9. McGee, "Nelson, Peter Christopher," 636–37.
10. McCafferty, "Study to Show Thyself Approved," 19.
11. Hoover, "Tragedy of Modern Theology," 7.

until they become our slaves and not our masters in life. A well-trained mind surely pleases God." However, as he experienced in his college education, he had his faith "derided by the professor of biology" for his rejection of evolution. In this landscape of doubt and theories about the Bible, Perkins declares, "God needs men and women with trained heads. But God first of all wants the hearts."[12] The head over heart was also the subject of A. G. Jeffries's critique of seminaries.

> For fifty years the American people have been cursed with head, and starved for heart preaching. Many churches have demanded of their ministers a classical education before ordination, and have little or no demands of them along spiritual lines. It has been all head and no heart.[13]

The answer to the problem of modernist theology and education was not to reject education, but to place the Bible in the center of education. What was needed, commented Jamieson, was an "educated ministry."

> Some conscientious people look upon education as a drawback to the gospel ministry, on the ground that the Holy Spirit will furnish the necessary education. . . . The Bible places no premium on the ignorance of the word. God chose Paul, a man of ability and scholarship . . . the great reformers, they were nearly all college men.[14]

In their minds, the church needed schools built on the authority of the Bible and in which the Holy Spirit was the lead teacher. More than that, Pentecostals saw the goal of college to be "moral formation" in the context of "the practical training behind the utilitarian approach to education."[15] They emphasized spiritual experiences, right practices, and missional action alongside biblical truth, life skills, and some basic educational frameworks in normal schools.

ESTABLISHING BIBLE SCHOOLS

To combat Modernism, the AG believed Pentecostal Bible schools were the perfect antidote to infidelity by training students to "contend for the

---

12. Perkins, "Higher Education, Lower Fidelity," 2.
13. Jeffries, "Limits of Divine Revelation," 6.
14. Jamieson, "Need of an Educated Ministry," 4.
15. Yong and Coulter, *Holy Spirit and Higher Education*, 98.

faith" and "defend the great fundamentals of the Christian religion."[16] One of the General Council's first goals was to establish "a general Bible Training School with a literary department for our people."[17] For the first decade of the Pentecostal movement (1906–16), short-term Bible schools were a popular way to train people for the task of end-time evangelism. The imminent return of Jesus meant that ministers needed only to be trained in what was necessary to reach lost people as soon as possible. T. K. Leonard advertised his Bible school in Findlay, Ohio, saying, "Time is too precious. Jesus is coming too soon. Traditional education has proved too futile."[18] Some Bible schools offered terms as short as one to three months, while others set indefinite terms, leaving the term to the direction of the Holy Spirit. Some literary schools were offered for young people as an alternative to public school education.[19] What they all had in common was the belief that there would be no teacher but the Holy Ghost and no better text than the Bible.[20]

Because many AG early leaders understood the value of education, there was a strong impulse to establish Pentecostal Bible schools to train pastors and missionaries in the Pentecostal worldview. J. R. Flower assisted D. Wesley Myland in establishing the Gibeah Bible School in Plainfield, Indiana, before joining the Pentecostal movement. T. K. Leonard started the first Bible school endorsed by the General Council, the Gospel School in Findlay, Ohio. A. P. Collins started a Bible school in Fort Worth, Texas, in 1917.[21] Samuel A. Jamieson founded the first General Council Bible School in 1920, the Midwest Bible School in Auburn, Nebraska, which closed shortly afterward for lack of support.[22] D. W. Kerr was instrumental in founding Glad Tidings Bible College in San Francisco and Southern California Bible College.[23] Frank Boyd was the principal at Bethel Bible Institute in 1918 before moving to Central Bible Institute. In 1922, the AG made a second attempt at launching a General Council-sponsored school

---

16. McCafferty, "Study to Show Thyself Approved," 19.

17. "General Convention of Pentecostal Churches," 1; *GC Constitution and Bylaws* (April 2–12, 1914), 4.

18. Leonard, "Gospel School, What Is It?," 3.

19. "Three Schools," 2.

20. Leonard, "Gospel School, What Is It?," 3; "Mount Tabor Bible Training School," 9.

21. "Announcement of Bible School," 14.

22. Bell, "Midwest Bible School," 8; Bell, "Bible School Assured," 2; Jamieson, "Need of an Educated Ministry," 4; Brumback, *Like a River*, 87.

23. Kerr, "Report from the Southern California," 9. See also Kerr, "Southern California Bible School," 11.

when D. W. Kerr launched his second Bible school, Central Bible Institute in Springfield, Missouri, which offered a three-year diploma. P. C. Nelson opened the Southwestern Bible Institute in Enid, Oklahoma, in 1927. The priority of organizing Bible schools by the first General Council was realized very quickly. By 1921, there were six Pentecostal Bible schools run by prominent AG leaders.[24]

The educational goal of Bible schools was scriptural knowledge of Bible doctrines, discipleship, and ministry training. Kerr described the Bible school as "a place where one may devote his whole time to gaining a practical working knowledge of the Scriptures in the shortest possible time consistent with thoroughness and efficiency."[25] The Gospel School of Findlay, Ohio, opened in October of 1915 and boasted of "no teacher but the Holy Spirit." However, the description of the curriculum was quite different. The advertisements boasted of E. N. Bell teaching "Old and New Testament" and O. E. McCleary teaching "Homiletics, Church History and Bible Geography."[26] Similarly, the Mount Tabor Bible Training School at Stone Church in Chicago offered an education where the Holy Spirit is the teacher, and the Bible is the textbook. But they also gave themselves to "the study of the Greek Language, Church History, of Speech and praying, music, and special attention to missionary training."[27] Kerr's Southern California school included "theology, dispensational studies, Synthetics, personal work, Church history, homiletics, missions and missionaries, Bible atlas, public speaking, English, and music."[28] Students not only studied, but they were also required to engage in practical social outreach such as street work, visiting hospitals, rescue work, and visiting the sick and needy.[29] Programs were later expanded to two to three years, concentrating on Bible doctrine, interpretation of Scripture, and Pentecostal ministry.

In 1921, the General Council decided to open a school in Springfield, Missouri.[30] Independent Bible schools were established all over the United States, but the General Council recognized they needed a General Council Bible school near the headquarters. Leading the charge were E. N.

---

24. "Pentecostal Bible Schools," 9.
25. Kerr, "Heart Talks on Bible Schools," 4.
26. Leonard, "Gospel School, What Is It?," 3.
27. "Mount Tabor Bible Training School," 9.
28. Kerr, "Report from the Southern California," 9.
29. Kerr, "Report from the Southern California," 9.
30. Brumback, *What Meaneth This?*, 86.

Bell, J. W. Welch, and D. W. Kerr.[31] Kerr's daughter comments, "Father Kerr would often speak of the longing of his heart to see a Bible institute at headquarters."[32] Kerr became the principal of Central Bible Institute in Springfield when it opened in 1921 in the basement of Central Assembly. Kerr invited Myer Pearlman to CBI to serve on the faculty, and soon after that, Frank Boyd came to help Kerr lead the college. Kerr was the senior and most respected teacher at the college. His specialties included theology, hermeneutics, and pastoral epistles.[33] When Kerr became sick, Frank Boyd took over as principal. Boyd reported, "Our students need to know theology, that is, the study of God. If our young people are well grounded in scriptural theology, there is no danger of them being overturned into the error."[34] While the opening of the school was good for the AG, it also meant that a half dozen other smaller schools would ultimately close.[35]

FROM BIBLE COLLEGES TO LIBERAL ARTS COLLEGES

As the movement matured and the eschatological fervor began to wane, Bible schools became pivotal for training ministers for the harvest and doctrinal preservation.[36] Over the next decade, endorsed Assemblies of God Bible schools were established, and more formal educational terminology and methods were used. By 1934, the leaders recognized the need for the AG to shift from Bible colleges and ministerial training to other forms of education. P. C. Nelson and the Executive Presbytery first called for expanding AG colleges to include other professions in 1934. Nelson says:

> Many believe that the hour has come for us to take an advanced step along educational lines. . . . A beginning has been made to provide Bible school training for prospective pastors, evangelists, missionaries, and other Christian workers. But as yet, nothing has been attempted by the General Council to provide education along other lines. All of our fine young people cannot be preachers, or

---

31. Welch, "Current Comments," 8; Wilson, "Kerr-Peirce Role in A/G Education," 21.
32. Christine Peirce, quoted in Brumback, *What Meaneth This?* 86.
33. "Obituary, D. W. Kerr," 3.
34. "Four Days with the Presbyters," 2.
35. Menzies, "Developing Educational Institutions," 3–4.
36. Kay, *Pentecostalism*, 300.

missionaries. But all need a good knowledge of the Bible and liberal education.[37]

As more Pentecostal young people enrolled in secular and non-Pentecostal institutions for liberal arts education, Bible schools suffered lower enrollment and underfunding. Some schools were forced to consolidate by 1945. Nelson and the Executive Presbytery desired to offer students an opportunity to be educated in all fields of study in schools that preserved their Pentecostal faith. In 1947, Irvine J. Harrison led the Education Committee's effort to begin converting the AG's Bible colleges into liberal arts colleges to meet the educational needs of Pentecostal youth, not just ministers.[38] By 1956, six schools offered four-year bachelor's degrees, and two had begun graduate degrees.[39]

The next decade saw attitudes toward higher education further develop. By the mid-1960s, nine AG colleges offered various bachelor's degrees, and several offered a fifth-year bachelor's in theology degree.[40] Yet, some were worried that regular four-year colleges would not maintain the standard of spirituality found in the Bible schools. Carlson argued that AG liberal arts colleges could keep the same spiritual environment as the Bible colleges. He says, "The Bible is the core of the curriculum in a Bible college. In the Pentecostal liberal arts college, the Bible is a guidebook in the basic work of seeking our truth in all fields of human knowledge."[41] For Carlson, education was not something to be feared but a tool of revealing truth in every area of life. He says:

> We Pentecostal ministers must not turn away from scholarship; even humanistic scholarship may have something to say to us. Further, some acquaintance with the wisdom of this world has its place. A knowledge of those whom we contact, and some measure of understanding of their beliefs, can be useful. But let us never forget to test scholarship against God's holy and infallible Word. ... Excellence of scholarship and spirituality are not in opposition to each other.[42]

---

37. Nelson, "Enlarging Our Educational Facilities," 7.
38. *General Council Minutes* (September 4–9, 1947), 16–21.
39. Chapman, "In Spirit and Truth," 50–51.
40. Scott, "Education in the Assemblies of God," 10–13. The bachelor's in theology is similar to the MDiv.
41. Carlson, "Pentecostal Dimension in Education," 12–13.
42. Carlson, "Place of Education," 22–23.

Carlson demonstrates a growing appreciation for fields of knowledge outside biblical subjects, as long as they align with biblical revelation.

As these colleges established graduate schools in theology, suspicion about higher education remained an issue. In 1961, the General Council established a Board of Education to oversee the AG colleges and consider the possibility of establishing a "theological seminary."[43] Feeling that the term "seminary" carried too many negative connotations, the 1971 General Council replaced "seminary" language in favor of the terminology of "graduate school of theology."[44]

William Kay argues that Pentecostal education was generated by a series of four factors: protection of doctrine, accreditation of ministers, ministerial training, and higher education.[45] The AG certainly followed that pattern. The Statement of Fundamental Truths, adopted two years after the AG was organized, became a doctrinal framework by which the theological culture of the fellowship was established. Periodicals and published doctrinal works further solidified doctrinal understandings of the fellowship and defined accepted methodologies for interpreting Scripture. Bible schools were founded for the preservation of Pentecostal doctrine and to train pastors and missionaries. The adoption of liberal education and accreditation led many to pursue terminal degrees. From the beginning, AG established a cautious but necessary relationship with education. The doctrine of the Assemblies of God has been preserved and articulated through these educational structures.

APPROACHES TO THEOLOGY AND DOCTRINE

One of the key issues with higher education was the tension between theology and doctrine. The AG had a strong orientation toward doctrine from its earliest days. Two of the five rationales for organizing the first General Council had to do with Pentecostal ministers uniting in sound doctrine and training. When the first council was called, one of the goals was to "better understand what God would have us teach that we may do away with so

---

43. *GC Constitution and Bylaws* (August 23–29, 1961), 20.

44. The 1971 resolution declares, "The significance of the word 'seminary' in present-day usage does not adequately express the type of graduate training that is being provided for those desiring graduate work in the field of Bible and religion." *GC Constitution and Bylaws* (August 19–24, 1971), 90.

45. Kay, *Pentecostalism*, 300.

many divisions in doctrines."[46] Squabbles over doctrine divided the Pentecostal movement, and the organizers believed the General Council could bring people into doctrinal unity. As crucial as was Pentecostal spirituality, the teaching and producing literature on sound Bible doctrine was among their highest priorities.

Despite objections by early AG ministers to having doctrinal statements, the impulse to identify core commitments is foundational to an organization's maturity and identity. Jaroslav Pelikan observes that this process of self-identification by which new confessional communities emerge follows a predictable historical pattern toward dogmatization through that which is "believed, taught, and confessed."[47] What is "believed" is an expression of how individuals experience God within the community context. What is "taught" is the biblical explanation or reconceptualization of that experience by the community through the didactic process of exegesis and teaching. What is taught is eventually codified into what is "confessed" as the official version of that teaching that members of the group are required to believe to be a member of the community. By the very act of organizing, the AG committed itself to the process of identifying as a confessional community. Adolf von Harnack points out, "The inclination to formulate the content of religion in *Articles of Faith* is as natural to Christianity as the effort to *verify* these articles with reference to science and history."[48] Because of this, doctrine should be seen as articulating a set of meanings and values shared by a particular theological community. As Richard Heyduck points out, doctrine is a speech act of the church or "grammar of the community" that communicates its self-identity.[49] Doctrine also acts as a line of social demarcation that defines the community by what it confesses.[50]

The primary approach of AG theology throughout history has been the "Bible doctrine" methodology rather than traditional theology.[51] Between 1930 and 1960, several important doctrinal volumes were produced that sought to outline the theology and doctrine of the AG. Douglas Jacobsen notes that these works nurtured second-generation Pentecostals

---

46. "General Convention of Pentecostal Churches," 1.
47. Pelikan, *Emergence of the Catholic Tradition*, 3–4.
48. Harnack, *Outlines of the History of Dogma*, 1; emphasis original.
49. Heyduck, *Recovery of Doctrine*, 67.
50. McGrath, *Genesis of Doctrine*, 37–52.
51. Stephenson, *Types of Pentecostal Theology*; Jacobsen, "Knowing the Doctrines," 90–99.

with a more moderate and systematic explanation of faith than the radical extremes of the early movement.[52] P. C. Nelson's classic *Bible Doctrines* was the first published doctrinal work in 1936. It was later republished by GPH in 1948 and continued in print until the 2000s. Several other doctrinal volumes followed, including Myer Pearlman's *Knowing the Doctrines of the Bible* and E. S. Williams's three-volume *Systematic Theology*. These works continued to be the standard for doctrine until 1993, when William Menzies and Stanley Horton produced *Bible Doctrines*, the doctrinal texts for AG ministers and Bible colleges. This section will examine the approaches to theology found in these important volumes.

Bible Doctrine as Theology

The Bible doctrines methodology is the primary way in which the AG articulated beliefs about the truths in the Bible.[53] Based on 2 Tim 3:16, the AG Constitution and Bylaws defined its doctrine as the plain teaching of the Bible as expressed in the Statement of Fundamental Truths.[54] J. R. Flower describes AG doctrine as the "skeleton structure which gives form and beauty to the body."[55] These doctrines were not theological tomes or creedal statements; they were propositional statements centered solely on biblical datum.[56] Myer Pearlman says, "Christian doctrine (the word 'doctrine' means literally 'teaching' or 'instruction') may be defined as the fundamental truths of the Bible arranged in systematic form."[57] Spittler characterizes AG doctrinal works not as theology but simply as "an organized summary of the teaching of the Bible set down in plain language."[58] Rather than engaging theological thinkers and arguments, Stephenson notes that they used a plain reading of Scripture, emphasized word study, and harmonized biblical verses describing doctrine without theological reflection.[59]

---

52. Jacobsen, "Knowing the Doctrines," 92.

53. The preamble of the constitution gives the purpose of the body the authority to "disapprove of all unscriptural methods, doctrines and conduct, and approve of all Scriptural truth and conduct." *GC Constitution and Bylaws* (April 2–12, 1914), 4.

54. *GC Constitution and Bylaws* (April 2–12, 1914), 1.

55. Flower, *Origin and Development*, 18.

56. Archer, "Pentecostal Way of Doing Theology," 306–7.

57. Pearlman, *Knowing the Doctrines*, 8.

58. Pearlman, *Knowing the Doctrines*, 8.

59. Stephenson, *Types of Pentecostal Theology*, 12.

Myer Pearlman echoes this approach, saying, "The doctrines of the New Testament as originally set forth, are simple, and may be simply derived."[60] This manner of reading of Scripture exhibits a Princeton epistemology and common-sense approach to scriptural interpretation that assumes the Bible is reducible to precise, clear propositional statements of truth.[61] Later doctrinal writers did not share this simplistic approach to writing doctrine, as seen in the works of Pearlman's *Knowing the Doctrine of the Bible* and E. S. Williams's three-volume *Systematic Theology*. Pearlman and Williams are more open to critically engaging with outside theological or philosophical views and cite sources.

The AG's official doctrine is expressed in the Statement of Fundamental Truths established by the General Council in 1916. The positions are the shared beliefs of its ministers and churches. However, the dogma of the AG is created when works are produced by the denomination that attempts to explain that doctrine. Dogma is the term within Christian doctrine that "designates that which is declared by the church to be revealed truth as a part of the universal teaching, or through a solemn doctrinal judgment."[62] For example, Russell Spittler describes P. C. Nelson's classic *Bible Doctrines* as "a sort of primitive dogmatics," treating doctrine based on the Statement of Fundamental Truths.[63] These attempts to articulate the "we believe" aspects of the fellowship are dogmatic. Whereas all dogma expresses doctrine, the two should not be considered synonymous. Dogma is the attempt to explain doctrine but is not canonical in fully setting out AG beliefs. That privilege is the prerogative of the Statement of Fundamental Truths alone. Therefore, like the Statement of Fundamental Truths, these works should be considered fallible in their interpretation. They should be seen as individual attempts to set forth common understandings among those in the General Council but can never authoritatively speak for the General Council. As former General Superintendent E. S. Williams insisted:

> It is not the prerogative of any one person to infallibly interpret for the entire General Council its doctrinal declaration ... Neither can a lone individual, though elected to office in the General Council, speak infallibly for the entire Council Fellowship in endorsing the

---

60. Pearlman, *Knowing the Doctrines*, 20. Pearlman often quoted Charles Hodge in reference to his views of inspiration.

61. Marsden, *Fundamentalism and American Culture*, 110–14.

62. McGrath, *Genesis of Doctrine*, 9.

63. Spittler, "Theological Style among Pentecostals," 298.

work of one person who seeks to interpret the meaning of the Fundamental Truths adopted by the body.[64]

Therefore, remembering the fallibility and contextualized construction of such works, these should be seen as interpretations of doctrine rather than the doctrines of the AG themselves. Despite this, ministers and denominational officials hold these classic works in high esteem in modern periods as articulated AG theology.

The Spirit and Interpretation of Doctrine

Because the AG wanted to avoid creedalism, the Bible was prioritized as the "rule of faith" rather than creeds. J. R. Flower comments, "It was thought best at the time to agree on the principle that the Scriptures themselves are the all-sufficient rule for faith and practice, with freedom for interpretation and development of truth left to the individual minister."[65] They took a position that entrusted the Spirit with the role of revealing truth, encouraging unity, and generating good faith among ministers. D. W. Kerr comments, "What men have said concerning the doctrines and facts of the Bible have their value, but we prefer to refer our students to the old-fashioned way of affirming and confirming. We believe the Bible is its own interpreter."[66] Private interpretation was the key to de-centralizing interpretation, which was a fundamental orientation that was adopted from the Evangelical Alliance.[67]

In that, the Holy Spirit, as the author of the word of God, had to take priority. Bell and Flower were committed to standing for "certain truths" without extremes. Yet they believed in the Spirit's ability to reveal new truths. They remark, "We must keep our sky-lights open so as not to reject any new light God may throw upon the old Word. We must not fail to keep pace in life or teaching from heaven."[68] This meant that theology is "by no means to be despised, or set aside, because it is, for the most part, written by men whose minds were illuminated by the Spirit of God."[69]

64. Williams, "Introduction," 3.
65. Flower, *Origin and Development*, 8.
66. Kerr, "Opening of Central Bible Institute," 4.
67. See chapter 4.
68. Bell and Flower, "In Doctrines," 2.
69. Bell and Flower, "In Doctrines," 2.

Similarly, Kerr recognizes that the Bible does not present theology in a systematic form. The best theology is that which the Holy Spirit enables the reader to learn through reading the narrative of Jesus.[70] This is what Kerr calls "Spontaneous Theology," which is theological truth about God revealed by the Holy Spirit through the narrative of Scripture.[71] This type of theology supersedes the opinions of man, the creeds, and the great theologians of the past. Kerr believed that the danger of creeds was not in the statement of doctrine but in the way it limited further truth from being revealed by the Holy Spirit. He says, "They have not stopped to consider that though the faith has once for all been delivered to the saints, there are yet many new jewels of truth to be drawn from the unsearchable riches of Christ."[72] Without new and further revelation, creeds can destroy spiritual life by becoming a "strait-jacket into which divine truth was painfully squeezed."[73] This is an important insight into how Pentecostals should view doctrine. If the Spirit leads into all truth, then the Spirit can give new insights that keep doctrine from becoming rigid and lifeless, which they saw as the problem with creedalism in modern denominations.

Bible Doctrines

In 1934, P. C. Nelson wrote *Bible Doctrines* as a "Handbook of Pentecostal Theology Based on the Scriptures and Following the Lines of the Statement of Fundamental Truths as Adopted by the General Council of the Assemblies of God."[74] Originally a Baptist preacher and evangelist, Nelson attended Denison University and later Rochester Theological Seminary, where he trained under Augustus H. Strong.[75] Nelson was baptized in the Spirit in 1920 and planted a church and Southwestern Bible School in Enid, Oklahoma, in 1927, which merged with another Bible school and moved to Waxahachie, Texas.[76] In 1934, Nelson published *Bible Doctrines* as a manual for teaching AG doctrine to college students. Calling it an "Elementary Pentecostal Theology," it was intended for ministers and lay people alike. It

---

70. Bell and Flower, "In Doctrines," 3.
71. Kerr, "Spontaneous Theology," 3.
72. Kerr, "Christian Creed and Life," 6.
73. Kerr, "Christian Creed and Life," 6.
74. Nelson, *Bible Doctrines* (1936), revised as Nelson, *Bible Doctrines* (1948).
75. McGee, "Nelson, Peter Christopher," 636–37.
76. Nelson, "Biographies."

was used so often as a text for defining AG doctrine that Gospel Publishing House republished it in 1948. As the first attempt to expound upon official AG doctrine, *Bible Doctrines* was recommended by E. S. Williams as a "clear exposition of the Statement of Fundamental Truths."[77] Thomas F. Zimmerman frames *Bible Doctrines* as a "brief exposition" of the Fundamental Truths.[78] Stanley Horton called it a "written commentary" on the Fundamental Truths.[79] The 1998 edition was the twenty-seventh edition, representing nearly sixty years of influence on AG ministers. Later editions were modified to match the changes to the Fundamental Truths following Nelson's death in 1942.

Nelson wrote his book just six years after affiliating with the AG. Having his own Bible school, he recognized that the AG lacked "a well-written Pentecostal textbook on theology."[80] Although this book would not be sufficient for such a task, he hoped it would be used as a catalyst for further studies and perhaps the type of volume he desired. The book progressed in several iterations with new and revised material. The 1936 edition was put together with the help of his Bible school students. The 1938 edition added more information not covered previously in response to a call from the General Presbytery mandating all AG Bible schools add a class on AG doctrine to their curriculum.[81] In 1971, the Executive Presbytery commissioned a new edition that included a different order of chapters based on the revised Statement of Fundamental Truths. To do this, J. R. Flower and Anthony Palma revised or created six chapters.[82]

Despite its focus on Scripture to build his "Bible doctrines," Nelson occasionally supports his interpretations by quoting various secondary sources when appropriate. For example, he draws from Eric Lund's *Hermeneutics*, which Nelson translated from Spanish and published in 1932.[83] William Oliverio Jr. notes that Nelson uses Lund's approach to hermeneutics to discover "the meaning of individual Scriptural texts in order to prepare for their systematic organization and application."[84] This supports the inter-

---

77. Williams, "Introduction."
78. Nelson, *Bible Doctrines* (1992), 3–4.
79. Menzies and Horton, *Bible Doctrines*, 13.
80. Nelson, *Bible Doctrines* (1936), "preface to first edition."
81. Nelson, *Bible Doctrines* (1938), "preface."
82. Nelson, *Bible Doctrines* (1992), 3.
83. Lund, *Hermeneutics*.
84. Oliverio, *Theological Hermeneutics*, 118.

textual approach of cobbling various texts together to support claims. That said, Nelson selectively draws from several sources in his explanation of the inspiration of the Bible.[85] The Holy Spirit chapter is the only other chapter where he engages the ideas of others and cites multiple commentaries that support Pentecostal understandings of the Spirit as empowering.[86] For most other topics, he makes no mention of sources, only Scripture citations.

Nelson exemplifies the Bible doctrines approach of brief, propositional concepts supported by proof texts. He gives little information on how he views theology or its development, or how Pentecostals might view these doctrines uniquely. However, as a dogmatic commentary on the Fundamental Truths, a couple of observations can be made about the success of such an endeavor. First, each chapter contains teachings related to a particular article of the Fundamental Truths, which is most often supported by supporting verses, reflecting the style of the Fundamental Truths. It faithfully expresses distinctive concepts such as Trinitarian Godhead, sanctification as both instantaneous and progressive, Spirit-baptism as subsequent work with speaking in tongues as evidence, and a finished work approach to divine healing in the atonement. However, a few chapters do not necessarily explain the various concepts in the article it represents. For example, the "Scriptures Inspired" chapter covers "inspiration" and gives other "proofs" of the Bible's divine origin. But Nelson ignores the article's last half, explaining how it is "superior to conscience and reason, but not contrary."[87] Information on his perspective of the interplay between reason and truth would have been a helpful insight into his theological epistemology. A more dramatic example is the "New Heavens and New Earth," which has seven sections giving additional information on the millennium but devotes little energy to explaining the truth except to quote the verse and mention that it will be a "remaking," not "annihilation."[88]

A second interesting observation is that his treatment of the final judgment is similar to what is found in the periodical literature.[89] Nelson prioritizes hell as a punishment for the devil and his angels, noting that

---

85. In one full-page footnote, Nelson mentions over a dozen works on the Bible from evangelicals such as William Evans, H. A. Strong, R. A. Torrey, Marcus Dodd, and S. E. Stowe. Nelson, *Bible Doctrines* (1948), 21.

86. Nelson, *Bible Doctrines* (1948), 87–90.

87. Nelson, *Bible Doctrines* (1948), 15–21. The wording of this chapter was preserved throughout the revisions to the later editions.

88. Nelson, *Bible Doctrines* (1948), 163–70.

89. Isgrigg, *Imagining the Future*, 61, 248–49.

the lake of fire "was not prepared for man, but for the punishment of the arch-enemy of God and man."[90] As most interpretations do, it emphasizes hell more so than the nature of the final judgment.

A third observation comes with the 1971 revision that corrected some of Nelson's claims. For example, in Nelson's original chapter on baptism, he claims, "With amazing unanimity, our Pentecostal people practice immersion in water in the name of the Father, Son, and Holy Ghost."[91] In doing so, he completely ignores the Oneness tradition that originated from a schism in the AG in 1916 over baptism in "Jesus' name." However, the revision changed the language to "most Pentecostal groups," making the statement more accurate.[92] Another observation is that the chapter on the church was completely rewritten from the original version by Anthony Palma. Nelson emphasizes using the term *assembly* as the proper expression of the biblical word *church*. Palma uses some of Nelson's sections but eliminates some of the "assembly" language where Nelson gives the rationales for the name used by early AG leaders.[93]

Knowing the Doctrines of the Bible

Myer Pearlman published *Knowing the Doctrines of the Bible* in 1937 at the request of the Gospel Publishing House.[94] Born in Scotland, Pearlman was a Jewish man who was converted at the Glad Tidings Mission in San Francisco, California. After conversion, he attended Central Bible Institute and, following graduation, joined the faculty. Although having earned only a Bible school education, he was well versed in several languages such as Hebrew, French, and Greek. Pearlman's *Knowing the Doctrines of the Bible* is the first AG book that attempts to treat Bible doctrines as theology. Spittler believes "the wide dissemination of [Pearlman's] book and its long life earn it top honors and senior status in the scantily populated ranks of Pentecostal theological writing."[95]

---

90. Nelson, *Bible Doctrines* (1948), 161–62.
91. Nelson, *Bible Doctrines* (1948), 61.
92. Nelson, *Bible Doctrines* (1992), 42.
93. Compare Nelson, *Bible Doctrines* (1948), 111–17, and Nelson, *Bible Doctrines* (1992), 80–86.
94. Pearlman, *Knowing the Doctrines*.
95. Spittler, "Theological Style among Pentecostals," 298.

Unlike Nelson, Pearlman begins his work with a chapter on the nature of theology and doctrine. For Pearlman, doctrine expresses "fundamental truths of the Bible arranged in systematic form."[96] However, Pearlman acknowledges there are different kinds of theology: exegetical theology, historical theology, dogmatic theology, biblical theology, and systematic theology. Pearlman's approach is what he considers to be a "combination of Biblical and systematic theology."[97] He attempts to arrange the great doctrines of the Bible following the major systematic themes such as the doctrine of God, man, Christ, salvation, etc. Pearlman does not claim that this is Pentecostal or AG doctrine specifically. Although many individuals and movements are mentioned, this work does not mention the Pentecostal movement itself. Likewise, Pearlman does not use Pentecostal sources for his content, preferring to use popular Methodists and fundamentalist authors to bolster his formulation of these doctrines.[98]

Pearlman engages vital figures and debates in the development of theological concepts. For example, in the chapter on salvation, he discusses the differences in the doctrine of election and predestination between Calvinistic and Arminian positions. After engaging in discourse using Augustine, John Calvin, Charles Finney, and John Wesley, Pearlman makes his argument for a "scriptural balance" between the views.[99] In his defense of initial evidence, he draws from liberal theologians and several Presbyterians rather than Pentecostals.[100] Pearlman's willingness to supplement scriptural texts with theological reflection and engagement shows the growth in theological reflection during the scholastic period.[101] The addition of a subject index also shows a growth in maturity of the theological nature of AG doctrinal texts.

---

96. Pearlman, *Knowing the Doctrines*, 8.
97. Pearlman, *Knowing the Doctrines*, 12.
98. Jacobsen, "Knowing the Doctrines of Pentecostals," 93.
99. Pearlman, *Knowing the Doctrines*, 267–76.
100. Pearlman, *Knowing the Doctrines*, 313–18.
101. This is contrary to Jacobsen who claims Pearlman had "little engagement," although because the wording is imprecise it is hard to evaluate the claim. Jacobsen, "Knowing the Doctrines of Pentecostals," 92–93.

Systematic Theology

In 1953, E. S. Williams published a three-volume *Systematic Theology*. Williams's volumes were an important theological development as it was the first critical engagement of AG doctrine with other theological or philosophical views. This volume was produced as AG Bible schools were transitioning to liberal arts colleges, and the G.I. Bill provided greater education opportunities for Pentecostals.[102] The transition that was taking place in the AG from Bible colleges to four-year colleges was mirrored by the transition from Bible doctrine to higher levels of theological reflection. This maturation is seen as Williams is open to engaging other ideas and thinkers so that his readers might consider multiple perspectives rather than "the theological thought of one school of interpreters only."[103] Williams believes Pentecostal doctrine should be understood in conversation with other ideas and traditions. He says, "Much good has come to me through reading the works of different writers. On some subjects I have seen things differently, but at the same time I have been enabled to understand the position of others better. This enables me to appreciate them more."[104] Each of his concepts is described by engaging with scholars from across the spectrum of evangelical theology.

In his chapter on theology and doctrine, Williams notes that theology is the "science" of discourse about God.[105] Systematic theology involves the arrangement of Biblical truth into theological categories, an approach he takes in the divisions of his book. For Williams, the study of theology is the process of "discovering and properly arranging the truths found in the Word of God."[106] Williams moves beyond the Bible doctrines perspective to engage in scholastic theology that compares views for his readers. For example, his chapters on divine decree, sovereignty, election, Rom 9–11, and Arminianism present various theological views and provide rebuttals of those views by other theologians. Further theological development can

---

102. *General Council Minutes* (September 4–9, 1947), 16–21.

103. Williams, *Systematic Theology*, 1:vii. Williams was a popular pastor and quickly rose to the level of General Superintendent in 1929 and served until 1949. Williams has no formal theological degrees. After leaving the position of Superintendent, Williams joined the faculty of CBC where he taught theology. The notes from his classes were compiled by Frank Boyd into this three-volume work.

104. Williams, *Systematic Theology*, 1:viii.

105. Williams, *Systematic Theology*, 1:155.

106. Williams, *Systematic Theology*, 1:157.

be seen in chapters on kenosis theory, engagements with evolution as anthropology, and explanation of atonement theories. Though Williams was far less educated than most of his peers, his willingness to engage in critical theology demonstrates a greater commitment to theological engagement than any Bible doctrine works.

Into All Truth

If Williams's systematic theology was a progressive step toward critical theology, Stanley Horton's 1955 book *Into All Truth* harkened back to the Bible doctrine genre.[107] Though one of the most recognized scholars in the AG, his approach intentionally avoids theological discussion, boasting of "no references to books other than the Bible."[108] Despite completing three theological degrees, including a ThD, Horton displays a suspicion toward theology. He laments, "For too long theologians and preachers have come to the Bible seeking to read into its teachings derived from human sources."[109] Horton believes Christian doctrine should be derived simply from what the Bible "actually teaches." Frank Boyd commends Horton for his work in articulating doctrine that is "stripped of technical theological terms" and free from "heavy tomes of creed and dogma."[110]

Rather than discuss the nature of theology and doctrine as Pearlman and Williams did, Horton assumes a propositionalist approach to define the "truths" contained in Scripture. He notes that his title *Into All Truth* could be "a little presumptuous." However, he argues that plainly seeing the truth in the Bible is possible because Jesus promised the Holy Spirit would guide believers "into all truth."[111] A dependence on the Holy Spirit is the key for Horton to bring about an understanding of Bible truths. This is especially important to Horton because he believes the world has moved away from notions of truth due to liberalism, which he blames on Christians trading education, science, and philosophy instead of the truth of God found in the revelation of Jesus Christ, the true one.[112]

---

107. Horton, *Into All Truth*. This book was featured regularly in early 1956 as the chosen training resource for Sunday School workers.
108. Horton, *Into All Truth*, "introduction."
109. Horton, *Into All Truth*, "introduction."
110. Horton, *Into All Truth*, "foreword."
111. Horton, *Into All Truth*, 1.
112. Horton, *Into All Truth*, 3–4.

Next, Horton uses this pneumatological approach to dig deeper into how the Holy Spirit brings about "progressive revelation" of truth. In the same way some early leaders expressed the Spirit's role in bringing certain doctrines to the forefront in each generation, Stanley Horton comments that the Holy Spirit emphasizes truth differently in different ages.[113] He is not suggesting that truth is evolving; rather, the Spirit is presently active in the church to illuminate truth because "the Spirit still desires to guide us into all truth."[114] In particular, Horton identifies the four-fold gospel as having been given particular emphasis by the Pentecostal Movement: salvation, healing, baptism in the Spirit, and the second coming of Christ. He says, "These four teachings have received special emphasis and illumination by the Holy Spirit during the present-day Pentecostal revival."[115] He believes the Spirit has "delighted to bring all of them into prominence." The rest of the book devotes two chapters to each of the four truths. Guided only by biblical texts and some exegesis of Bible words, Horton lays out his understanding of these truths from various angles, yet his interpretation is the only one presented.

Understanding Our Doctrine

In 1971, William Menzies published a Sunday school worker's curriculum called *Understanding Our Doctrine*.[116] This resource is not widely known, but it is one of the most influential doctrinal works as it was the basis for the later *Bible Doctrines: A Pentecostal Perspective* by Menzies and Horton. With no introduction chapter, there is little to indicate Menzies's approach to doctrine and theology. Still, it is arranged as explanations of the articles of the SFT, which are mentioned at the beginning of each chapter. However, he combines some articles and creates chapters for other divisions not in the Fundamental Truths. For example, he chooses to make a chapter on the deity of the Holy Spirit (not a Fundamental Truth). Then, he combines the two on baptism in the Holy Spirit with sanctification into one chapter entitled "Life in the Spirit." He also combines the church, ministry, and ordinances into one chapter. Additionally, he consolidates the four eschatological fundamentals into two lessons on the "second coming of Christ"

113. Horton, *Into All Truth*, 13.
114. Horton, *Into All Truth*, 13.
115. Horton, *Into All Truth*, 13.
116. Menzies, *Understanding Our Doctrine*.

and "Last Things." Each lesson begins with the article from the Statement of Fundamental Truths and then provides explanations of each doctrine in the Bible doctrines method. The reasoned approach gives a biblical explanation for each aspect addressed. There are no citations, but Menzies does bring in nuanced conversations about theological concepts, including textual transmission, eternal subordination, the nature of the soul, and atonement. He also occasionally references outside perspectives such as Reinhold Niebuhr, when dealing with sin and corporate evil.[117]

Bible Doctrines

In 1993, Logion Press (the academic imprint of Gospel Publishing House) published *Bible Doctrines: A Pentecostal Perspective* by William Menzies and Stanley Horton.[118] Widely recognized as the standard on AG doctrine for ministers and AG universities, it has affirmed Horton as the "shaper of Pentecostal theology" more than any other doctrinal text.[119] However, it is not widely recognized that most of the text is taken from word-for-word from Menzies's *Understanding Our Doctrine*. Horton compiled Menzies's content and contributed new chapters for those Fundamental Truths that he had combined or revised. Horton contributed the most information on eschatology. Menzies's version includes the second coming, the rapture, the tribulation, and the final judgment. Horton also fills out what Menzies fails to cover on the doctrine of the millennium as well as new heavens and new earth.

Horton opens the book with a chapter reaffirming the Bible doctrines approach to AG doctrine. Horton notes, "Our purpose, however, is not to promote Assemblies of God doctrines, but to bring out the biblical basis and applications of these fundamental Bible truths."[120] At the same time, the title asserts that these doctrines are from a "Pentecostal perspective." By asserting an unbiased biblical interpretation, Horton reinforces the conflation of contextualized Pentecostal interpretations of the Bible with universal biblical truth. Whereas Menzies recognizes the contextual nature of his study by naming it "Our Doctrines," Horton re-roots his contextualized Pentecostal expressions of Biblical interpretation as "Bible Doctrines."

117. Menzies, *Understanding Our Doctrine*, 32.
118. Menzies and Horton, *Bible Doctrines*.
119. Olena, *Stanley M. Horton*.
120. Menzies and Horton, *Bible Doctrines*, 8.

The problem with Horton's method is that he also admits that the content of the study is influenced by previous Bible doctrine works. For example, he added content from the Position Papers created by the Commission on Doctrinal Purity directly into the chapters. Horton also added several footnotes to various other GPH-published works, including previous doctrinal books, his works, and various other books. Specifically, most of the chapters related to eschatology, especially the rapture, were drawn from previous articles and books by Horton such as *It's Getting Late* and *Ultimate Victory*.[121] Therefore, this is clearly a dogmatic representation of teachings within the AG rather than objectively derived biblical truths.

Systematic Theology

In tandem with Horton's release of *Bible Doctrines* came the first multi-author systematic theology created with the goal of "seriously and earnestly" seeking to articulate theological perspectives on AG doctrine.[122] This edited volume contains essays by AG faculty members with doctoral degrees. Unlike *Bible Doctrines*, the essays seek to do more than compile Scripture but to "address various views and their strengths and weaknesses" in defense of the AG's Pentecostal perspective. The volume chapters follow the Statement of Fundamental Truths in structure but are more systematic and critical than previous volumes. The text was intended to fill a gap in theological texts from a Pentecostal perspective for AG colleges and universities. Each scholar takes a biblical theology approach to articulate AG beliefs through engaging scholarship as support, including Pentecostal scholars in the AG and other Pentecostal traditions. The result is a thoughtful, well-researched, and reasoned "defense" of the AG's theological perspectives.

CONCLUSION

Analyzing the development of AG theology illustrates the tensions between their biblical commitments and the role of critical theology. The AG certainly believed in education. They established Bible schools and eventually liberal arts colleges where Pentecostals could gain deeper understanding and training. AG educators moved from Bible school degrees to advanced

---

121. Menzies and Horton, *Bible Doctrines*, 216–26.
122. Horton, *Systematic Theology*, "introduction," back cover.

Aspects of Theology and Education

degrees in theology and other fields. While AG ministers drew significantly from the teachings of learned people within Evangelicalism, they most often articulated their theology in the form of Bible doctrines where AG views are not critically engaged as much as expressed as plain truths of the Bible. While theological development made significant progress in the works of Pearlman and Williams, Horton (and to some degree Menzies) sought to preserve the Bible doctrines approach while at the same time producing the first academic systematic theology.

As highly educated scholars, Horton and Menzies demonstrate the definite tension in appealing to authoritative works to undergird the interpretation of biblical truths while at the same time posturing that it is the plain, universal meaning of Scripture unaffected by the theological or cultural horizons of those who are interpreting such data. As Christopher Stephenson points out, the weakness in this model is that the authors do not acknowledge the influence of theological and philosophical development, nor do they acknowledge the sources of that understanding they present as "truths."[123] As was demonstrated in chapters 4 and 5, Pentecostals read widely and drew from many evangelical sources to understand biblical truth. Yet, the Bible doctrines method does not acknowledge that influence and creates the illusion that Bible truths are self-evident when read without human interpretation. When the hermeneutical horizons of the interpreter are not considered, there tends also to be no consideration of what would make this theology "Pentecostal" because it refuses to acknowledge that any hermeneutical lens is warranted. As shown, these Bible doctrine works do not strive to be expressions of Pentecostal or AG doctrine. Instead, they claim they express only what the Bible teaches, a position that lacks theological humility and creates issues with ecumenical relations.

The AG has a right to articulate and defend its doctrine as a unique expression of its theological orientation. This is accomplished when its ministers and scholars have the tools to critically engage the unique perspectives of this community. Acknowledging that higher education and critical approaches to theology can strengthen the AG's beliefs is growing in its ranks. This was demonstrated with the edited volume *Systematic Theology: A Pentecostal Perspective* in 1994. As more clergy seek graduate and terminal degrees, the AG must continue to develop greater theological maturity and better articulation of its theology and doctrine.

---

123. Stephenson, *Types of Pentecostal Theologies*, 24–26.

Chapter 8

Aspects of Social Engagement

INTRODUCTION[1]

DURING THE LATE NINETEENTH century, Evangelicalism experienced a shift in eschatological views from postmillennialism to premillennialism. For most of the nineteenth century, evangelicals worked for the reversal of societal ills such as poverty and slavery, and were advocates of women's rights and public welfare.[2] The shift to premillennialism led to the "great reversal" from Christian activism in society to missionary activity focused on saving as many souls as they could before Jesus comes.[3] For the evangelical tradition, this meant the world that was perceived as getting worse and was soon to end. Therefore, the emphasis and energy must be prioritized on saving souls rather than fixing society. As a premillennial tradition, Pentecostals were very much oriented toward this prioritization of souls over social issues. Because of this, Pentecostal scholars have critiqued Pentecostal eschatology as the source of escapism and indifference to meeting society's social needs.[4] For example, Murray Dempster called dispensational premillennialism "a major, perhaps the major, theological factor that has sparked and perpetuated the controversy over the social

---

1. This chapter is a revision of Isgrigg, "Interpreting the Signs of the Times."
2. Dayton, *Discovering an Evangelical Heritage*, 121–29.
3. Dayton, "Pentecostal Studies," 170–71.
4. For a good survey of the issues expressed by Pentecostal scholars, see Althouse, "Landscape of Pentecostal," 1–21.

Aspects of Social Engagement

involvement of the church."[5] Because of this, some Pentecostal scholars argue for alternative eschatological models that encourage social engagement and are more compatible with Pentecostal spirituality.

The AG is firmly rooted in premillennial and dispensational eschatology. They took a strong stance from the beginning that Jesus was coming soon. The *Pentecostal Evangel* expressed eschatological perspectives and commentary on social issues. The AG believed that the outpouring of the Spirit was a sign pointing to his near return, but they also interpreted war, world political changes, and other social issues equally as "signs of the times."

Like most early Pentecostal periodicals, emphasis on the return of Jesus was evident throughout every issue of the *Pentecostal Evangel*. The picture these articles paint of the future is pessimistic.[6] The world was rapidly changing as they watched society decline morally, economically, and politically, which convinced them that society was not getting better; the world was indeed getting worse.[7] Pentecostals criticized human attempts at "progress" since they produced social regress, particularly the global conflict of WWI.[8] They were not just critical of the moral state of the world; they criticized the church relying on the social gospel and progressive reforms of society. Additionally, prayer and waiting on the Lord were deemed more valuable than social work. A. G. Ward comments, "Remember that your Bridegroom is much more concerned about your waiting upon Him and satisfying His heart than He is about your going around working in your own energy."[9]

This chapter explores how the AG's premillennial beliefs affected how they interpreted economic, racial, political, and social issues. To aid in this task, articles in the *Pentecostal Evangel* will be analyzed through the first two generations of the AG (1914–42). It will demonstrate that although the

---

5. Dempster, "Eschatology, Spirit Baptism," 155–88.

6. To the charges that their view of the end times was too pessimistic the writer comments, "'A very pessimistic picture,' you say. Perhaps so, but it is not one of my own invention, but of God's revelation." "Great War and the Speedy Return," 2. This same argument was made verbatim in "Light on This Present Crisis," 7.

7. "Is the World Growing Better," 3. Also see "Further Signs of the Last Days," 1; "Signs of the Approaching End," 8; McAlister, "Startling Signs of the End," 1–3; S., "Signs of the Times," 8.

8. Russell, "Prophecy and Present Day Events," 8; "Good News of the Lord's Appearing," 8.

9. Ward, "Soul Food for Hungry Saints," 1.

AG was skeptical of human progress before the return of Jesus, they were motivated by the needs of hurting people and the call to preach the gospel in various social aspects.

ECONOMIC JUSTICE

As a movement whose early adherents were among the poor and marginalized, one social issue Pentecostals recognized was income inequality. The advent of industrialization in America created a new set of economic realities in which individuals were acquiring unprecedented wealth. For early Pentecostals, wealth was not a sign of God's blessing but rather a sign of judgment. The wealth gained was nothing more than "miseries for rich men" that were being "hoarded for the last days."[10] They were particularly critical of the rich because wealth was included in prophetic scriptures as a "sign of the times."[11] S. A. Jamieson criticized the "greed and corruption" of the government and the banking industry for the rising poverty in America. He says, "To enrich themselves they run up the cost of living so that a great many people cannot reach it. I call this bad economics, but Christ will right things soon."[12] Pentecostals noticed that while the rich were experiencing unprecedented wealth, the latter rain of the Spirit fell on the poor. As one writer said, "The phenomenon of the Latter Rain coincides with the phenomenon of the increasing world riches."[13] Riches amassed by millionaires were seen as a sign of judgment, but the outpouring of the Spirit was interpreted as God's answer to economic equality. One writer comments, "The Lord says, 'Upon my servants, I will pour out my Spirit!' Handmaidens! In the millionaire's home, it is the millionaire of the cook who goes to the Pentecostal meeting."[14] As marginalized believers, they were content to be the "down-trodden, the defrauded, the cheated" because they knew their rewards were in heaven.[15]

During the Great Depression, some in the AG criticized the economic injustice in the US. The critique of wealth became a justification for criticism of worker exploitation and income inequality resulting from the Great

10. "Miseries for Rich Men," 4–5.
11. "Significant Sign," 5.
12. Jamieson, "Seven Fears and Seven Cheers," 3.
13. "Significant Sign," 5.
14. "Significant Sign," 5.
15. "Significant Sign," 5.

Aspects of Social Engagement

Depression.[16] Some drew attention to various ways the wealthy had encouraged the systematic institutional exploitation of the vulnerable. One article condemned crooked salesmen, bankers, stockbrokers, and large industrialized farm corporations that were driving local farmers into poverty.[17] This reinforced the narratives of marginalization among Pentecostals as signs of identification with Christ. One writer comments, "As the ruthless hand of passing events strips the veil of illusion from earthly prosperity, the child of God will rejoice in the fact that he has laid up a treasure in heaven that no person and no circumstance can take from him."[18] Yet, even with these critiques, their belief in the coming of God's rule on earth in the millennial kingdom kept them from addressing systemic economic issues in society. At the same time, they were ardent opponents of socialism and the growing threat of Communism in the US.[19]

As the country emerged from the Great Depression, Pentecostals moved up in the social strata and were forced to wrestle with the eschatological implications of wealth. These second-generation Pentecostals of the 1930s and 1940s built permanent churches.[20] As they did, attitudes shifted from wealth as a "sign of the times" to an issue of stewardship. This more positive perspective on wealth was shared by Superintendent E. S. Williams, who says, "It is wrong when people frown on persons just because they are rich. Some of them are the most beautiful of characters. God bless them."[21] Instead of seeing wealth as a "sign of the times," which will receive the judgment of God, wealth was seen as a tool to advance the Christian mission, mainly to fund missions and help the needy.[22]

---

16. Frodsham, "Coming of Christ," 1.
17. "When the Son of Man Comes," 2.
18. "Uncertainty of Riches," 2.
19. Another issue that led to discussion of wealth was the rise of Communism. Communist attitudes toward wealth and poverty were seen as an end-time evil and counterfeit Millennium. Fredrick Childe comments, "Communism looks forward to the ideal social state that has no class distinctions, and without private ownership of property. Now we know that that all sounds very nice when we talk about it, but that ideal is far too ideal for the Communists or any other man to undertake to bring about because of the nature of selfish man. Nobody but the Lord Jesus Christ will ever bring in a condition like that! When He returns He will establish such an ideal social state." Childe "Christ's Answer to the Challenge," 1, See also "Red Terror," 5.
20. Menzies, *Anointed to Serve*, 144–49.
21. Williams, "Jesus Advises a Rich Man," 5.
22. Isgrigg, *Imagining the Future*, 134–35.

RACIAL JUSTICE

The development of industrialization in the US created not only economic inequality but also growing issues surrounding racial inequality.[23] The Azusa Street Revival symbolized the alternative vision of Pentecost that emphasized the Spirit being poured out on all flesh and washing away all social and racial distinctions. The AG, however, was relatively silent on the issue of racial inequality and made seemingly no attempt to embrace the racial vision present at the Azusa Street Mission.

One minister who conveyed overtly racist views was W. F. Carothers, a close associate of Goss and Bell who shared Parham's views against racial mixing.[24] Carothers argued that different races were "God's intention," a claim he believed was not motivated by "prejudice nor any other evil intent" but was necessary to "preserve racial purity and integrity."[25] He argued that the American South "selfishly" mixed the races for their financial gain through slavery, which was the primary reason for racial tensions in America. However, these white supremacist views were not necessarily shared by others in the AG. E. N. Bell was asked if "Negros" were created by the curse of Cain. He responded, "I don't think this is the origin of the Negro." Instead, he says the reason for the dark skin tone was from being from Africa.[26]

Fellowship between blacks and whites in the AG was not common in the Jim Crow South. But sometimes white AG ministers fellowshipped with and ministered to black Pentecostal believers. F. A. Hale reported in 1917 that he visited the "negro tabernacle" in San Antonio where the worship and freedom inspired him in the Spirit.[27] Next, he visited a Mexican mission where again he was in awe of the testimonies of Spirit baptism among the believers. Zola Taylor also felt called to minister to the African American population in Arkansas and shared how much she loved the "precious people" in that community.[28] In 1917, Nellie Wright reported that she was

---

23. Donovan, *White Slave Crusades*, points out that during the turn of the century, fears surrounding growing immigration and industrialization led to "whiteness" and "colored" becoming class-oriented concepts used by anti-industrialization proponents to preserve the social order.
24. Martin, *Charles Fox Parham*, 151–68.
25. Carothers, "Attitude of Pentecostal Whites," 2.
26. Bell, "Questions and Answers," Dec. 28, 1918, 9.
27. Hale, "Word from San Antonio," 14.
28. Taylor, "Line from Zola Taylor," 16.

conducting an interracial revival in Coffeyville, Kansas, with Ozero Jones. Bishop O. T. Jones, as most know him, was one of the founding bishops of the Church of God in Christ. Wright reported "turning over" the work to Jones to lead the continuing revival and to establish a permanent work.[29]

That said, Howard Kenyon notes that in the AG, "few champions of civil rights and human rights were to be found."[30] He found only one instance addressing racial justice or equality.[31] But there are two additional stories that better illustrate the Spirit's power to break prejudice for people in the AG. The first is the testimony of Jonathan Ellsworth Perkins, a Methodist Episcopal pastor reared in Virginia in deeply rooted prejudice toward blacks. Before joining Pentecost, he attended a Pentecostal mission in Wichita, Kansas, where Pentecostal spirituality took over. He recalls, "One old colored Auntie got up and began to praise God and soon gave hilarious vent to her religious ecstasy." Perkins felt prejudice stir up in him, and he stormed out, declaring, "I was not called upon to worship God with 'n____.'"[32] Perkins believes God punished him for his act of prejudice. In 1923, Perkins became ill and hungry for the baptism in the Holy Spirit and healing. He was invited to a Pentecostal mission in Wichita led by a black minister who asked him to preach since he was a minister. As he told his story of his prejudice, he admitted to the congregation, "I had never been around Pentecostal folks since that colored woman had scared me away." With deep remorse over his prejudice, he shared his need for the baptism in the Spirit. That night, he received the fullness of the Spirit and spoke in tongues. He recalls, "I turned down the Pentecostal truth fourteen years before because of a black-skinned woman, but I had to wade through a whole campmeeting of them when I got the baptism. God surely broke me over the wheel of my prejudice."[33]

The second testimony is of Vida B. Baer, who had a black female servant named Eliza. Baer admitted she was very harsh with Eliza. But one day, God spoke to her and told her to apologize for being harsh. Eliza said her husband was not providing for her, and her kids were hungry. God's love melted her heart, and Baer offered to pay her rent and feed her kids. She realized that Eliza was not a servant but a fellow believer. This ignited in her

29. Wright, "Coffeyville, Kansas," 14.
30. Kenyon, *Ethics in the Age*, 132–33.
31. Kenyon, *Ethics in the Age*, 71.
32. Perkins, "My First Sermon," 6.
33. Perkins, "My First Sermon," 7.

a sense that she needed to be baptized in the Spirit to change her attitude. Then, one day, surrounded by "a Mexican woman on one side of [her], a colored woman on the other," she was baptized in the Spirit.[34]

These aspects demonstrate how the majority of white Pentecostals that make up the AG were comfortable with segregated ministry but also enjoyed fellowship with black Pentecostals, especially in revival meetings. This legacy would persist in the succeeding decades as racial issues became more pronounced.[35] The AG continued to be a predominantly white fellowship until the decades that followed the civil rights movement.

SOCIAL JUSTICE

Though AG ministers did not address the issue of prejudice and racism, early AG ministers were aware of the growing problem of human trafficking.[36] The issue of the "white slave trade" was the name given to the trafficking of white women across state lines for prostitution.[37] Bell called the trafficking of women "one of the worst wickedness in the nation" and warned his readers about the dangers of human traffickers.[38] Exaggerated claims made by the producers of racially motivated "white slave" literature were intended to create moral panic. AG ministers utilized these narratives as justification that the coming of the Lord was near.[39] Even though the idea of "white slave" was racist, early Pentecostals felt compassion for trafficked women and opened rescue homes where women could be saved

---

34. Baer, "Latter Rain," 3.

35. See Kenyon, *Ethics in the Age*, 74–71; Rodgers, "Assemblies of God and the Long Journey," 55.

36. See Isgrigg, "'Rescued Women,'" 443–61, for a complete history of Pentecostals and the rescue home movement for victims of sex trafficking.

37. Donovan, *White Slave Crusades*, investigated the "white slavery" campaigns, which sought to protect women and the "morality and purity" of American culture during a time when the age of industrialization was producing racial and social anxiety. Dramatic stories of white women being lured into prostitution rings were often exaggerated and repeated in various books and even films. The unintended consequences of this movement were the emergence of "colored" and "white" as racial language, as well as the rise of white masculinity and degradation of femininity. Much of the "morality and purity" literature surrounding this issue came out of Chicago, a center for Midwest Pentecostals.

38. Bell, "Questions and Answers," Apr. 14, 1917, 9; "White Slave Craft," 3.

39. Donovan, *White Slave Crusades*, 19. See Pope, "Morphine Tablets of Hell," 5; Pope, "Crying Need of the Hour," 9–12.

and restored to society.[40] One such rescue mission in Arkansas was led by Bell and Goss, who took over a home in 1917 and invited AG ministers to support the work of helping women come out of the white slave trade.[41] Bell encouraged his readers to give offerings to "help save girls and send them to the Home where they can get saved and get on their feet again and lead a clean life."[42] While the legacy of this work is complicated due to its overt racial emphasis and how it reinforced holiness codes about women's dress, it demonstrates a willingness of early AG leaders to address the exploitation and violence against women, empowering them toward better lives.

Rescue homes were not just for trafficked women, but they often helped many at-risk people, including orphans, the hungry, and those suffering from addiction. R. L. Cotham's rescue home in Sapulpa, Oklahoma, was open to all: the indigent, homeless, or any vulnerable person who needed help.[43] The famous Pisgah Rescue home welcomed "any unfortunate soul that has lost health and home and happiness and hope."[44] Compassion for the down and out is one of the characteristics of Pentecostal ministry. Florence Burpee criticized believers in the US for having large homes with many rooms but treating people without housing like the innkeeper in the Christmas story. She says, "There are helpless little children in our orphan asylums who once had a home and kind parents, but when cruel death took their loved ones away, they had to depend on the kindness of the world. Many rich, or comparatively poor people, might give them a home if they would."[45] Sven Lidman shared how the homeless of Philadelphia broke his heart. He exhorted, "I feel we need so much more love for the homeless."[46] However, most of the advocacy for the homeless was from missionaries who started orphanages and many other homeless ministries for people abroad.

40. Isgrigg, "'Rescued Women,'" 16–19.
41. Bell, "Bethel Rescue Home," 1.
42. Bell, "Bethel Rescue Home," 1.
43. Cotham, "Pentecostal Rescue Home," 6.
44. Frodsham, "Pisgah as I Have Seen It," 2–4.
45. Burpee, "No Room in the Inn," 3.
46. Lidman, "Priestly Service before God," 3.

POLITICAL ENGAGEMENT

Another aspect of social engagement that eschatology significantly shaped was their outlook on engagement in politics. In 1917, Woodrow Wilson shared his vision that the promotion of democracy was a divine global mission given to America to save the nations and promote liberty, prosperity, order, and justice.[47] Early Pentecostals strongly disagreed for several reasons. First, they believed democracy elevated the ability of people to reform society as a secular form of postmillennialism. James McAlister comments, "Democracy means to govern without Christ, and will therefore prove the biggest failure of all forms of government. It will land this world in a welter of blood and death unparalleled."[48] Second, they believed that sinful people would vote for reform without God. Stanley Frodsham believed that the democratic value of exercising voting rights was often fruitless and antithetical to fundamental Christian convictions. Therefore, the political process itself was corrupt. He says, "The world says: 'Of two evils, choose the lesser.' The saint says: 'Seeing two evils, avoid both.'"[49] Similarly, W. T. Gaston declared, "I am going to sing and shout and vote for Jesus, I have no enthusiasm for anybody else."[50] On the other hand, Bell proudly supported Pentecostals using the right to vote. He says, "I feel it right for me to vote. I vote the man, not for the party. I never mix in party politics."[51] But he did not feel it right for the AG to advocate either way.

Similarly, the AG's apolitical eschatological orientation was instrumental in the stance on pacifism.[52] For many, war was antithetical to Christian morals and was nothing more than a political tool. As one writer says, "The War belongs to the world, and it has served to illustrate the association of the highest civilization with the deepest wickedness."[53] As WWI began, readers of the *Pentecostal Evangel* wondered which "Christian nation" should be supported in the war. But one article argued that truly "Christian nations" would have "made such a war impossible."[54] In fact, the

---

47. Studebaker, *Pentecostal Political Theology*, 33–37.
48. McAlister, "Startling Signs of the End," 1.
49. Frodsham, "Politics from the Pentecostal Viewpoint," 3.
50. Gaston, "Coming for and with His Saints," 3.
51. Bell, "Questions and Answers," Oct. 14, 1922, 5.
52. See Alexander, *Peace to War*; and Kenyon, *Ethics in the Age*.
53. "Good News of the Lord's Appearing," 8.
54. "Good News of the Lord's Appearing," 8.

Aspects of Social Engagement

AG rejected the notion that any nation could be classified as a "Christian nation" since the church is scattered throughout all nations. As one writer put it, "A little clear and logical thinking, accompanied by an intelligent knowledge of God's Word, will easily dispose of the fallacy that this war is being waged between Christian nations, for it is impossible for us to find in this dispensation a whole Christian town, village or congregation, not to mention a Christian nation."[55] With this, they were also skeptical of nationalism and patriotism. Stanley Frodsham notes, "The school children of every nation are nurtured in national pride from the day they begin to read their history books; but national pride, like every other form of pride, is an abomination in the sight of God."[56] Frodsham emphasized that being a "Citizen of Heaven" involved pledging allegiance to the Prince of Peace, the leader of all nations, not the leaders of nations who would wage war.[57]

Because of this, the AG took an official stance of pacifism in 1917 related to armed conflict that the General Council ratified. It declared:

> We, as a body of Christians, while purposing to fulfill all the obligations of loyal citizenship, are nevertheless constrained to declare we cannot conscientiously participate in war and armed resistance which involves the actual destruction of human life since this is contrary to our view of the clear teachings of the inspired Word of God, which is the sole basis of our faith.[58]

On the one hand, Spirit-filled Christians are not "those who delight in war, but those who are so permeated by the Spirit of the Prince of Peace."[59] On the other hand, war was a sign of the times that Jesus prophesied.[60] John Goben mentions, "We are living in a time when the churches are advocating no more war. I don't like war: but, my brother, there will be war as long as the devil is loose and rules in the hearts of men."[61] Pentecostal participation

---

55. "Light on This Present Crisis," 6–9.
56. Frodsham, "Our Heavenly Citizenship," 3.
57. Frodsham, "Our Heavenly Citizenship," 3.
58. *GC Combined Minutes* (1914–1917), 11–12.
59. "Crisis," 7.
60. Goben, "Millennial Reign," 2, declares, "We are living in a time when the churches are advocating no more war. I don't like war: but, my brother, there will be war as long as the devil is loose and rules in the hearts of men." Also, "Great War and the Speedy Return," 1.
61. Goben, "Millennial Reign," 2.

was discouraged not only for the moral issues of killing but also because the wars were part of the plans that would produce the anti-Christ.

Yet there were definite tensions from taking this pacifist position for loyalty and good citizenship. In 1915, Frank Bartleman wrote a scathing article that the greed and materialism of the nations fueled war. He did not spare his criticism of America saying, "The United States has a score of kings where European countries have but one. That is about the only difference. We are ruled by the money gods."[62] A few years later, after America joined WWI, Bell issued an apology for the article and told readers to "destroy this tract" as it was "entirely too radical for war times."[63] Bell was concerned that the government would perceive ministers as disloyal as citizens. Earlier that year, Bell warned ministers, "All preachers should be careful to be and act in loyalty to our country in this great crisis and not say a word in opposition to the authorities."[64] He affirmed the right to be "opposed personally to taking human life, even in war," but warned not to "preach against our Government going to war." For Bell, loyalty to the government was a priority, and that religious conviction should not be a matter of public policy. Nearly every district council passed resolutions of loyalty to the US government in 1918.[65] Bell even suggested that AG ministers buy war bonds in support.[66] In 1919, Bell was asked if it is insulting if Pentecostals do not salute the American flag. Bell replied, "Yes. . . . Salute to the Flag is not worship; it only indicates our love for our country."[67] Between Frodsham and Bell, there were two conflicting visions of the role of US citizenship among AG members.

As the Second World War approached, questions of citizenship again came to the forefront. E. S. Williams reminded ministers to vote. "As citizens of our nation it is both the privilege and the duty of a Christian to utilize his right as a citizen."[68] He encouraged ministers also to express their support or opposition to legislation. But he warned against turning the church forsaking its mission to be a political lobby. He says, "Shall the Church leave its place in the Kingdom of God to dabble in the affairs of men? To do so

---

62. Bartleman, "Present Day Conditions," 3.
63. Bell, "Destroy This Tract," 4.
64. Bell, "Preachers Warned," 4.
65. Bell, "Loyalty Bonds," 8.
66. Bell, "Questions and Answers," Jan. 26, 1918, 9.
67. Bell, "Questions and Answers," July 12, 1919, 5.
68. Williams, "Christian and Politics," 2.

Aspects of Social Engagement

would prove it to be a feeble failure. What is the primary duty of Biblical Christianity?"[69] Williams appeals to the "separation of church and state" as the guiding principle that will keep the church in its "proper sphere." When ministers in the AG recognized that WWII was changing the attitudes toward non-combatant positions, the issue was raised with the AG leadership. In 1942, Flower wrote to the fellowship about ministers and the "difficulties encountered by them to reconcile their calling as servants of Christ with the militaristic spirit that is necessary to fight and win a war."[70] On the one hand, some AG ministers were fearful that the AG would change its conviction with conscientious objectors actively paying a price for not answering the draft and being sentenced to work camps. On the other hand, there were AG ministers and church members who were joining as combatants or in non-combat positions. Flower notes the need for the General Council to support all positions on this issue.

CONCLUSIONS

It is clear from this brief study that belief in the nearness of the coming of Christ had both negative and positive consequences on social engagement. On the positive side, the AG's eschatological interpretations engendered an apolitical attitude that insulated them from the trappings of looking for political answers to solve society's issues. Their suspicion of the democratic ideal was fueled by a conviction that political systems were tools of the coming antichrist. This meant that believers needed to exercise discernment in political involvement and should identify more as citizens of the Kingdom of God than citizens of the United States. This eschatological perspective on politics would be a welcome perspective in the current political and religious entanglement issues.[71] The separation of the AG from political allegiances also enabled the AG's commitment to non-violence and pacifism, an impulse that is important to a new generation of scholars.[72] Yet

---

69. Williams, "Christian and Politics," 2.

70. Flower, "AG Ministers Letter."

71. Studebaker, *Pentecostal Political Theology*, 22–37. The great irony of present-day Evangelicalism (and Pentecostalism) is that though they primarily hold premillennial views of eschatology, they hold postmillennial visions of culture that seek to see America as a Christian nation and politics as a way to reform society.

72. Pipkin and Beaman, *Early Pentecostals on Nonviolence*; Alexander, *Pentecostals and Nonviolence*; Beaman, *Pentecostal Pacifism*.

most of the literature about Pentecostal pacifism ignores the eschatological motivations that fueled these beliefs. Both social aspects are encouraged by premillennial pessimism.

A second positive aspect of the AG's eschatological interpretation is how they viewed income inequality. The assumption that Pentecostals have not engaged with the poor must be qualified based on this short survey of the AG. Because wealth was a "sign of the times," they believed that those who had amassed wealth had done so by exploiting the poor. Wealth or affluence was not something to aspire to because it was part of the world system and often was at the expense of the vulnerable. They believed the outpouring of the Spirit was a critique of the current economic injustices by heralding and anticipating the coming institution of true economic equality in Christ's kingdom. Pentecostals also identified with the plight of the poor because they shared their financial status. I think David Lewis may be right that Pentecostals could not minister to the poor because many were poor themselves.[73] However, when the AG began to climb the social strata, the attitudes had to shift to change the narrative about wealth so that giving to people experiencing poverty was possible.

Based on these observations about meeting the felt needs of those they ministered to, it is clear their eschatology did not inherently encourage passivity. Instead, like Murray Dempster, it suggests that eschatology certainly has the "potential" for escapism, but it did not necessarily encourage escapism in the AG.[74] The belief in the imminence of Christ's return fueled the AG's missionary impulse, not just to "snatch from the fire" but to meet practical needs such as compassion ministry, orphanages, and rescue homes.[75]

Unfortunately, whatever engagement was seen in these early years is qualified because the AG was often selective in the types of social issues they chose to engage in. This is particularly the case with the AG's silence

---

73. Lewis declares, "Are we to be indicted for lack of social consciousness in those days? We were those that others should have been socially conscious about." Lewis, "Premillennarian Rapture Believers," 12–13.

74. Dempster, "Eschatology, Spirit Baptism," 157.

75. Satyavrata, *Pentecostals and the Poor*, believes that there is "adequate support" within the global Pentecostal "tradition" to make a case for a Pentecostal "tradition" of engagement with the poor. Dempster argues, "Responding to human need within a global context with its various cultural matrixes became a practical component in gaining a hearing for the good news of God's salvation and has generated a staggering proliferation of social programs in all sectors of the Pentecostal movement." Dempster, "Eschatology, Spirit Baptism," 158.

and passivity toward racial equality in the early years. Suffice it to say that racial attitudes do not seem to be eschatologically interpreted in the same way as other social issues. This fact proves that the motivation to get involved in social issues was complicated in the AG.

Chapter 9

Aspects of Further Research

This volume has explored various issues concerning the AG's origins, theology, and identity in the early years. Each chapter addressed an issue or question raised within the Pentecostal academy. While this book is primarily retrospective, it is also essential to look forward to other issues that need to be addressed in AG scholarship. This chapter suggests areas of research that could deepen our understanding of AG history and theology.

The first opportunity for new research would be to produce an updated systematic theology volume by AG scholars addressing contemporary theological issues. The AG's *Systematic Theology* (1994), edited by Stanley Horton, was a suitable systematic text, yet it is now nearly three decades old. A more recent attempt at systematic theology is Amos Yong's *Renewing Christian Theology*, which looks at theology through the eleven-point World Assemblies of God Fellowship doctrinal statement.[1] Yong's work is a helpful and constructive look at these theological tenets. But with a new generation of AG scholars in our midst, a more mature and updated theological text that is not bound by the limited topics covered in the Statement of Fundamental Truths is needed. A text like this is vital to the continuing theological development of the fellowship and its educational institutions.

There is also a need for major academic studies of individual AG doctrinal beliefs. Just as there is now a robust history of AG eschatology, more studies utilizing reception history[2] are needed to examine the development of other theological disciplines, including healing, baptism, pneumatology

---

1. Yong, *Renewing Christian Theology*.
2. See Isgrigg et al., *Receiving Scripture in the Pentecostal Tradition*.

Aspects of Further Research

(broader than tongues), and other theological issues. For example, a robust study of AG soteriology seems warranted as one of the core doctrines of the fellowship. Coming out of the finished work tradition, the AG leaned toward evangelical reformed influences for expressing their soteriology despite having a Wesleyan-based Arminian view of salvation. A study is needed to explore the effects of Reformed thought on AG soteriology and how the rise of neo-Reformed theology has influenced AG ministers and theology. In 1993, Blumhofer suggested that the growing educational level of ministers is influencing the overall theology of AG ministers. Many younger pastors are drawn to the neo-Reformed movement for theological stability. But what consequences does that have on the Pentecostal orientation of AG ministers? An empirical study on this is needed as to the effects on views on women in ministry, grace and election, and operation of the *charsimata*.

Another needed area of research is in Pentecostal biographies of AG figures. Some recent ones are Joshua Ziefle on David du Plessis, David Ringer on J. R. Flower, and Lois Olena on Stanley Horton. But many others could be explored, such as E. N. Bell, S. A. Jamieson, Stanley Frodsham, E. S. Williams, and Thomas Zimmerman, among many others. In addition, there is undoubtedly a need for biographies of notable female ministers such as Alice Flower, Elizabeth Sisson, and Alice Luce. Also, a study of female child healing evangelists, such as Louise Nankeville and Edna Jean Green Horn, could shed light on this uniquely Pentecostal phenomenon. There is also a need for academic histories of most AG colleges and institutions.

Another area that has received very little academic treatment is AG publishing efforts through the Gospel Publishing House. The GPH has had a profound impact on providing AG ministers with access to doctrinal materials. What they have produced has shaped the AG's understanding of itself and its doctrines. More research is needed into the internal editorial philosophy and stages of development in shaping that legacy. One interesting area to explore is the prevalence of two genres in GPH history: poetry and junior fiction novels. It is remarkable how many poems were published in the *Pentecostal Evangel* and how many AG ministers published Christian poetry books. What might be the relationship between poetry and the Spirit-filled imagination? There could also be a literary analysis study of junior fiction novels the GPH published in the 1950s. What was behind their publication? Were they reflective of the Victorian era conduct novel that sought to represent the idealistic roles of children? What messages are embedded in these works about gender roles, societal issues, and family dynamics? These questions would make a great interdisciplinary study combining literature and religious conduct.

Finally, there is a need for more regional and local AG histories. I am inspired by the district histories of the Oklahoma District by Robert Burke and North Dakota by Darrin Rodgers. But every district has a story to tell that could enhance and nuance the greater story of the AG. With that, the histories of significant localities are important. My book *Pentecostalism in Tulsa* unearthed important information on the early years, since Tulsa was a key location for the early white COGIC meetings. Studies of other major hubs, such as Chicago, Dallas, Houston, and others, are also needed. Not only are micro-histories needed, but globally based national histories are also needed. With most AG adherents outside the US, many of the AG World Fellowship National Fellowships stories have not been told.

As the Pentecostal academy continues to grow, so do the aspects of Assemblies of God origins that need to be explored. I pray this volume will inspire a new generation of scholars to find new stories to tell and new ways to examine the narratives that occupy our collective memory of the Assemblies of God.

Bibliography

PRIMARY SOURCES

"Announcement of Bible School." *Christian Evangel*, Feb. 24, 1917, 14.
"Assemblies Superintendent Named NAE Head." *Pentecostal Evangel*, July 10, 1960, 14.
"Back to Fundamentals." *Weekly Evangel*, Sept. 23, 1916, 7.
Baer, Vida B. "The Latter Rain." *Pentecostal Evangel*, Mar. 4, 2022, 3.
Bartleman, Frank. "Present Day Conditions." *Weekly Evangel*, June 5, 1915, 3.
Bell, E. N. "Bethel Rescue Home." *Word and Witness*, June 1913, 1.
———. "Bible School Assured." *Pentecostal Evangel*, July 10, 1920, 2.
———. "Churches in Christ." *Christian Evangel*, Feb. 13, 1915, 2.
———. "Cleansing and Holiness." *Word and Witness*, Aug. 20, 1912, 2.
———. "Destroy This Tract." *Christian Evangel*, Aug. 24, 1918, 4.
———. "Doctrinal Statement." *Christian Evangel*, June 28, 1919, 8.
———. "A Few Questions about Books." *Pentecostal Evangel*, Nov. 1, 1919, 12.
———. "The Finished Work." *Word and Witness*, Apr. 20, 1914, 2.
———. "For Strangers. Who Are We?" *Word and Witness*, May 20, 1914, 1–2.
———. "General Council Special." *Word and Witness*, May 20, 1914, 1.
———. "Loyalty Bonds." *Christian Evangel*, June 1, 1918, 8.
———. "The Midwest Bible School of the Assemblies of God." *Pentecostal Evangel*, Jan. 10, 1920, 8.
———. "Notes on Modern Bibles." *Christian Evangel*, June 1, 1918, 5.
———. "Notice about Parham." *Word and Witness*, Oct. 1912, 3.
———. "Not Missions, but Churches of God in Christ." *Word and Witness*, Aug. 20, 1912, 2.
———. "Preachers Warned." *Christian Evangel*, Jan. 5, 1918, 4.
———. *Questions and Answers*. Springfield, MO: Gospel Publishing House, 1923.
———. "Questions and Answers." *Christian Evangel*, Apr. 14, 1917, 9.
———. "Questions and Answers." *Weekly Evangel*, Jan. 26, 1918, 9.
———. "Questions and Answers." *Christian Evangel*, Mar. 30, 1918, 9.
———. "Questions and Answers." *Christian Evangel*, Dec. 28, 1918, 9.
———. "Questions and Answers." *Pentecostal Evangel*, Feb. 8, 1919, 5.
———. "Questions and Answers." *Christian Evangel*, Mar. 22, 1919, 5.

BIBLIOGRAPHY

———. "Questions and Answers." *Weekly Evangel*, July 12, 1919, 5.
———. "Questions and Answers." *Christian Evangel*, Dec. 27, 1919, 5.
———. "Questions and Answers." *Pentecostal Evangel*, June 25, 1921, 2.
———. "Questions and Answers." *Pentecostal Evangel*, Oct. 14, 1922, 5.
———. "The Second Blessing." *Word and Witness*, Dec. 20, 1913, 2.
———. "The Second Coming Near." *Christian Evangel*, Sept. 12, 1914, 1.
———. "Seventh Day Trouble." *Christian Evangel*, Jan. 11, 1919, 9.
———. "Testimony of a Baptist Pastor." *Pentecostal Testimony* 1.1 (Mar. 1911) 9.
———. "War! War!! War!!!" *Christian Evangel*, Aug. 15, 1914, 1.
———. "What Is the Bride?" *Weekly Evangel*, Oct. 18, 1915, 1.
Bell, E. N., and J. R. Flower. "In Doctrines." *Christian Evangel*, Aug. 1, 1914, 2.
"Bible Study Course by Correspondence." *Pentecostal Evangel*, Feb. 12, 1927, 15.
Blackstone, W. E. *Jesus Is Coming*. Chicago: Revell, 1916.
———. "Times of the Gentiles." *Weekly Evangel*, May 13, 1916, 6.
Boddy, A. "Preliminary Meetings." *Confidence* 3 (June 18, 1908) 4–6.
"The Book of Revelation." *Weekly Evangel*, Feb. 3, 1917, 15.
"The Book of Revelation." *Weekly Evangel*, Mar. 24, 1917, 12.
"Books on Prophecy and the Lord's Return." *Pentecostal Evangel*, June 30, 1934, 16.
Boyd, Frank. *Ages and Dispensations*. Springfield, MO: Gospel Publishing House, 1955.
———. *Introduction to Prophecy*. Springfield, MO: Gospel Publishing House, 1948.
———. *The Budding Fig Tree*. Springfield, MO: Gospel Publishing House, 1925.
———. *Prophetic Light*. Springfield, MO: Gospel Publishing House, 1968.
———. *Signs of the Times*. Springfield, MO: Gospel Publishing House, 1950.
Brumback, Carl. *Like a River*. Springfield, MO: Gospel Publishing House, 1977.
———. *Suddenly . . . From Heaven*. Springfield, MO: Gospel Publishing House, 1961.
———. *What Meaneth This?* Springfield, MO: Gospel Publishing House, 1947.
Burnett, C. C. "Forty Years Ago." *Pentecostal Evangel*, Mar. 28, 1954, 3, 12–13.
Burpee, Florence L. "No Room in the Inn." *Weekly Evangel*, Dec. 23, 1916, 3.
Carlson, G. Raymond. "The Pentecostal Dimension in Education." *Pentecostal Evangel*, Sept. 23, 1962, 12–13.
———. "Place of Education in the Pentecostal Ministry." *Pentecostal Evangel*, Dec. 20, 1964, 22–23.
Carothers, W. F. "Attitude of Pentecostal Whites to the Colored Brethren in the South." *Christian Evangel*, Aug. 14, 1915, 2.
Childe, Fredrick. "Christ's Answer to the Challenge of Communism and Fascism." *Pentecostal Evangel*, Oct. 31, 1931, 1, 7–8.
Collins, A. P. "A Baptized Baptist Preacher." *Christian Evangel*, Jan. 23, 1915, 1.
———. *Sign of the Son of Man: Sermons on the Second Coming of Christ*. Houston: United Prayer and Workers League, 1919.
"Convention Notices." *Bridegroom's Messenger*, Nov. 1, 1911, 2.
Cotham, R. L. "A Pentecostal Rescue Home." *Weekly Evangel*, Apr. 7, 1917, 6.
"The Council Roll." *Weekly Evangel*, Oct. 21, 1916, 11.
"Crisis." *Weekly Evangel*, Apr. 21, 1917, 7.
Darby, J. N. *Synopsis of the Books of the Bible*. Vol. 4. London: G. Morrish, 1877.
"Doctrinal Statement." *Christian Evangel*, June 28, 1919, 8.
Drummond, Henry. *A Defense of the Students of Prophecy in Answer to the Attack of the Rev. Dr. Hamilton*. London: James Nisbet, 1828.

Bibliography

Durham, William H. "A Chicago Evangelist's Pentecost." *Apostolic Faith* 1.6 (Feb.–Mar. 1907) 4.
———. "Editorial." *Pentecostal Testimony* 1.5 (July 1910) 1–4.
———. "The Great Battle of Nineteen Eleven." *Pentecostal Testimony* 2.1 (Jan. 1912) 6.
———. "The Great Crisis Number Two." *Pentecostal Testimony* 1.5 (July 1910) 4.
———. "The Great Revival at Azusa Street Mission—How It Began and How It Ended." *Pentecostal Testimony* 1.8 (Aug. 1911) 7–11.
———. "An Open Letter to My Brother Ministers in and out the Pentecostal Movement." *Pentecostal Testimony* 1.8 (Aug. 1911) 12.
———. "Our Pentecostal Book." *Pentecostal Testimony* 1.5 (July 1910) 16.
———. "Sanctification." *Pentecostal Testimony* 1.8 (June 1911) 1.
———. "Some Other Phases of Sanctification." *Pentecostal Testimony* 2.3 (1912) 9–11.
———. "Speaking in Tongues Is the Evidence of Baptism in the Holy Spirit." *Pentecostal Testimony* 2.2 (May 1912) 10.
———. "The Two Great Experiences." *Pentecostal Testimony* 1.8 (Aug. 1911) 5.
———. "What Is the Evidence of Baptism in the Holy Ghost." *Pentecostal Testimony* 2.1 (Jan. 1912) 4–5.
———. "The Work of God in Los Angeles." *Pentecostal Testimony* 1.8 (Aug. 1911) 10–12.
"The Evangel Book Shelf." *Weekly Evangel*, May 31, 1919, 16.
"An Experience of Divine Guidance." *Christ's Ambassadors* 1.3–4 (June 1926) 1.
Fletcher, John. *The Works of the Rev. John Fletcher*. Vol. 1. London: Thomas Allman, 1836.
Flower, J. R. "AG Ministers Letter." March 16, 1943. Flower Pentecostal Heritage Center, Springfield, MO.
———. "The Basis Unity of Evangelical Christianity." *Pentecostal Evangel*, June 19, 1943, 8.
———. "History of the Assemblies of God." Notes from Church Orientation, Central Bible College, Springfield, Missouri, 1949. Holy Spirit Resource Center, Oral Roberts University, Tulsa, OK.
———. *In the Last Days . . . An Early History of the Assemblies of God*. Springfield, MO: Assemblies of God, 1962.
———. *The Origin and Development of the Assemblies of God*. Springfield, MO: Gospel Publishing House, 1938.
———. "The Present Position of Pentecost." *Pentecostal Evangel*, June 13, 1925, 8.
———. "Why We Joined the NAE." *Pentecostal Evangel*, Mar. 29, 1947, 12.
Flower, J. R., to M. M. Pinson. Letter, January 4, 1950. Pinson File, Flower Pentecostal Heritage Center, Springfield, MO.
"Four A/G Officials Elected." *Pentecostal Evangel*, June 8, 1969, 28–29.
"Four Days with the Presbyters." *Pentecostal Evangel*, June 7, 1924, 2.
Frodsham, S. H. "The Coming of Christ and Our Gathering to Him." *Pentecostal Evangel*, June 2, 1928, 1.
———. "The Coming Revival and the Coming Christ." *Pentecostal Evangel*, May 17, 1924, 4.
———. "Disfellowshipped." *Pentecostal Evangel*, Aug. 18, 1928, 7.
———. "Fifth Annual Convention of the NAE." *Pentecostal Evangel*, May 10, 1947, 6–7.
———. "Fundamentalist Plus." *Pentecostal Evangel*, July 12, 1924, 4.
———. "Letter to Readers, March 29, 1924." *Pentecostal Evangel*, Apr. 5, 1924, 15.
———. "Politics from the Pentecostal Viewpoint." *Pentecostal Evangel*, Oct. 30, 1920, 3.
———. "Pisgah as I Have Seen It." *Weekly Evangel*, Mar. 17, 1917, 2–4.

Bibliography

———. "Our Heavenly Citizenship." *Weekly Evangel*, Sept. 11, 1915, 3.

———. "Things Which Must Shortly Come to Pass." *Weekly Evangel*, Nov. 25, 1916, 6.

———. *Things Which Must Shortly Come to Pass*. Springfield, MO: Gospel Publishing House, 1928.

———. "Why We Know the Present Pentecostal Movement Is of God." *Christian Evangel*, Aug. 9, 1919, 4–5.

———. *With Signs Following*. Springfield, MO: Gospel Publishing House, 1926.

"Fundamentalism." *Pentecostal Evangel*, Oct. 27, 1928, 3–5.

Funk, A. E. "In the Heavenlies." *Alliance Witness* 32.10 (Feb. 3, 1904) 2–3.

"A Further List of Helpful Books." *Pentecostal Evangel*, Dec. 1, 1923, 32.

"Further Signs of the Last Days." *Weekly Evangel*, Apr. 10, 1915, 1.

Gaston, W. T. "Coming for and with His Saints." *Pentecostal Evangel*, Sept. 27, 1924, 3.

GC Combined Minutes. 1914–1917. Consortium of Pentecostal Archives. https://pentecostalarchives.org/?a=p&p=home&e=-------en-20--1--img-txIN-general+council+Minutes+1914–1917-----------.

GC Constitution and Bylaws. April 2–12, 1914. Consortium of Pentecostal Archives. https://pentecostalarchives.org/?a=p&p=home&e=-------en-20--1--img-txIN-general+council+Constitution+and+Bylaws+April+1914-----------.

GC Minutes. September 4–9, 1947. Consortium of Pentecostal Archives. https://pentecostalarchives.org/?a=d&d=GCMC1947-Minutes.1.3&srpos=1&e=-------en-20--1--img-txIN-general+council+Minutes+1947-----------.

"The General Council Reading Course." *Pentecostal Evangel*, Jan. 5, 1924, 8.

"The General Council Reading Course." *Pentecostal Evangel*, Feb. 14, 1931, 15.

"The General Council Reading Course." *Pentecostal Evangel*, Feb. 17, 1934, 16.

"Glory and Unity at the Eureka Springs Camp!" *Word and Witness*, Aug. 20, 1912, 1.

Goben, John. "The Millennial Reign." *Pentecostal Evangel*, Feb. 21, 1925, 2.

"The Good News of the Lord's Appearing." *Pentecostal Evangel*, July 23, 1921, 8.

Gortner, J. Narver. *Are the Saints Scheduled to Go through the Tribulation?* Springfield, MO: Gospel Publishing House, 1930.

Goss, Ethel. *The Winds of God: The Story of the Early Pentecostal Days (1901–1914) in the Life of Howard A. Goss*. New York: Comet, 1958.

Goss, Howard, and E. N. Bell. "State Encampment." *Pentecostal Testimony* 1.5 (July 1910) 10.

"A Great Move Forward." *Pentecostal Evangel*, May 1, 1926, 3.

"The Great War and the Speedy Return of Our Lord." *Weekly Evangel*, Apr. 10, 1917, 2.

Hale, F. A. "A Word from San Antonio." *Weekly Evangel*, Dec. 22, 1917, 14.

Hoover, J. N. "The Tragedy of Modern Theology." *Pentecostal Evangel*, Dec. 7, 1929, 7.

Horton, Stanley M. *Bible Prophecy: Understanding Future Events*. Springfield, MO: Gospel Publishing House, 1995.

———. *Into All Truth*. Springfield, MO: Gospel Publishing House, 1955.

———, ed. *Systematic Theology*. Springfield, MO: Logion, 1995.

"Hot Springs Assembly; God's Glory Present." *Word and Witness*, Apr. 20, 1914, 1.

"The Impending World Judgment and the Only Place of Shelter." *Christian Evangel*, Jan. 25, 1919, 9.

"Important Books on the Book of Revelation." *Christian Evangel*, Sept. 7, 1918, 3.

"Interstate Campmeeting to Be Held This Year in Meridian, Miss." *Word and Witness*, Feb. 20, 1913, 1.

"Is the World Growing Better or Worse?" *Pentecostal Evangel*, May 1, 1915, 3.

Bibliography

Jamieson, S. A. "Five Judgments." *Weekly Evangel*, Mar. 11, 1916, 7.
———. "His Coming Draweth Nigh." *Pentecostal Evangel*, Nov. 28, 1925, 10–11.
———. "How a Presbyterian Received the Baptism." *Pentecostal Evangel*, Jan. 31, 1931, 2.
———. "Need of an Educated Ministry." *Pentecostal Evangel*, Dec. 25, 1920, 4.
———. "The New Heaven and New Earth." *Pentecostal Evangel*, Sept. 30, 1922, 6.
———. *Pillars of Truth*. Springfield, MO: Gospel Publishing House, 1926.
———. "The Second Coming of Christ." *Weekly Evangel*, Feb. 26, 1916, 6.
———. "Seven Fears and Seven Cheers." *Pentecostal Evangel*, Feb. 13, 1926, 2–3.
———. "Sign of the Times." *Pentecostal Evangel*, Apr. 4, 1931, 1–2.
———. "Sign of the Times." *Pentecostal Evangel*, Apr. 11, 1931, 6–7.
———. "Who Are the Departed Dead." *Pentecostal Evangel*, Mar. 8, 1930, 8–9.
Jeffries, A. G. "The Limit of Divine Revelation." *Pentecostal Evangel*, Mar. 18, 1916, 6.
Kelly, William, ed. *The Collected Writings of J. N. Darby*. Vol. 3. London: G. Morrish, 187?.
Kerr, D. W. "Christian Creed and Life." *Pentecostal Evangel*, Sept. 7, 1929, 6.
———. "Fundamentals of the Faith 'Plus.'" CBI Correspondence Course 8, 1926. Flower Pentecostal Heritage Center, Springfield, MO.
———. "Heart Talks on Bible Schools." *Pentecostal Evangel*, May 27, 1922, 4.
———. "The Ministry of Christ." *Living Truths*, July 1903, 3.
———. "Opening of Central Bible Institute." *Pentecostal Evangel*, Sept. 30, 1922, 4.
———. "Report from the Southern California Bible School." *Pentecostal Evangel*, Feb. 19, 1921, 9.
———. "The Southern California Bible School of Los Angeles." *Pentecostal Evangel*, Apr. 16, 1921, 11.
———. "Spontaneous Theology." *Weekly Evangel*, Apr. 17, 1915, 3.
———. "The Two-Fold Aspect of Church Life: Will the Church Go through the Tribulation?" *The Latter Rain Evangel* (Oct. 1919) 2–6.
———. *Waters in the Desert*. Springfield, MO: Gospel Publishing House, 1927.
Kerr, D. W., and Willard C. Peirce. "Outlines Studies in the Chart of the Ages." Kerr, D. W. File, Flower Pentecostal Heritage Center, Springfield, MO.
Kerr, Mattie. "All May." *Pentecostal Report* 11.7 (Jan. 1916) 8–9.
King, J. H. *Passover to Pentecost*. Franklin Springs, GA: Pentecostal Holiness Church Publishing House, 1955.
Lawrence, B. F. *Apostolic Faith Restored*. Springfield, MO: Gospel Publishing House, 1916.
———. "The Assembly of God." *Christian Evangel*, May 9, 1914, 5–6.
———. "The Works of God." *Weekly Evangel*, May 27, 1916, 4.
Leonard, T. K. "The Gospel School, What Is It?" *Word and Witness*, Oct. 1, 1914, 3.
Lewis, David A. "Premillennarian Rapture Believers: Are They Socially Irresponsible Escapists?" *Pentecostal Evangel*, Aug. 16, 1987, 12–13.
Lidman, Sven. "Priestly Service before God." *Pentecostal Evangel*, Mar. 1, 1924, 2–3.
"Light on This Present Crisis." *Pentecostal Evangel*, July 1, 1916, 6–7, 9.
Luce, Alice. *Little Flock and the Last Days*. Springfield, MO: Gospel Publishing House, 1927.
Lund, Eric. *Hermeneutics: Or, The Science and Art of Interpreting the Bible*. Translated by P. C. Nelson. Enid, OK: Southwestern, 1932.
Macchia, Frank. "Struggle for Global Witness: Shifting Paradigms in Pentecostal Theology." In *The Globalization of Pentecostalism: Religion Made to Travel*. Edited by Murray W. Dempster et al., 8–29. Oxford: Regnum, 1999.
"The Man God Calls a Fool." *Pentecostal Evangel*, Dec. 23, 1944, 1, 4–5.

BIBLIOGRAPHY

Mason, C. H. *The History and Life Work of Bishop C. H. Mason.* Memphis: n.p., 1924.

McAlister, James. "Startling Signs of the End." *Pentecostal Evangel*, Second Coming Supplement, Sept. 10, 1920, 1–3.

McAlister, R. E. "The Pentecostal Movement." *Pentecostal Evangel*, May 13, 1922, 5.

McCafferty, W. B. "My Pastor." *Pentecostal Evangel*, July 9, 1921, 4–5.

———. "Study to Show Thyself Approved." *Pentecostal Evangel*, Feb. 19, 1921, 19.

Menzies, William W. *Understanding Our Doctrine.* Springfield, MO: Gospel Publishing House, 1971.

Menzies, William, and Stanley Horton. *Bible Doctrines: A Pentecostal Perspective.* Springfield, MO: Logion, 1994.

"Minutes of the Annual Convention of the Church of God in Christ, Dothan Alabama. October 27, 1913." Assemblies of God History File, Holy Spirit Resource Center, Oral Roberts University, Tulsa, OK.

"Minutes of Church of God, Slocomb, AL." February 10, 1911. Assemblies of God History File, Holy Spirit Resource Center, Oral Roberts University, Tulsa, OK.

"Miseries for Rich Men." *Pentecostal Evangel*, Nov. 27, 1926, 4–5.

Montgomery, Carrie Judd. "Faith's Reckonings." *Triumphs of Faith* 1.1 (Jan. 1881) 1.

"Mount Tabor Bible Training School." *Weekly Evangel*, Feb. 12, 1916, 9.

Myland, D. W. "The Book of Revelation." *Latter Rain Evangel* 3.8 (May 1911) 13–17.

———. "The Book of Revelation." *Latter Rain Evangel* 3.9 (June 1911) 4–9.

———. "The Book of Revelation." *Latter Rain Evangel* 3.10 (July 1911) 6–10.

———. "The Book of Revelation." *Latter Rain Evangel* 3.11 (Aug. 1911) 5–13.

———. "The Book of Revelation." *Latter Rain Evangel* 3.12 (Sept. 1911) 14–19.

———. "The Book of the Revelation of Jesus Christ." *Latter Rain Evangel* 3.4 (Jan. 1911) 5–12.

———. "The Book of the Revelation of Jesus Christ." *Latter Rain Evangel* 3.5 (Feb. 1911) 2–6.

———. "The Book of the Revelation of Jesus Christ." *Latter Rain Evangel* 3.6 (Mar. 1911) 2–6.

———. "The Book of the Revelation of Jesus Christ." *Latter Rain Evangel* 3.7 (Apr. 1911) 3–7.

———. "The Fifth Latter Rain Lecture." *Latter Rain Evangel* 1.12 (Sept. 1909) 13–19.

———. *The Latter Rain Covenant and Pentecostal Power.* Chicago: Evangel Publishing House, 1910.

———. "The Latter Rain Covenant." *Latter Rain Evangel* 1.9 (June 1909) 15–22.

———. "The Latter Rain Covenant." *Latter Rain Evangel* 1.10 (July 1909) 2–3, 15–22.

———. "The Latter Rain—Its Designs and Operations." *Latter Rain Evangel* 2.11 (Aug. 1909) 11–18.

———. "Literal and Spiritual Rain Falling Simultaneously." *Latter Rain Evangel* 2.1 (Oct. 1909) 17–23.

———. "Revelation of Jesus Christ." *Latter Rain Evangel* 4.3 (Dec. 1911) 19–22.

———. *The Revelation of Jesus Christ.* Chicago: Evangel Publishing House, 1911.

Nelson, P. C. *Bible Doctrines: A Handbook of Pentecostal Theology Based on the Scriptures and Following the Lines of the Statement of Fundamental Truths as Adopted by the General Council of the Assemblies of God.* Enid, OK: Southwestern, 1936.

———. *Bible Doctrines.* Rev. ed. Springfield, MO: Gospel Publishing House, 1948.

———. *Bible Doctrines.* Rev. ed. Springfield, MO: Gospel Publishing House, 1992.

BIBLIOGRAPHY

———. "Biographies." Unpublished manuscript. Nelson, P.C. file, Holy Spirit Resource Center, Oral Roberts University, Tulsa, OK.

———. "Enlarging Our Educational Facilities." *Pentecostal Evangel*, June 16, 1934, 7.

"Obituary, D. W. Kerr." *Springfield Leader*, Apr. 3, 1927, 3.

"Ordained Ministers in the Churches of God in Christ." August 1, 1912. Flower Pentecostal Heritage Center, Springfield, MO.

"Outlines Studies of the Book of Revelation." *Weekly Evangel*, Oct. 20, 1917, 11.

"Our Pentecostal Books." *Pentecostal Evangel*, Dec. 17, 1927, 16.

"Parham Is Rallying Forces: Split Is Threatened in the Apostolic Faith Movement." *Houston Daily Post*, May 22, 1907, 5.

Pearlman, Myer. *Knowing the Doctrines of the Bible*. Springfield, MO: Gospel Publishing House, 1937.

———. *Windows into the Future*. Springfield, MO: Gospel Publishing House, 1941.

"Pentecostal Bible Schools." *Pentecostal Evangel*, Mar. 19, 1921, 9.

Perkin, Noel. "I Remember." *Pentecostal Evangel*, Jan. 19, 1964, 9.

Perkins, Jonathan E. "Higher Education, Lower Fidelity." *Pentecostal Evangel*, Dec. 6, 1924, 2.

———. "My First Sermon That I Did Not Preach." *The Pentecostal Evangel*, Mar. 22, 1924, 6–7.

Pinson, M. M. "The Finished Work of Calvary." *Pentecostal Evangel*, Apr. 5, 1964, 7, 26–27.

———. "From Los Angeles World-Wide Campmeeting." *Word and Witness*, May 20, 1913, 1.

———. "Sanctified in Christ." *Word and Witness*, Jan. 20, 1913, 4.

Pinson, M. M., to J. R. Flower. Letter, January 10, 1951. Pinson File, Flower Pentecostal Heritage Center, Springfield, MO.

———. Letter, December 19, 1950. Pinson File, Flower Pentecostal Heritage Center, Springfield, MO.

Pinson, M. M., et al. "General Convention of the Pentecostal Saints and Churches of God in Christ." *Word and Witness*, Dec. 20, 1913, 1.

Pope, Willard. "The Crying Need of the Hour." *Latter Rain Evangel* 24.2 (Nov. 1931) 9–12.

———. "Morphine Tablets of Hell." *Latter Rain Evangel* 11.3 (Dec. 1918) 5.

"Prophecy." *Pentecostal Evangel*, Jan. 24, 1925, 15.

Record of the International Conference on Divine Healing and True Holiness. London: 1885.

"The Red Terror." *Pentecostal Evangel*, Feb. 2, 1924, 5.

Riggs, Ralph. *The Path of Prophecy*. Springfield, MO: Gospel Publishing House, 1937.

Russell, R. M. "Prophecy and Present Day Events." *Pentecostal Evangel*, Apr. 16, 1921, 8.

S., A. E. "Signs of the Times." *Pentecostal Evangel*, Dec. 15, 1923, 8.

Scofield, C. I, ed. *The Scofield Reference Bible*. New York: Oxford University Press, 1909.

"Scofield Reference Bibles." *Weekly Evangel*, Dec. 9, 1916, 16.

"The Scofield Reference Bible." *Weekly Evangel*, September 15, 1917, 16.

Scott, Chas H. "Education in the Assemblies of God." *Pentecostal Evangel*, Sept. 1, 1963, 10–13.

"Second Coming and Prophecy." *Pentecostal Evangel*, July 10, 1926, 15.

Seerist, J. S. "Jesus Is Coming Soon." *Christian Evangel*, Oct. 10, 1914, 3.

Seiss, Joseph A. *Lectures on the Apocalypse*. New York: Charles Cook, 1869.

———. *The Parable of the Ten Virgins: In Six Discourses and a Sermon on the Judgeship of the Saints*. London: Smith, English, 1862.

"Significant Sign of the Lord's Near Return." *Pentecostal Evangel*, Jan. 8, 1927, 5.

BIBLIOGRAPHY

"Signs of the Approaching End." *Weekly Evangel*, Sept. 8, 1917, 8.
"Signs Shall Follow." *Apostolic Faith* 1.2 (Dec. 1906) 2.
Sisson, Elizabeth. "Application for Ordination." December 18, 1917. Sisson Files, Flower Pentecostal Heritage Center, Springfield, MO.
———. "The Coming Glory." *Pentecostal Evangel*, Nov. 26, 1927, 3.
———. "The End Not Yet." *Latter Rain Evangel* (Jan. 1917) 6-9.
———. *Faith Reminiscences and Heart to Heart Talks*. Springfield, MO: Gospel Publishing House, 1927.
———. *Foregleams of Glory*. Chicago: Evangel Publishing House, 1912.
———. "The Great Tribulation." *Weekly Evangel*, Feb. 9, 1918, 2.
———. "The Holy Ghost and Fire." *Latter Rain Evangel* 1.8 (May 1909) 6-10.
———. "A Man Born Blind Now Begins to See." *Confidence* 7.6 (June 1914) 109-10.
———. "May We Tarry Till The Lord Comes?" *Pentecostal Evangel*, May 5, 1917, 6.
———. "A Sign People." *Pentecostal Evangel*, Jan. 11, 1919, 2-3.
———. "These Wars! Why?" *Latter Rain Evangel*, July 1916, 17.
———. "Three Aspects of the Great Tribulation." *Latter Rain Evangel*, June 1913, 16-17.
"Soon Coming of Christ." *Weekly Evangel*, Nov. 3, 1917, 1.
Standifer, Jewell. "Testimony for Jesus." *Church of God Evangel*, June 15, 1910, 5.
"State Camp Meeting." *Tulsa Tribune*, July 31, 1913, 7.
Taylor, Zola. "A Line from Zola Taylor." *Weekly Evangel*, Dec. 2, 1916, 16.
"Therefore Ye Also Be Ready." *Pentecostal Evangel*, Mar. 9, 1935, 16.
"Three Schools." *Weekly Evangel*, Sept. 5, 1914, 2.
Tomlin, Wayne. "Dothan Camp Good." *Word and Witness*, Nov. 20, 1913, 1.
Turner, C. W. M. *Outline Studies in the Book of the Revelation and Key to the Chart of the Ages*. Plain City, OH: C. M. Turner, 1916.
Turner, W. H. *The Finished Work of Calvary or the Second Blessing—Which?* Franklin Springs, GA: Pentecostal Holiness Church Publishing House.
"Twelfth General Council Meeting." *Pentecostal Evangel*, Oct. 8, 1927, 2-10.
"The Uncertainty of Riches." *Pentecostal Evangel*, Apr. 1, 1933, 2.
Ward, A. G. "Soul Food for Hungry Saints." *Pentecostal Evangel*, Aug. 23, 1919, 1.
Ward, C. M. *Waiting*. Springfield, MO: Gospel Publishing House, 1959.
Welch, J. W. "Current Comments." *Pentecostal Evangel*, Nov. 14, 1931, 8.
"Wesley on Wealth." *Pentecostal Evangel*, July 1, 1944, 9.
"When the Son of Man Comes." *Pentecostal Evangel*, Apr. 21, 1928, 2.
"White Slave Craft." *Word and Witness*, Jan. 1914, 3.
Williams, E. S. "The Christian and Politics." *Pentecostal Evangel*, June 24, 1939, 2.
———. "Introduction." In *Bible Doctrines*, by P. C Nelson, 3. Springfield, MO: Gospel Publishing House, 1948.
———. "Jesus Advises a Rich Man." *Pentecostal Evangel*, Dec. 13, 1947, 5.
———. *Systematic Theology*. 3 vols. Springfield, MO: Gospel Publishing House, 1953.
"With Christ." *Pentecostal Evangel*, Oct. 22, 1971, 28.
Worrell, A. S. *Full Gospel Teachings*. Louisville, KY: Charles T. Dearing, 1900.
———, ed. *The New Testament*. Louisville, KY: Self-published, 1904.
———. "Wonderful Times Coming." *Bridegroom's Messenger*, Mar. 1, 1908, 2.
"Worrell's New Testament." *Pentecostal Evangel*, Dec. 22, 1923, 7.
Wright, Nellie. "Coffeyville, Kansas." *Weekly Evangel*, Oct. 6, 1917, 14.

Bibliography

SECONDARY SOURCES

Alexander, Estrelda. *Black Fire: One Hundred Years of African American Pentecostalism.* Downers Grove, IL: Intervarsity, 2011.

Alexander, Kimberly E. *Pentecostal Healing.* JPTS 29. Blandford, UK: Deo.

Alexander, Paul. *Peace to War: Shifting Allegiances in the Assemblies of God.* Telfor, PA: Cascadia, 2009.

———, ed. *Pentecostals and Nonviolence: Reclaiming a Heritage.* Eugene, OR: Pickwick, 2010.

Althouse, Peter. "The Landscape of Pentecostal and Charismatic Eschatology: An Introduction." In *Perspectives in Pentecostal Eschatology: World without End*, edited by Peter Althouse and Robby Waddell, 1–21. Eugene, OR: Pickwick, 2010.

———. "Left Behind—Fact or Fiction: Ecumenical Dilemmas of the Fundamentalist Millenarian Tensions in Pentecostalism." *Journal of Pentecostal Theology* 13.2 (2005) 187–207.

———. *Spirit of the Last Days: Eschatology in Conversation with Jürgen Moltmann.* London: T&T Clark, 2003.

Althouse, Peter, and Robby Waddell, eds. *Perspectives in Pentecostal Eschatology: World without End.* Eugene, OR: Pickwick, 2010.

Archer, Kenneth J. "The Making of an Academic Pentecostal Theological Tradition: The Cleveland School." A paper presented at Society of Pentecostal Studies, San Dimas, CA, March 2016.

———. *A Pentecostal Hermeneutic: Spirit, Scripture and Community.* Cleveland, TN: CPT, 2009.

———. *A Pentecostal Hermeneutic for the Twenty-First Century.* London: T&T Clark, 2004.

———. "A Pentecostal Way of Doing Theology." *International Journal of Systematic Theology* 9.3 (2007) 301–14.

Beaman, Jay. *Pentecostal Pacifism.* Eugene, OR: Wipf & Stock, 2009.

Bebbington, David W. *The Dominance of Evangelicalism: The Age of Spurgeon and Moody.* Downers Grove, IL: Intervarsity, 2005.

Bixler, Virgil. "Founding Issues." *Reflections* 1 (1993) 16–20.

Blumhofer, Edith L. *The Assemblies of God: A Chapter in the Story of American Pentecostalism.* 2 vols. Springfield, MO: Gospel Publishing House, 1989.

———. *Restoring the Faith.* Urbana: University of Illinois Press, 1993.

———. "William H. Durham: Years of Creativity, Years of Dissent." In *Portraits of a Generation*, edited by James R. Goff Jr. and Grant Wacker, 123–42. Fayetteville: University of Arkansas Press, 2002.

Brunner, Emil. *Eternal Hope.* Philadelphia: Westminster, 1954.

Burgess, Stanley, and Gary B. McGee, eds. *Dictionary of Pentecostal and Charismatic Movements.* Grand Rapids, MI: Zondervan, 1988.

Cerillo, Augustus, Jr. "Interpretive Approaches to the History of American Pentecostal Origins." *Pneuma* 19.1 (Spring 1997) 29–54.

Chapman, P. Douglas. "In Spirit and Truth: Higher Education in the Assemblies of God." *Assemblies of God Heritage* 31 (2011) 50–51.

———. "Thomas King Leonard: A Truly Indispensable Man." *Assemblies of God Heritage* (Mar. 2014) 16–25.

Bibliography

Clayton, Alan "The Significance of William Durham for Pentecostal Historiography." *Pneuma* 1.1 (1979) 27–42.

Clemmons, Ithiel C. *Bishop C.H. Mason and the Roots of the Church of God in Christ.* Bakersfield, CA: Pneumalife, 1996.

Crutchfield, Larry V. *The Origins of Dispensationalism: The Darby Factor.* Lanham, MD: University Press of America, 1992.

Daniels, David D. "Charles Harrison Mason: The Interracial Impulse." In *Portraits of a Generation,* edited by James R. Goff and Grant Wacker, 254–70. Fayetteville: University of Arkansas Press, 2002.

Dayton, Donald W. *Discovering an Evangelical Heritage.* New York: Harper and Row, 1976.

———. "From Christian Perfection to the 'Baptism of the Holy Ghost.'" In *Aspects of Pentecostal-Charismatic Origins,* edited by Vinson Synan, 41–52. Plainfield, NJ: Logos, 1975.

———. "Pentecostal Studies." In *From the Margins: A Celebration of the Theological Work of Donald W. Dayton,* edited by Christian T. Collins Winn, 156–57. Eugene, OR: Pickwick, 2007.

———. "Re-Thinking Evangelicalism." In *From the Margins: A Celebration of the Theological Work of Donald W. Dayton,* edited by Christian T. Collins Winn, 257–60. Eugene, OR: Pickwick, 2007.

———. *Theological Roots of Pentecostalism.* Peabody, MA: Hendrickson, 1987.

Dempster, Murray W. "Eschatology, Spirit Baptism, and Inclusiveness: An Exploration into the Hallmarks of a Pentecostal Social Ethic." In *Perspectives in Pentecostal Eschatology: World without End,* edited by Peter Althouse and Robby Waddell, 155–88. Eugene, OR: Pickwick, 2010.

Donovan, Brian. *White Slave Crusades: Race, Gender, and Anti-Vice Activism 1887–1917.* Chicago: University of Illinois Press, 2005.

Faupel, D. William. *The Everlasting Gospel: The Significance of Eschatology in the Development of Pentecostal Thought.* Sheffield, UK: Sheffield Academic, 1996.

———. "Whither Pentecostalism?" *Pneuma* 15.1 (Spring 1993) 22–25.

Friezen, Aaron. *Norming the Abnormal.* Eugene, OR: Pickwick, 2013.

Gibson, Scott. *A. J. Gordon, American Premillennialist.* Lanham, MD: University Press of America, 2001.

Goff, James R., and Grant Wacker, eds. *Portraits of a Generation.* Fayetteville: University of Arkansas Press, 2002.

Gohr, Glenn. "The Assemblies of God: A Good Name." *Assemblies of God Heritage* (Fall 1994) 11–15.

———. "An Early A/G Leader: Samuel A. Jamieson." *Assemblies of God Heritage* (Feb. 1991) 9–10.

Harnack, Adolf von. *Outlines of the History of Dogma.* Boston: Starking, 1957.

Harrison, Irvine J. "A History of the Assemblies of God." ThD thesis, Berkley Baptist Divinity School, 1954.

Hart, Trevor, and Richard Bauckham. *Hope against Hope.* Grand Rapids, MI: Eerdmans, 1999.

Heyduck, Richard. *The Recovery of Doctrine in the Contemporary Church.* Waco, TX: Baylor University Press, 2002.

Hollenweger, Walter. "The Black Roots of Pentecostalism." In *Pentecostals after a Century,* edited by Allan H. Anderson and Walter J. Hollenweger, 33–44. Sheffield, UK: Sheffield Academic, 1999.

Bibliography

———. "The Pentecostal Elites and the Pentecostal Poor: A Missed Dialogue?" In *Charismatic Christianity as a Global Culture*, edited by Karla Poewe, 200–14. Columbia: University of South Carolina, 1994.

———. *Pentecostalism: Origins and Developments Worldwide*. Peabody, MA: Hendrickson, 1997.

Hummel, Daniel G. *The Rise and Fall of Dispensationalism: How the Evangelical Battle over the End Times Shaped a Nation*. Grand Rapids: Eerdmans, 2023.

Isgrigg, Daniel D. "The Charismatic Origins of the Rapture: Re-assessing the 'Uneasy' Relationship between Dispensationalism and Pentecostal Eschatology." A paper presented at the 53rd Meeting of the Society for Pentecostal Studies, Atlanta, GA, March 2024.

———. "The First ORU Seminary: An Experiment in Unity without Uniformity." *Spiritus: ORU Journal of Theology* (Fall 2023) 179–89.

———. *Imagining the Future: The Origin, Development, and Future of Assemblies of God Eschatology*. Tulsa, OK: ORU Press, 2021.

———. "Interpreting the Signs of the Times: How Eschatology Shaped Assemblies of God Social Ethics." A paper presented at the 47th Annual Meeting of the Society for Pentecostal Studies, March 2018.

———. "The Latter Rain Revisited: Exploring the Origins of the Central Eschatological Metaphor in Pentecostalism." *Pneuma* 41.3-4 (2019) 439–57.

———. "Luce, Alice Eveline." In *Brill's Encyclopedia of Global Pentecostalism Online*, edited by Michael Wilkinson et al. Leiden: Brill, 2020. DOI: 10.1163/2589-3807_EGPO_COM_041675.

———. "The Pentecostal Evangelical Church: The Theological Self-Identity of the Assemblies of God as Evangelical 'Plus.'" A paper presented at the 42nd Meeting of the Society for Pentecostal Studies, St. Louis, MO, March 9–11, 2017.

———. *Pentecost in Tulsa: The Revivals and Race Massacre That Shaped the Pentecostal Movement in Tulsa*. Lanham, MD: Seymour, 2021.

———. "'Rescued Women': Early Pentecostal Responses to Sex Trafficking." *Pneuma* 44.3-4 (2022) 443–61.

Isgrigg, Daniel D., et al. *Receiving Scripture in the Pentecostal Tradition: A Reception History*. Cleveland, TN: CPT, 2021.

Jacobsen, Douglas. "Knowing the Doctrines of Pentecostals." In *Pentecostal Currents in American Protestantism*, edited by Edith Blumhofer et al., 90–107. Urbana: University of Illinois Press, 1999.

———. *Thinking in the Spirit: Theologies of the Early Pentecostal Movement*. Bloomington: Indiana University Press, 2003.

Jenkins, Phillip. *The Great and Holy War*. San Francisco: HarperOne, 2014.

Johns, Cheryl Bridges. "The Adolescence of Pentecostalism: In Search of a Legitimate Sectarian Identity." *Pneuma* 17.1 (1995) 3–17.

———. "Partners in Scandal: Wesleyan and Pentecostal Scholarship." *Pneuma* 21.1 (Fall 1999) 183–97.

Johnson, Robin. *Howard A. Goss: A Pentecostal Life*. Hazelwood, MO: Word Aflame, 2010.

Kay, William K. *Pentecostalism*. London: SCM, 2009.

———. "Three Generations On: The Methodology of Pentecostal History." *EPTA Bulletin* 11.1 (1992) 58–70.

Kendrick, Klaude. *The Promise Fulfilled: A History of the Modern Pentecostal Movement*. Springfield, MO: Gospel Publishing House, 1961.

Bibliography

Kenyon, Howard N. *Ethics in the Age of the Spirit: Race, Women, War, and the Assemblies of God*. Eugene, OR: Pickwick, 2019.

King, Gerald W. *Disfellowshipped: Pentecostal Responses to Fundamentalism in the United States, 1906–1943*. PTMS 164. Eugene, OR: Pickwick, 2011.

King, Paul. "Pentecostal Roots and the Christian and Missionary Alliance." *Assemblies of God Heritage* (2004) 12–16.

Knight, Henry L., III, ed. *From Aldersgate to Azusa: Wesleyan, Holiness, and Pentecostal Visions of the New Creation*. Eugene, OR: Pickwick, 2010.

Kraus, C. Norman. *Dispensationalism in America*. Richmond, VA: John Knox, 1958.

Kuykendall, Michael. "A. S. Worrell's *New Testament*: A Landmark Baptist-Pentecostal Bible Translation from the Early Twentieth Century." *Pneuma* 29.2 (2007) 254–80.

Land, Steven J. *Pentecostal Spirituality: A Passion for the Kingdom*. JPTSup 1. Sheffield, UK: Sheffield Academic, 1993.

Lewis, Paul. "Why Have Scholars Left Classical Pentecostal Denominations?" *Asian Journal of Pentecostal Studies* 11.1 (2008) 69–86.

Lonergan, Bernard. *Method in Theology*. New York: Seabury, 1979.

Lovett, Leonard. "Black Origins of the Pentecostal Movement." In *Aspects of Pentecostal Origins*, edited by Vinson Synan, 123–41. Plainfield, NJ: Logos International, 1971.

Macchia, Frank D. *Baptized in the Spirit: A Global Pentecostal Theology*. Grand Rapids: Zondervan, 2006.

———. "Pentecost as the Power of the Cross: The Witness of Seymour and Durham." *Pneuma* 30.1 (2008) 1–3.

———. *Spirituality and Social Liberation*. Metuchen, NJ: Scarecrow, 1993.

Marsden, George M. *Fundamentalism and American Culture*. New York: Oxford University Press, 1980.

Martin, Larry. *Charles Fox Parham: The Unlikely Father of Modern Pentecostalism*. New Kensington, PA: Whitaker, 2022.

McGee, Gary B. "Historical Background." In *Systematic Theology: A Pentecostal Perspective*, edited by Stanley M. Horton, 9–38. Springfield, MO: Logion, 1995.

———. "Luce, Alice Eveline." In *Dictionary of Pentecostal and Charismatic Movements*, edited by Stanley Burgess and Gary B. McGee, 543–44. Grand Rapids: Zondervan, 1988.

———. "More Than Evangelical." *Pneuma* 25.2 (Fall 2003) 289–300.

———. "Nelson, Peter Christopher." In *Dictionary of Pentecostal and Charismatic Movements*, edited by Stanley Burgess and Gary B. McGee, 636–37. Grand Rapids: Zondervan, 1988.

McGrath, Alister E. *The Genesis of Doctrine: A Study in the Foundation of Doctrinal Criticism*. Grand Rapids: Eerdmans, 1997.

McQueen, Larry D. *Toward a Pentecostal Eschatology*. JPTSup 39. Dorset, UK: Deo, 2012.

Menzies, Glen. "Tongues as 'The Initial Physical Sign' of Spirit Baptism in the Thought of D. W. Kerr." *Pneuma* 20.2 (Fall 1998) 175–89.

Menzies, Glen, and Gordon Anderson. "D. W. Kerr and Eschatological Diversity in the Assemblies of God." *Paraclete* (Winter 1993) 8–16.

Menzies, William W. *Anointed to Serve*. Springfield, MO: Gospel Publishing House, 1971.

———. "Developing Educational Institutions." *Assemblies of God Heritage* (Summer 1983) 3–4.

———. "Non-Wesleyan Pentecostalism: A Tradition the Influence of Fundamentalism." *Asian Journal of Pentecostal Studies* 14.2 (2011) 199–211.

Bibliography

———. "The Reformed Roots of Pentecostalism." *PentecoStudies* 6.2 (2007) 78–99.
Minter, Terry N. "Antecedents to the Assemblies of God." PhD diss., Regent University, 2011.
Miskov, Jennifer A. *Life on Wings: The Forgotten Life and Theology of Carrie Judd Montgomery (1858–1946)*. Cleveland, TN: CPT, 2012.
Moltmann, Jürgen. *The Coming of God*. Minneapolis: Fortress, 2004.
Newman, Raybon Joel. *Race and the Assemblies of God*. Youngstown, NY: Cambria, 2007.
Olena, Lois. *Stanley M. Horton: Shaper of Pentecostal Theology*. Springfield, MO: Gospel Publishing House, 2009.
Oliverio, L. William, Jr. *Theological Hermeneutics in the Classical Pentecostal Tradition: A Typological Account*. Leiden: Brill, 2012.
Olsen, Roger E. "Pentecostalism's Dark Side." *Christian Century*, Mar. 7, 2006, 27–30.
Owen, Michael G. "Five Ohio Bible Schools—Forerunners of Today's Colleges." *Assemblies of God Heritage* 9.4 (Winter 1989) 5.
Pelikan, Jaroslav. *The Emergence of the Catholic Tradition*. Chicago: University of Chicago Press, 1971.
Pipkin, Brian, and Jay Beaman. *Early Pentecostals on Nonviolence and Social Justice*. Eugene, OR: Pickwick, 2016.
Poloma, Margaret. "The Future of American Pentecostal Identity: The Assemblies of God at a Crossroad." In *The Work of the Spirit*, edited by Michael Welker, 147–68. Grand Rapids: Eerdmans, 2006.
Poloma, Margaret, and John Green. *The Assemblies of God: Godly Love and the Revitalization of American Pentecostalism*. New York: New York University Press, 2010.
Prosser, Peter. *Dispensationalist Eschatology and Its Influence on American and British Religious Movements*. Lewiston: Edwin Mellen, 1999.
Qualls, Joy E. *"God Forgive Us for Being Women": The Rhetorical Negotiations and Renegotiations of the Role of Women in the Assemblies of God*. Eugene, OR: Pickwick, 2018.
Roebuck, David G. "Church of God, Cleveland." In *Brill's Encyclopedia of Global Pentecostalism Online*, edited by Michael Wilkinson et al. Leiden: Brill, 2022. DOI: 10.1163/2589-3807_EGPO_COM_044875.
Rodgers, Darrin. "The Assemblies of God and the Long Journey toward Racial Reconciliation." *Assemblies of God Heritage* (2008) 50–61.
Rosdahl, Bruce. "The Doctrine of Sanctification in the Assemblies of God." PhD diss., Dallas Theological Seminary, 2008.
Sandeen, Ernest R. *The Roots of Fundamentalism: British and American Millenarianism 1800–1930*. Chicago: University of Chicago Press, 1970.
Satyavrata, Ivan. *Pentecostals and the Poor*. Eugene, OR: Wipf & Stock, 2017.
Schaff, Philip, and David S. Schaff, eds. "Doctrinal Basis of the Evangelical Alliance A.D. 1846." In *Creeds of Evangelical Protestant Churches*, vol. 3 of *The Creeds of Christendom: With a History and Critical Notes*, 827–30. Grand Rapids: Baker, 2007.
Sheppard, Gerald T. "Pentecostals and the Hermeneutics of Dispensationalism: The Anatomy of an Uneasy Relationship." *Pneuma* 6.2 (Fall 1984) 5–33.
Spittler, Russell. "Are Pentecostals and Charismatics Fundamentalists?" In *Charismatic Christianity as a Global Culture*, edited by Karla Poewe, 103–16. Columbia: University of South Carolina Press, 1994.

BIBLIOGRAPHY

———. "Theological Opportunity before the Pentecostal Movement." In *Aspects of Pentecostal-Charismatic Origins*, edited by Vinson Synan, 235–44. Plainfield, NJ: Logos, 1975.

———. "Theological Style among Pentecostals and Charismatics." In *Doing Theology in Today's World*, edited by John D. Woodbridge and Thomas Edward McComiskey, 291–98. Grand Rapids: Zondervan, 1991.

Stephenson, Christopher A. *Types of Pentecostal Theology*. New York: Oxford University Press, 2013.

Sterling, Larry, Jr. "Are Pentecostals Evangelicals?" A paper presented at the 2011 meeting of the Society for Pentecostal Studies, Memphis, TN, March 2011.

Studebaker, Steven M. *A Pentecostal Political Theology for American Renewal: Spirit of the Kingdoms, Citizens of the Cities*. New York: Palgrave Macmillan, 2016.

Synan, Vinson, ed. *Aspects of Pentecostal-Charismatic Origins*. Plainfield, NJ: Logos, 1975.

———. *The Holiness-Pentecostal Tradition*. Grand Rapids: Eerdmans, 1997.

Synan, Vinson, and Charles R. Fox, Jr. *William J. Seymour: Pioneer of the Azusa Street Revival*. Alachua, FL: Bridge-Logos, 2012.

Tackett, Zachary. "The Embourgeoisement of the Assemblies of God: Changing Perspectives on Scripture, Millennialism, and the Roles of Women." PhD diss., Southern Baptist Theological Seminary, May 1998.

———. "More Than Fundamentalists: Fundamentalist Influences within the Assemblies of God, 1914–1942." A paper presented at the 26th Annual Meeting of the Society for Pentecostal Studies, Oakland, CA, March 13–15, 1997.

Van De Walle, Bernie. *The Heart of the Gospel: A.B. Simpson, the Fourfold Gospel, and Late Nineteenth-Century Evangelical Theology*. Eugene, OR: Pickwick, 2009.

Waldvogel, Edith L. "The 'Overcoming' Life: A Study in the Reformed Evangelical Contribution to Pentecostalism." *Pneuma* 1.1 (Spring 1979) 7–19.

———. "The 'Overcoming Life': Study in the Reformed Evangelical Origins of Pentecostalism." PhD diss., Harvard University, 1977.

Warner, Wayne. "A Call for Love, Tolerance, and Cooperation." *Assemblies of God Heritage* (Fall 1994) 4.

Weaver, Elton H., III. *Bishop Charles H. Mason in the Age of Jim Crow: The Struggle for Religious and Moral Uplift*. Lanham, MD: Lexington, 2020.

White, Charles E. *The Beauty of Holiness: Phoebe Palmer as Theologian, Revivalist, Feminist, and Humanitarian*. Eugene, OR: Wipf & Stock, 1986.

Wilkinson, Michael, et al., eds. *Brill's Encyclopedia of Global Pentecostalism Online*. Leiden: Brill, 2022.

Wilkinson, Paul Richard. *For Zion's Sake: Christian Zionism and the Role of John Nelson Darby*. Milton Keynes, UK: Paternoster, 2007.

Wilson, Lewis. "The Kerr-Pierce Role in A/G Education." *Assemblies of God Heritage* 10.1 (Spring 1990) 6–8, 21.

Winn, Christian T. Collins, ed. *From the Margins: A Celebration of the Theological Work of Donald W. Dayton*. PTMS 75. Eugene, OR: Pickwick, 2007.

Wood, Lawrence W. *The Meaning of Pentecost in Early Methodism*. Lanham, MD: Scarecrow, 2002.

Yong, Amos. *Renewing Christian Theology: Systematics for Global Christianity*. Waco, TX: Baylor University Press, 2014.

———. *Spirit-Word-Community: Theological Hermeneutics in Trinitarian Perspective*. Aldershot, UK: Ashgate, 2002.

Bibliography

Yong, Amos, and Dale M. Coulter. *The Holy Spirit and Higher Education*. Waco, TX: Baylor University Press, 2023.

Ziefle, Joshua R. *David du Plessis and the Assemblies of God: The Struggle for the Soul of a Movement*. Boston: Brill, 2012.

Index

Adams, L. P., 21
Archer, Kenneth, 56–57

Bell, E. N., 12–15, 18, 20, 24–25, 32–33, 39–40, 48, 63, 65, 69, 85, 87–89, 116, 119, 126, 142, 144, 146, 148, 153
Bible doctrines, 65, 123–31, 135–38
Blumhofer, Edith, 1, 9–10, 16, 27, 35, 45, 49, 60, 153
Boyd, Frank M., 101–2, 104, 105–6, 112, 118, 120, 133

Carlson, G. Raymond, 121–22
Carothers, W. F., 13, 142
Central Bible College (Institute), 8, 15, 17, 50, 94, 118–20, 130
Church of God in Christ (C. H. Mason), 12–26
Church of God in Christ (white), 12–26, 154
Christian & Missionary Alliance, 45, 73, 75, 93
Collins, A. P., 14, 18, 21, 33–34, 69, 81, 85–87, 112, 116, 118

Darby, J. N., 34, 61–62, 65, 66
Dispensationalism, 40–41, 45, 49, 59–78, 79–113, 138–39
Durham, William, 12–26, 27, 32–33, 85, 142, 145

Flower, J. R., 12, 15–22
Frodsham, Stanley, 4–5, 40, 48, 50–51, 54

Fundamentalism, 8, 10, 42, 44, 49–51, 53–55, 56, 58, 60, 66, 131

Gospel Publishing House, 7, 17, 69, 78, 79, 81, 88, 90, 96, 100, 105, 111–12, 124 130, 135, 136, 153
Goss, Howard, 12–26, 27, 32–33, 85, 142, 145

human trafficking, 144–145
higher education, 8, 114–37
higher criticism, 48, 91, 114, 116, 148
Horton, Stanley, 112, 124, 128, 133–34, 135–37, 152, 153

Jamieson, S. A., 81, 89–93, 116, 117, 118, 140, 153

Kay, William K., 35, 122,
Kendrick, Klaude, 7–9, 15–16
Kenyon, Howard N., 10, 19, 143
Kerr, D. W., 50, 71, 93–96, 118–20, 126

Lawrence, B. F., 4, 25
Luce, Alice, 96–100, 153

Macchia, Frank, 34, 38, 115
Mason, C. H., 12–26, 27
Menzies, Glen, 95
Menzies, William, 8, 15, 27, 94, 134–136, 137
Myland, D. W., 68, 73–78, 93, 118

National Association of Evangelicals (NAE), 10, 53–55

Index

Nelson, P. C., 65, 116, 119, 120–21, 125, 127–30

Parham, Charles, 8, 11, 13, 24, 25, 27, 32, 67, 142
Premillennialism, 9, 41, 45, 48–49, 51, 58, 59–62, 65, 69, 79, 82, 95, 111, 138–39, 149
Pearlman, Myer, 106, 109–11, 112, 120, 124, 125, 130–31, 133, 137
Pinson, M. M., 13–14, 17–18, 20–21, 22–27, 33, 96
politics, 87, 98, 101, 103, 111, 139, 146–51

rapture (of the church), 59–78, 79–113
racism, 16, 21, 22, 26, 28, 97, 142–44, 145, 151
Riggs, Ralph, 105, 106–9, 112
Rodgers, Darrin, 22, 144, 154

Scofield Reference Bible, 62–63, 66–67, 72, 78
Seiss, J. A., 63–64, 73, 78, 92
Sheppard, Gerald, 60
Sisson, Elizabeth, 80–85, 112, 114, 153
social justice, 138–51
Statement of Fundamental Truths, 34, 35, 46–48, 52, 79, 80, 88, 90, 92, 93, 103, 122, 124–25, 128, 135, 136, 152

tribulation, 61, 64, 68, 70, 72, 76–78, 79–113, 135

Williams, E. S., 52, 125–26, 128, 132–34, 148, 149, 153

Zimmerman, Thomas, 54–55, 128, 153

www.ingramcontent.com/pod-product-compliance
Lightning Source LLC
Chambersburg PA
CBHW071457150426
43191CB00008B/1374